# CTRL HATE DELETE

"Powerfully exposes the full scale of today's anti-feminist backlash, which is more impactful and more harmful than ever before … a well-researched and moving account of today's mainstreaming of male supremacy. It is a must-read for men and women on either side of the culture wars."

**Julia Ebner, author of *Going Dark* and *Going Mainstream***

"The collision of gender with technology is amongst the most powerful forces shaping society, right now. Read this book."

**Carl Miller, Demos Centre for the Analysis of Social Media**

"An incisive exploration of the rising anti-feminist backlash, illuminating how online misogyny threatens gender equality and inspiring action to combat it."

**Charlotte Proudman, barrister, campaigner and academic**

# CTRL HATE DELETE

## The New Anti-Feminist Backlash and How We Fight It

Cécile Simmons

First published in Great Britain in 2025 by

Policy Press, an imprint of
Bristol University Press
University of Bristol
1-9 Old Park Hill
Bristol
BS2 8BB
UK
+44 (0)117 374 6645
bup-info@bristol.ac.uk

Details of international sales and distribution partners are available at
policy.bristoluniversitypress.co.uk



British Library Cataloguing in Publication Data
A catalogue record for this book is available from the British Library

ISBN 978-1-4473-7484-8 paperback
ISBN 978-1-4473-7485-5 ePub
ISBN 978-1-4473-7486-2 ePdf



Cover design: Sarah-Louise Deazley

## CONTENT WARNING

Due to its subject matter, this book deals with sensitive issues including abuse, violence, coercion, harassment and sexual assault.

To my late father, Jean-Claude,
who supported me unconditionally.

# Contents

# Glossary

**Accelerationism** ideology promoted by white supremacists and other extremist groups which consists in accelerating the collapse of current societies and structures to rebuild new white ethnonationalist societies.

**Ethnonationalism** ideology which promotes the segregation of people according to ethnicity.

**Great Replacement** a conspiracy theory which posits that white Christian European populations are being erased through orchestrated immigration.

**Great Reset** a conspiracy theory related to an initiative of the same name launched in June by the World Economic Forum to improve societies post-COVID-19. Proponents of the conspiracy argue that international elites are orchestrating lockdowns and want to implement various nefarious agendas under the guise of health emergencies.

**Maxxing** different strategies adopted by incels to self-improve and escape their status. Looksmaxxing is among the most popular ones and includes pseudoscientific techniques to improve one's looks.

**MRAs (Men's Rights Activists)** male supremacist activists and groups who believe that men are disadvantaged by feminism and that women have the upper hand in society. Some MRAs openly advocate dismantling key advances in women's rights to restore men's power.

**Mythopoetic movement** a men's self-help movement which emerged in the US in the early 1980s as a response to men's feminist movements and the emerging Men's Rights Activists movement. Through therapeutic workshops and retreats in nature, proponents of the movement believe men can achieve a form of mature masculinity.

**PUAs (Pickup Artists)** male supremacist communities and coaches who teach men how to trick women into sex.

PUAs advocate coercion, and some openly justify rape and sexual violence.

**QAnon** a political movement and conspiracy theory which claims that Donald Trump is fighting a cabal of Satanic paedophiles dominated by liberal elites and Hollywood.

**Sexual Market Value** theory which posits that dating and romantic relationships function like a market and that each individual has a designated sexual value within that market. Male supremacist communities have been at the forefront of promoting pseudoscientific theories about Sexual Market Value to provide a justification for their grievances and resentment towards women.

**Social Justice Warrior** pejorative term used to describe individuals who promote progressive and liberal ideas, including multiculturalism, feminism and LGBT+ rights. The term appeared on 4chan and Reddit and was widely adopted by the architects of Gamergate in 2014 and what would become the alt-right.

**Soyboy** pejorative term used to describe men who are deemed not to be conventionally masculine. The term was adopted by sections of the alt-right and is based on the pseudoscientific idea that soy decreased men's testosterone.

# Acknowledgements

This book owes its existence to the knowledge and kindness of the many experts, activists and researchers who have agreed to speak with me and share their thoughts. The generosity of the women and men I have spoken to and their dedication to their work have given me hope that there is a way out of despair and cynicism.

I would like to thank my excellent editor Ginny Mills, Ellen Mitchell and the team at Bristol University Press for their trust. My gratitude also goes to my agent Charlotte Atyeo at Greyhound for championing this project. Special thanks to the Institute for Strategic Dialogue for granting me a sabbatical to write this book and to my talented and passionate colleagues, from whom I learn every day.

I am especially indebted to Julia Ebner and Tim Squirrell, for their thoughtful and detailed feedback on the draft. Thank you to my friend Aisling Fowler, who read the book and made valuable suggestions.

Last but not least, thank you to my family and friends for their support throughout this enterprise and for their encouragement in times of hardship and doubt. Many conversations with them have been a source of inspiration and have allowed me to see the material for the book in a new light. To Immy, Josh, Marie-Laure, Maud, Natalie and Olivier, your friendship means the world to me.

Thank you to Richard for his love and support. This book would not exist without him.

# Prologue: My friend, the male supremacist

I have a friend whose name is Will. It isn't actually, but that's what we'll call him. He's in his mid-40s and has a good job in the creative industries in London. He has sandy-blonde hair, cropped short, stubble, and a penchant for flat caps and beanie hats which sit atop a pleasant, friendly-looking face.

We must have known each other for nearly ten years. I met him through a friend, who in turn met him at work. We didn't socialise one-on-one, but he was a regular at our social circle's group gatherings, nights out, birthdays and weddings. Sitting on the Tube or in an Uber as we headed back home after running into him, I'd often say: 'Will is a sweet man.' I always found him considerate, respectful and well-intentioned.

The pandemic happened and I didn't see Will for a couple of years. But as the parties and nights out gradually returned, so did he. Now, though, the conversations we had were more troubling and made our common group of friends uneasy. It started with various, not very subtle, hints. Will liked slipping in comments about how, contrary to what 'mainstream' society would have you believe, domestic abuse affects men as much as women, but 'the government is lying about it.' He expressed concerns for the 'many men' who are 'falsely accused of rape'. The comments were isolated enough that although they were red flags, people could ignore them, laugh them off and dismiss Will as the mild conspiracy theorist in the group – after all, post-pandemic, who doesn't have someone in their circle who is 'just asking questions'?

One night, after one too many glasses of wine, the conversation drifted onto personal relationships. Will had recently got out of a bad break-up. The discussion turned into a debate, then an argument, then a row. Then it reached breaking point. Will's final opinion, among other things, included that there is a 'widespread cover-up of male rape by women' and that 'women should not be allowed to have an abortion without a man's consent.' One of my female friends – let's call her Sarah – left the room and never saw him again.

'I never realised he was such a hardened misogynist. How could I have missed that?' she later told me. When she said this, I immediately thought: 'He's not a misogynist.' The word did not feel right, although there is no denying that what Will said was distressing and overtly misogynistic and he is, by the strict definition of the term, what Sarah says he is. But more than an ordinary misogynist, I saw him as someone who had become radicalised into a dangerous ideology that is spreading and becoming normalised in many corners of the world.

Will's strident beliefs sparked confusion among his social group, but for me the picture was clearer, because I study the exact ideas he is espousing and I know where they come from. I work for a think tank that studies online radicalisation and conspiracy theories. In the last few years, I have spent long coffee-fuelled days following extremist communities down their various rabbit holes. I have tracked lies about climate policies, followed the rise and decline of QAnon – the pro-Trump conspiracy theory which claims that Satanic elites are sucking the blood of children – and witnessed how COVID-19-era health conspiracies have taken on new shapes.

By the time of the incident, it had been clear to me for a little while that Will had been sucked deep into the so-called 'manosphere', a growing collection of anti-feminist communities and their associated podcasts, blogs, forums and influencers, although I didn't know just how deep. The manosphere, though diverse, is united by an overarching belief: contrary to mainstream messaging, men are oppressed by a feminised society and are at a disadvantage over women in virtually all areas of life, ranging from dating and relationships to workplace opportunities and custody battles. Related to this idea is the notion that this oppression is a deliberate and malign plot orchestrated by feminists and their allies, who conspire to conceal the truth of men's oppression.

The rift that happened between my friend Will and our social circle is a sad and familiar story to many. Conspiracy theories are everywhere now. The flat-earthers and moon landing truthers who earnestly spouted their ideas on the street corners of a pre-internet world seem quaint compared to the movements that blossomed during COVID-19. A 2023 poll by King's College London and the BBC revealed that a third of the UK population believe in the conspiracy theory that 15-minute cities – urban planning efforts to enhance people's access to services in their local area – are an effort to lock people down in their own neighbourhoods. A similar proportion believe in the 'Great Replacement', the idea that white European populations are being replaced through migration.[1]

If the pandemic showed how much conspiracy theories have flourished, the years since have shown the impact of such beliefs on public health, personal and community relationships, and democratic discourse. It has become impossible to ignore: lives lost because of fear of vaccines, attacks on religious and ethnic minorities, the assault on the US Capitol by pro-Trump protesters who believed the 2020 election had been stolen. Away from the headlines, in millions of houses across the world, from small bedsits to grand mansions, the descent of individuals into the 'rabbit hole' often feels more intimate and personal. As phones and laptops flicker into life, relationships sputter and die.

Will believes there is a conspiracy against men. He believes that our societies are not patriarchal and never were, because the very concept of patriarchy is a fabrication. According to him, official statistics about rape are fabricated. I know this because although my friend Sarah vowed to never speak with Will again, I later sat down with him to talk about his life and the development of his beliefs. These beliefs have cost him relationships with people who have known him for decades. They have also given him new relationships with like-minded individuals who go to great lengths to say they care about the issues dear to him. Overall, they have left him more isolated and alienated and have not made his life easier in any way.

In *Down Girl* (2017) feminist scholar Kate Manne has conceptualised misogyny as the behaviours and actions that enforce patriarchal norms and police women. These behaviours take many forms, from the spectacular to the mundane. While misogyny is the air we breathe, Will's beliefs are one of the many manifestations of a reactionary political project that is developing and growing across many parts of the world. This project is about policing and enforcing patriarchal norms, for sure, but it is also about reasserting men's dominance, superiority and control over women and undoing decades of progress towards women's autonomy and gender equality.

There are different ways to name this project. You could call it a backlash. In her 1991 classic, *Backlash*, Susan Faludi argued that any advance in women's rights leads to a counter-offensive from those who oppose it. While Faludi was writing about the 1980s reaction against the second-wave feminism of the late 1960s and 1970s, she argued that misogynistic flare-ups follow any progress towards gender equality.

In many parts of the world, we have entered a new era of anti-feminist backlash and support for right-wing authoritarian and far-right politics, of which the 2016 election of 'pussy grabbing' Donald Trump as US president was one of the first spectacular manifestations. Hostile misogyny, far from being an incidental element, was the defining ingredient of the reactionary movement that propelled Trump to the White House. An Ipsos UK/King's College London survey found that over half of British men thought that women's rights had gone 'too far' and resulted in discrimination against men.[2] Polling in the US showed that 62 per cent of young Republican men thought that feminism has 'done more harm than good' and 46 per cent of their Democratic counterparts agreed.[3]

The year 2022 saw the overturning of *Roe v. Wade* in the US. It saw Andrew Tate, a violent misogynist who is also accused of being a rapist and a pimp, gain a cult following among young men across the English-speaking world in a matter of months, sparking waves of harassment in schools. It saw a presidential candidate win the election in South Korea by overtly preying on men's resentment towards feminism and the country's #MeToo movement. *Rolling Stone* declared misogyny to be 'back in fashion'.[4] Misogyny has only become more fashionable since. Abuse of women running for office has become the new norm in every election. Around the world, authoritarian misogynists who promise to dismantle women's rights are winning elections or getting increasingly close to it.

The new anti-feminist backlash we are currently experiencing bears a resemblance to the ones that came before. Like the backlash that Faludi described, it targets women's bodily and reproductive autonomy at the same time as it undoes social safety nets. Like previous backlashes, it also wages a communication war and seeks to accuse feminism, a movement in favour of equality between men and women, of the ills it perpetuates.

It is, however, different in several ways. As recent decades have been marked by the greatest strides in history towards gender equality, the backlash we are now experiencing is the strongest. It is in large part driven by social media platforms and their opaque algorithms and curation systems. It is transnational and driven by complex webs of political influences and financial interests. And it operates in a world that feels increasingly out of control.

The COVID-19 pandemic, which took our lives even more online than before, was a turning point. The social fragmentation, loneliness and atomisation that it fuelled endure in multiple forms. It has left behind itself a trail of conspiracy theories, which are gripping ever more of us. In a world of interlocking crises, many of us are feeling that, as conspiracy theorists like to say, 'nothing is as it seems' and no collective structure is equipped to help us. We are also in the midst of an accelerating climate crisis, steaming at full speed towards the melting iceberg.

Of all the conspiratorial and extremist communities I have followed, the so-called 'manosphere' has felt the most perniciously dangerous. It is not just because I am a woman who can experience the chilling effect of hearing a man I thought I knew suggest that women should not be allowed to have an abortion without a man's permission. It is also because anti-feminism is often the entry point to other forms of radicalisation that has been consistently underestimated by governments, policy makers and researchers and is misrepresented in media coverage. It immediately threatens the integrity and rights of half of the world's population by normalising coercion, control and violence.

Although the term 'manosphere' is most often used by researchers, myself included for convenience in this book, and in media coverage, it is somewhat deceptive as it captures only part of the story and fails to fully articulate what is at stake. Talk of the manosphere conjures up the image of a few men behind their keyboards peddling disturbing views and suggests that only men are involved. In fact, it is a political movement whose goals and effects on women need to be named: it is a male supremacist project.

This book uses a definition adapted from the work of Emily K. Carian and Alex DiBranco and their colleagues at the Institute for Research on Male Supremacism, the first think tank of its kind dedicated to studying male supremacism.[5] In this book, I define male supremacism as, first, an ideology based on the essentialist belief in the superiority of cisgender men over all others, and their right to subjugate and control them, and, second, a movement that actively aims to re-establish traditional gender norms and undo progress towards gender equality.

This book was written in the run-up to the 2024 US presidential election. Donald Trump, who was found legally liable for sexual assault, ran a campaign which, through its rhetoric and policy promises, overtly aimed to restore men's dominance over women. The male supremacist slogan 'your body, my choice' which spread online in the hours after his victory reflected the fact that though Trump's gender politics is not the sole reason he won the popular vote, the young men whose vote he courted liked what they heard and supported him not despite of but because of who he is. The young white men, and a growing proportion of Latino men, who voted for Trump were not alone in handing him victory. A majority of white women supported a convicted felon who boasted being the architect of the overturning of *Roe v. Wade* and told them he would protect them 'whether they like it or not'.

This book is about how male supremacy is gaining ground and can be countered. It primarily focuses on the Global North, particularly English-speaking countries, where male supremacist ideology as I define it here has been most predominant and has grown alongside far-right movements and politics. While I mostly provide examples from the US and the UK, I also make reference to other countries, particularly France, where I was born. The choice of examples is determined by my research and the geographical contexts I know best. However, what I describe in this book is also increasingly happening in the Global South. From Kenya to India, and elsewhere, male supremacist influencers and groups are quickly building audiences online and support offline, preying on young men's resentment towards women and hard fought-for progress towards gender equality.[6]

Although male supremacy is not mere misogyny, it benefits from and weaponises existing patriarchal structures and norms to spread its message. Its recipe for mainstreaming its message includes a few ingredients: male supremacists blend ideology with predatory business models that monetise discontent. They promote pseudoscientific views which offer simple solutions to the complexities of contemporary gender politics and neoliberal discontent. They exploit the perceived or real failures of collective structures and the divisions and shortcomings of progressive movements. They have their mouthpieces, amplifiers and complicit allies. For many people, what they offer feels increasingly attractive amid a perception that there is no better alternative.

Male supremacists have worked for many years to bring their ideas into the mainstream. If they look one step ahead, it is because they are: they have honed their playbook over many years and have learned what works and what doesn't. They benefit from governments' apathy, from tech giants' lack of incentives to deal with radicalisation and polarisation and from new technologies which are developing faster than society's ability to cope with them. The views they promote are also an extension of normalised misogynistic violence against women in our societies.

I wrote this book because of my frustration at seeing male supremacist ideas spread, seemingly unstoppably, and because I'm worried about how easily we can become desensitised to them. I have witnessed first-hand how they can shape men's beliefs, influence policies and normalise the notion that women's basic rights are up for grabs. I have also realised that although there have been excellent books on anti-feminism generally, there is not much in the way of nuanced examination of how we can collectively respond to this problem from different angles.

Part I of the book examines the new faces of male supremacy. It looks at the influencers who have brought male supremacy into the mainstream, the new post-#MeToo witch-hunts, the shape of the backlash against women's reproductive health and autonomy, the rise of anti-feminist women's movements and the exploitation tactics used by male supremacists to capture resources, votes and attention. We can do something about this.

Part II explores how we can fight back. I've spoken to influencers, campaigners, experts and innovators who invite us to consider nuanced solutions to a problem that is increasingly good at dividing its adversaries. There are progressive men who are trying to help their fellow men find meaning in their lives and in doing so wrest them away from the call of male supremacists. There are lone individuals who have taken it upon themselves to counter the lies that spread online and organisations that look to educate young people. They are faced with hard questions: how far should we bend towards those we fight? Should women be working with men to address their discontent? Do any of these initiatives actually work?

Male supremacists offer easy answers. I can't. This is a battle being fought on multiple fronts, against people who are determined and quick to adapt. It will be a long process, but there is hope that the male supremacist project can be countered.

# PART I

# The new faces of male supremacy

# 1

# One click away: male supremacy at the fingertips

Looking at him, you might not think my friend Will was the type of person who'd have much time for anti-feminist conspiracy theories. He's a good-looking man who's had partners, although by the time he started getting deeper into the manosphere, he had just come out of a bad break-up. He's well-educated and has a good job in the media and a mortgage. He is, by all measures, a functioning adult. But all of us have points of vulnerability that can be exploited. I am no exception. Later on I'll talk about my own. But I'll start with Will.

After the incident that broke our group of friends apart, I dropped him a message. His radicalisation troubled me. This was the time when the violent male supremacist Andrew Tate, who said that women should 'bear responsibility' for their rape and who spoke of hitting and choking them, had started amassing billions of views on TikTok, appealing to legions of mesmerised teenage boys. In my work, I have seen extreme misogyny grow, having studied abuse campaigns against women in public life for several years, but for the first time this hit very close to home.

I wanted to understand his radicalisation path and appeal to him. He was keen to talk.

Will grew up with his younger brother in London in a setting he described as 'progressive and woke-y'. His upbringing was overshadowed by his parents' dysfunctional relationship. After their divorce, Will became estranged from his mother. A few years later, his father admitted to physical violence against her. The revelation was devastating, but it did not take Will down the path you would expect. Far from turning him against his father, it brought Will closer to him. He could not accept the idea that his father – 'one of the nicest guys [he] had ever met' – could do such a thing. 'I reject this concept that my dad is the baddie; it doesn't sit with me,' he told me. He decided to blame his mother instead. Later, his younger brother went through a difficult divorce and battled for custody of his child. During the divorce proceedings, it seemed as if the whole order of things was arranged against men.

This is Will's point of vulnerability when it comes to questions of gender roles and norms: his family story. His experiences with his parents provided a background for personal pain and grievances, he chose to interpret information given to him in a certain way (unsurprisingly given his and everyone else's socialisation in a world where violence against women is discounted and disbelieved), and his brothers's custody woes acted as the tipping point for his involvement in male supremacist ideology. He describes his path down this road in terms reminiscent of a spiritual awakening: 'Now I have started on this journey, I can't turn back and unsee.' Unless one spends a lot of time immersed in manosphere communities, one would not necessarily be expected to recognise this sort of language for what it is: the language of the 'red pill'.

## Is everyone red-pilled?

Around the turn of the millennium there was a website called sixsixfive.com, run by an individual known only as JSP. It was in effect one of the internet's early blogs: an eclectic mix of daily content including JSP's own writing and surreal cartoons (his 'Safety Tips from Anubis' would go viral on *Buzzfeed* many years later), funny pictures he had found online and his musings on early internet culture. On one occasion he discovered a group who believed that the concept of the 1999 sci-fi film *The Matrix* – that the reality we experience is in fact a computer simulation and humanity is unknowingly enslaved – was true. He got a day's worth of content by sending messages to its members and fooling them into believing he was a figure interested in extracting them from the simulation and bringing them back to the real world. JSP observed that the internet was bringing together similar individuals who would previously have had no way of connecting to construct a shared delusion and also correctly predicted that their fantasies would only become more convoluted and bizarre given time. He viewed these groups with detached amusement, but what he couldn't have known was that the odd but essentially harmless behaviour he was witnessing in a tiny online forum contained the seeds of what would one day become a worldwide hate movement.

With its themes of technology, hidden knowledge and philosophical reflection on the nature of reality, right from the beginning *The Matrix* appealed to a certain breed of highly online individuals, mostly young men, with a penchant for conspiracy theories. In the film the protagonist, Neo, is offered a choice between taking a blue pill and living out his life in a simulated dream world or taking a red pill and having his eyes opened to reality. While it began as a nerdy pop culture reference, the 'red pill' became a way for the early online manosphere of the 2010s, which congregated on the imageboard websites 4chan and 8chan, obscure blogs and forums and the Reddit r/TheRedPill community, to describe their awakening to a hidden truth: that men are oppressed by a feminised society and that women have the upper hand in everything, from dating and sex life to workplace recruitment and custody battles. The red pill has in recent years become the reference of choice for virtually every far-right and conspiratorial movement around the world to describe their awakening to various hidden truths.

Once confined to fringe ultra-misogynistic and far-right communities, the notion of red-pilling has become part of internet slang and entered mainstream culture, reaching a level of absurdity in the process. As a piece in *The Atlantic* noted, one can now be 'coconut-oil-pilled' (unable to resist the urge to put coconut oil in every dish) or 'Rory Gilmore-pilled' (compelled to act like a character from the TV show *Gilmore Girls*).[1] When conspiracy theorists talk about being red-pilled, many do so with a level of self-awareness that doesn't extend to much else they say. Other concepts developed by male supremacist communities have spread too. Once upon a time, terms like *alpha* and *beta* were merely Greek letters and Chad was a country in Central Africa. Now, tell a section of teenagers in your local high school that 'girls prefer chads', and they will nod knowingly.

Annie Kelly began researching the contemporary manosphere when it emerged in the early 2010s. In the space of just a few years, she has seen its vocabulary and arguments find new audiences and unprecedented reach. 'A few years ago, you were able to map out the manosphere, you could count and name the blogs and websites,' she tells me. 'Today, it's impossible because the arguments of these groups are everywhere online.'[2] If that's the case, it is not just because internet trends spread or because language becomes diluted: it is because more and more people are becoming a little bit, and sometimes very, red-pilled.

Men increasingly subscribe to the red pill view the world male supremacist communities have tried to convey for many years – that men are now systematically disadvantaged and that it is a perilous time to be a man – and that feminism is to blame. A 2024 poll discovered that 22 per cent of British men think it's harder to be a man than a woman today, with young men the most likely to feel this way.[3]

One development has greatly contributed to this normalisation: the rise of charismatic influencers with outsized social media audiences. These influencers differ in personality but they have one thing in common: their anti-feminism is not a side dish. It is the main ingredient in an online recipe for radicalisation. They convey the ideas of fringe male supremacist communities in palatable terms and monetise them by packaging them as lifestyle-oriented content targeting men in search of meaning. Male supremacy can then become the entry point into other forms of radicalisation. r/TheRedPill discussion group on Reddit became a key force in the Make America Great Again (MAGA) movement, which helped propel Donald Trump to the White House in 2016,[4] turning the feeling that men are oppressed by women into a political movement.

While others have provided a detailed analysis of the different corners of the manosphere, including Laura Bates in *Men Who Hate Women* (2020), it's impossible to talk about the manosphere without a quick introductory overview. While these communities seem neatly delineated – sometimes even disavowing each other – their beliefs often overlap. Their main characteristics are their misogynistic views, the use of pseudoscience or disinformation to justify them and the endorsement of coercion, manipulation and abuse of women.

On 23 May 2014, 22-year-old Elliot Rodger stabbed 3 men to death in his apartment, shot 3 further people and wounded 14 in Isla Vista, California, before turning the gun on himself. Before doing so, he posted a video on YouTube and emailed a 140-page document to acquaintances in which he detailed his hatred of women. He called the rampage his 'Day of Retribution'. It was not the first example of contemporary terrorism motivated by misogyny: in 1989, Marc Lépine killed 14 women at the École Polytechnique in Montréal, stating that he was 'fighting feminism', but it was the first example of contemporary terrorism associated with incels.

Incels (short for involuntary celibates) are an online community of men united by their inability to find a sexual partner, their resentment towards women and their entitlement to sex. Rodger had spent time on incel forums including PUAHate.com where men vented their frustration and hatred of women. In the decade since Isla Vista, more attacks have followed, including one in Toronto in April 2018 where an incel terrorist drove a car into pedestrians, killing 11 people and citing Rodger as his hero.

The threat of misogynistic terrorism, while receiving greater attention in recent years, has long been underestimated by law enforcement and government and is not clearly tracked. Many attacks appear to have been motivated by misogyny but are not classified as incel or male supremacist terror incidents unless they meet a certain threshold, for example the perpetrator leaving behind a manifesto. In August 2021, a 22-year-old who spent a lot of time on incel forums gunned down five people in Plymouth, UK. Despite being strongly linked to the incel movement, and despite the perpetrator making various comments about women's 'low IQ', the attack was not classified as terrorism and was blamed on the perpetrator's mental health.

Visits to incel forums rose sixfold after the Plymouth attack,[5] and references to violence increased eightfold in incel forums between 2016 and 2022.[6] The full extent to which male supremacist ideology underpins terrorism remains unknown but is probably underestimated. In April 2024, a man stabbed six people in a shopping mall in Sydney, five of whom were women. While his motives are difficult to know with certainty in the absence of clear statements of intent, the New South Wales police commissioner told Australian media that it's 'obvious' that the 'offender focused on women and avoided the men'. When questioned by media outlets, the killer's father said 'he wanted a girlfriend' and 'was frustrated out of his brain'.[7]

Incel communities are obsessed with the idea that men's success with women is biologically predetermined and that relationships function like a market where individuals have a socio-sexual value and where sexual hierarchies prevail. To conceptualise these hierarchies, they have popularised an ever-expanding lexicon that is hard to keep up with. In their world, *alpha* males (or *Chads*) are sexually successful and attract *Stacys* (their female equivalents), while *betas* are less favoured by nature and less likely to find a partner. Pseudoscientific theories based on dubious interpretations of evolutionary psychology abound in incel communities, including modified versions of the Pareto principle (20 per cent of men get 80 per cent of women), the idea that women are naturally 'hypergamous' or want 'higher' status men.

Anyone taking a virtual walk through incel discussion groups will see the self-loathing and simultaneous dehumanisation of women that prevail in them. To deal with their situation, incels adopt different strategies. Some attempt self-improvement (*maxxing*). These can include fairly harmless, if dubious, activities such as *mewing* (doing tongue exercises for a stronger jawline) as well as genuinely good ideas like getting a better haircut. But at the extreme end of the spectrum there is *hardmaxxing*, which can include using steroids, resorting to cosmetic surgery or even smashing one's own facial bones to achieve the kind of chiselled look women supposedly desire. Those who have abandoned the dream of escaping inceldom can *LDAR* (lay down and rot) and fellow community members will give them advice on how to commit suicide. Most extreme of all, a section of the incel movement advocates for the *rapepill*: raping women as a remedy to one's sexual frustration.

Maeve Park, who works for Groundswell, a counter-extremism organisation that does prevention training around male supremacy, says incels have worked hard to normalise their ideas and recruit more men. 'Incels online are interested in talking to each other but they want to talk to others too,' Park says. They have crept out from their shady forums and moved to mainstream social media platforms. Wherever young people congregate online, there are incels. A study by Dr Lisa Sugiura found widespread incel content on TikTok, which uses memes and appealing viral videos to appeal to young men.[8] 'When they first emerged, incels wanted to show they were uniquely worse off, now they want to say: "We're like every other guy, all men are being rejected",' Park adds. It's this message that, if it takes hold, adds a level of danger that goes beyond widely publicised terrorist attacks. As my colleague at the Institute for Strategic Dialogue (ISD) Tim Squirrell puts it: 'The problem is that ideology has become quite pervasive. There is a genuine threat to women and girls, which is normalised through manosphere ideologies, and then normalised further when those things get into the mainstream.'

From being a niche discussion topic in incel forums, looksmaxxing has become a TikTok trend driven by influencers quickly building audiences off fears they have greatly contributed to manufacturing and telling teenage boys and young men that they are inadequate. The aim is to look like the Australian model Jordan Barrett, whose canthal tilt (the angle your eyes slant at) is deemed to be irresistible to women, or Patrick Bateman, the serial killer from *American Psycho*, who is venerated in male supremacist communities as an example of the pseudoscientific sexual archetype of the 'sigma male', first forwarded by the far-right science-fiction writer and blogger Theodore Robert Beale on a fringe nationalist website in 2010.

My friend Will isn't an incel. He is involved in the world of Men's Rights Activists, or MRAs. This movement is the 'think tank' of the manosphere. MRAs articulate real problems that affect men – men's physical and mental health struggles, suicide and loneliness – but these issues provide a shield for an anti-feminist world view steeped in the belief that feminism has created a society which oppresses men. To prove their points, MRAs will cherry-pick niche studies not indicative of broader trends and cite controversial and decontextualised data. One of the most prominent groups is A Voice for Men, the website-cum-business founded by Paul Elam. Will 'quite likes' Elam and thinks he does 'good work' although he acknowledges some of his methods are 'problematic'. What he finds problematic he won't say: perhaps Elam declaring October 'bash a violent bitch month' and stating that women would not be raped if they didn't carry an 'I'M A STUPID, CONNIVING BITCH – PLEASE RAPE ME neon sign glowing above their empty little narcissistic heads'.[9]

There are myriad advocacy groups, websites and social media accounts dedicated to advancing MRA talking points. Take for example an Instagram account like @TheTinMen. With its over 66,000 followers at the time of writing, it presents itself as a reflection of the 'unpopular other half of gender equality' and purports to discuss men's health. Its highly curated posts include stock pictures of good-looking men staring at distant sunsets with reassuring messages ('You are not toxic') and innocent conversation starters ('What's it like to be a man?'). At first glance, the posts can be difficult to distinguish from the work of organisations promoting social justice. Look closer though, and you'll soon realise the account is primarily dedicated to exposing 'misandry' (hatred of men), alleged widespread violence and prejudice against men and attacking feminism. An example of a post describes feminism as 'an angry and persistent fly; that instead of advocating for women and girls, seems more interested in whining, ranting and shaming men'.[10] Swat that fly, and men can get on with the important job of staring at those lovely sunsets.

MRAs are professional disinformation peddlers who are adept at the game of 'two truths and a lie'. Debunking them is a painstaking exercise.[11] They spend a lot of time crafting their arguments and campaigning, and because they have a veneer of credibility they are able to achieve communication and policy wins. Gillette, otherwise known for its broadly progressive campaigning, including a 2019 pro-#MeToo advertising campaign which triggered its own right-wing backlash,[12] launched a public relations (PR) campaign in France in 2021 on International Men's Day, failing to recognise that the said 'international day' is not an official one, despite its Wikipedia page, and was founded by an MRA activist located in Trinidad and Tobago.[13] In the same campaign, Gillette inadvertently cited data from French MRA groups.

Will, I discovered after a quick look at his Facebook account (which I confess I didn't pay much attention to before), is not someone who has just stumbled upon an MRA website and is dipping his toes in the movement. He has produced YouTube videos about the 'conspiracy against men' and is well connected to major figures in the movement. Like many MRAs, Will feels strongly about the two key issues of the movement: alleged systemic physical and sexual violence against men (perpetrated by women) and fathers' rights, which he says are non-existent. Will believes in widespread data cover-ups about discrimination against men. 'Men don't want to admit they are abused,' he says; 'If a man gets hit by his girlfriend, it doesn't get measured, and it's not understood to be as bad if a woman did it.' Angered by his brother's experience, Will has formed the belief that men do not have equal rights when it comes to child custody, although independent legal studies have found no bias against fathers.

At the beginning of our conversation Will tells me that he is 'probably a feminist' and only wants equal rights. Minutes later, he says that 'the domestic abuse industry was a chance for feminist organisations to get political power with their ideological agenda.' While there is no bias against fathers, individual men may have perceived or real grievances in custody battles and may experience real pain. I am not an insider in Will's brother's custody battle and don't know whether justified grievances played a part in his radicalisation, but it is quite clear that he has taken this experience to run to dark places. He has also made rationalisations for domestic violence. That tells me a lot.

While incels rage at hypergamous women and MRAs compile statistics and try to undermine feminism one campaign at a time, Pickup Artists, or PUAs, teach men how to subjugate women and trick them into sex. Early examples of these male supremacist seduction coaches include Roosh V, who ran a now defunct website called Return of Kings in the early 2010s where he explained 'why women should not be allowed to vote', as well as the journalist Neil Strauss, who in his book *The Game* recounted his undercover work in elite PUA communities (becoming a participant in the movement in the process). Contrary to ordinary relationship coaches, PUAs use pseudoscience to encourage various forms of manipulative, coercive and predatory behaviour, with many arguing that men can dispense with consent because, as Roosh V wrote in a piece that suggested rape should be legal in non-public places, 'Her No Means Yes'.[14]

Taking the almost opposite attitude to the pickup artists are the Men Going Their Own Way (MGTOW), the men's separatist movement which advocates for the rejection of our 'feminist' society and encourages men to disengage from women as much as possible: from rejecting long-term relationships to completely avoiding contact with them. They too subscribe to a mix of pseudoscientific ideas that overlap with other male supremacist communities: like incels, MGTOWs subscribe to the idea of female hypergamy, but like MRAs they believe there is widespread discrimination against men and false rape accusations. The movement's arguments gained popularity after #MeToo when MGTOW saw an opportunity to exploit misogynistic misconceptions about how easy it is for women to make false accusations, despite the fact that a man is 230 times more likely to be raped than to be falsely accused of rape.[15]

These distinctions have become somewhat less relevant in recent years as influencers seek to create their own 'brand' and differentiate themselves from others (who are peddling the exact same ideas). They will mix and match and borrow language from different sub-groups, with sometimes a dominant strand: some red pill rhetoric mixed with PUA and a smattering of MGTOW, for instance. They package this as self-help and use rhetorical and marketing tricks to capture attention.

## Building recruitment machines: the charismatic scammers

Sophie thought she knew her boyfriend of nine years. One day, though, he began to change. He started criticising her clothes, saying she was unfeminine. He started calling her a 'low value' woman. Sophie's boyfriend, as she revealed to *Vice*, was watching videos of Andrew Tate. Today, Tate is infamous. A study by Hope not Hate in the UK found more 16- and 17-year-old boys had watched his videos than had heard of the prime minister.[16] Another found that more than a quarter of UK men aged 18 to 29 agreed with his opinions on women.[17]

And those opinions are abhorrent. Tate has claimed that women are their husband's property and that women in relationships should stay at home. In 2016, he was kicked off reality show *Big Brother* after a video emerged showing him repeatedly striking a woman with a belt. More footage showed Tate describing how he would deal with a woman who accused him of cheating: 'It's bang out the machete, boom in her face and grip her by the neck. Shut up bitch.'[18] By the time social media platforms banned him in the summer of 2022, he had already amassed a legion of fans among teenage boys.

The speed at which Tate went from failed reality TV contestant to an influencer who sparked waves of harassment in schools baffled many commentators,[19] especially those who were not Tate's target audience. Yet the appeal is not so hard to understand: Tate achieved fame by promising to give young men muscular bodies, big cars and sexy girls – everything that mainstream society has always told them they should want. He uses hyperbolic and hubristic language that entertains and attracts some with its self-confidence: 'I never ever fail. This is why I am the greatest man alive. I'm never, ever wrong.'[20]

By the time of his arrest in Romania in December 2022 on sex trafficking charges, Tate had more followers on social media than Kim Kardashian and Donald Trump combined and had exposed millions of men like Sophie's partner to his worldview. He had also sucked thousands into an online course which combines scamming with cultic dynamics, all steeped in violent male supremacist rhetoric.

The story of the rise and fall of Tate is a classic tale of the kind of 'get rich quick' scam that pervades the internet, but it is also a story of grooming and cultic manipulation. He ran The Real World (formerly Hustlers University), an online programme that aims to be an alternative to mainstream education and purportedly teaches young men how to earn six-figure salaries, become alphas and escape the Matrix. Journalists who went undercover on the course described it as a largely empty operation dedicated to the cult of 'Top G',[21] as Tate calls himself, that provides a shallow feeling of community and uses elements of gamification to lure men into Tate's money-making machine. One of the key ways in which participants can make money in Tate's scheme is by recruiting more men into the operation.

Tate's followers love him. At the height of his success, his fans produced thousands of videos explaining how he 'changed their lives'. This isn't surprising given the cultic dynamics used by Tate: he promises to expose a hidden reality, and his online community creates closed spaces where men can be brainwashed and cut off from alternative narratives, with its own rituals and rules ('41 Tenets' for men) and its insider language and codes, including a hand gesture inspired by yoga.[22]

While Tate was the one who became a household name, there are hundreds of charismatic male supremacist influencers thriving in the influencer economy by hooking men with a similar mix of misogyny, self-improvement promises and cultic manipulation. While Tate is what writer Benjamin Fogel calls an 'open scammer',[23] or someone who doesn't work to hide to disguise his con, others like him are exploiting men more subtly – and they know that nothing quite helps generate subscriptions like incendiary rhetoric about how feminism has destroyed men.

Take the smooth-talking Adrian Markovac, who has seven million followers on YouTube and over three million on TikTok. Markovac is a smarter version of Tate. His TikToks, aimed at the same audience, are a series of anti-public education videos telling young British men that school has nothing to offer them. He too has an alternative school for boys, the 'Winners Academy' ($20 per month), which looks a tad sharper than Tate's fake university and teaches them how to win in the new online economy. Markovac also encourages young men to give up medical care and medication for mental health conditions thereby ensuring that the young men who follow him are separated from social support structures. He has a new name for taking the red pill: 'battling the conditioning'. Hamza Ahmed, whose own 'school' promises to turn men into 'Adonises', is a self-described 'cult leader'. The Russian-born Iman Gadzhi, who presents himself as a self-made millionaire, has produced videos about 'How feminism is destroying men?',[24] and in others he is encouraging the boys to drop out of school and join the online course he runs within his 'marketing agency'.[25]

## Building a political movement: the contrarian culture warriors

The sharp-suited psychologist Jordan Peterson seems worlds away from tattooed ex-kickboxer Tate. Peterson does not use misogynistic slurs or suggest that men should hit women. His trajectory from relatively unknown psychology academic with an interest in myth to self-help guru with millions of followers on social media, a bestselling book and a devoted audience that seems to withstand his mental health breakdowns was the result of a winning formula for engagement that combined intellectually repackaged male supremacist ideas with self-help advice and a bite-sized reactionary political discourse that works well in the format of a YouTube video and also appeals to anyone fatigued with 'identity politics' and the perceived 'wokeness' of our societies.

Peterson rose to prominence in 2016 after producing a three-part YouTube series ('Professor against Political Correctness') where he opposed a federal amendment to add gender identity to the Canadian Human Rights Act and condemned his university's plans to introduce compulsory anti-bias training. The same year, a Channel 4 interview about feminism and the gender pay gap went viral online. This signalled his allegiance to a new club: he attracted praise from the far-right conspiracy theorist Paul-Joseph Watson and Gavin McInnes, the founder of the Proud Boys, the violent far-right male supremacist militia group which featured prominently in the January 6 Capitol insurrection.

Peterson has claimed that 'the idea that women were oppressed throughout history is an appalling theory' and become a compassionate voice for disillusioned young men and misunderstood incels. In a TV interview with Piers Morgan, he cried when asked if he was a hero to the incel community: 'All these men who are alienated, it's like they're lonesome and they don't know what to do and everyone piles abuse on them' he said. Using dubious insights from evolutionary psychology and extrapolating from Jungian psychology, Peterson has argued that hierarchies and divisions in human societies are partly rooted in nature and provide fundamental truths, providing a veneer of intellectual credibility to basic male supremacist arguments about socio-sexual hierarchies.

The men who follow Peterson speak about him with the same wide-eyed admiration as Tate's disciples. For all the justifiable criticism that can be levelled at him, Peterson does seem to care at least a little bit about men's plight. A clinical psychologist, he delivers the kind of advice that men could hear in therapy. The insights he dispenses encourage self-responsibility and basic forms of self-care. He has counselled men to make their bed, stand up straight and treat themselves with respect, the kind of sage wisdom that has led to him being labelled 'Gwyneth Paltrow for incels'.[26] Of course, men do not need to turn to culture warriors to be told to make their beds or stand up straight. 'As uncomfortable as this reality is', Kelly tells me, 'it's the misogyny that is the most compelling ingredient.' By telling men that they can be in control of their lives, Peterson implicitly acknowledges that men were not in control before and that feminism and 'wokeness' are to blame.

Peterson remains a leading voice in a constellation of culture warriors who have turned reactionary politics, anti-feminist ideas and opposition to 'cancel culture' into a recipe for online engagement. They present themselves as brave iconoclasts who challenge accepted orthodoxy and act as bulwarks against more serious forms of extremist rhetoric. Former *New York Times* journalist Bari Weiss hailed them as the 'Intellectual Dark Web' in a 2018 article, listing Peterson among other 'iconoclastic thinkers, academic renegades and media personalities' shunned by mainstream institutions and building 'their own mass media channels'.[27] Weiss herself appears to have seen the professional potential in this: after accusing *The New York Times* of censoriousness and resigning, she launched her own media platform, *The Free Press*, announced the establishment of an 'anti-cancel-culture' university and hosted a sold-out debate about whether the 'sexual revolution has failed women', with tickets selling for $165.

Far from acting as a bulwark against anything, the YouTube channels of the anti-identity politics culture warriors are often the first stop for social media platforms' algorithms. A report by ISD, for instance, found that Australian boys and men were recommended male supremacist and anti-abortion content by YouTube's algorithms regardless of their expressed political interests.[28] Within hours of their creation, accounts set up to look like they belong to young men were recommended videos of Jordan Peterson 'taking down' feminists. Liking and engaging with Peterson's videos led to more overtly male supremacist content. Setting up an account belonging to a 19-year-old man and following YouTube recommendations led to the user being recommended videos about male serial killers of women within 90 minutes of being created, overtly male supremacist content by day two and content glorifying Hitler by day four, showing that if you're a young man tuning into English-speaking YouTube, things can escalate very quickly indeed.

This constellation of contrarians who are voicing 'unpopular opinions', particularly around gender and race and supposedly 'natural' hierarchies and realities, has shifted the Overton window of acceptable conversation. These figures have established their own sprawling ecosystem of YouTube channels, media outlets, podcasts and Substack newsletters where they profile each other. This includes the supposedly left-wing 'Red Scare' podcast, which has come to be associated with the New Right (a movement which seeks to reshape American conservatism along social conservative, economically protectionist and nationalist lines) and which presents itself as a critique of mainstream feminism, #MeToo and the current state of capitalism, increasingly paying lip service to the latter so it can concentrate on the former. Or the anti-identity politics magazine *Compact*, which promotes greater state intervention and seemingly pro-workers policies alongside anti-abortion views. Peter Thiel, the billionaire founder of PayPal, has emerged as a major funder of some of these anti-identity politics initiatives.[29] In addition to funding Weiss's new university, he also funds the anti-feminist and far-right women's magazine *Evie* and a related cycle tracking app.[30]

The centrality of the podcast format in this constellation is embodied by Joe Rogan, who once tweeted that he hoped men calling themselves feminists would 'choke to death on vegan pizza while crying over a Lady Gaga song'.[31] His mega podcast (which receives 11 million streaming downloads per episode) features a range of guests, which have included Jordan Peterson and Gavin McInnes who said appearing on the podcast boosted recruitment. Rogan himself, who interviewed and endorsed Trump during the 2024 campaign, has been caught uttering racist and sexist remarks (for which he has later apologised) alongside more broadly anti-feminist rhetoric, saying for instance that feminist men are 'sneaky and unattractive'.[32] None of this sounds particularly pleasant or subtle, but compared to other male supremacists these are 'soft' anti-feminist views which flatter young men's worldviews and allow Rogan to maintain plausible deniability.

## Exploiting health and body anxieties: the wellness influencers

'I believe men and women are not created equal; that's why a man is called a man and a woman is called a woman. I believe that we are complementary opposites. I believe that men are purpose-built to fight, to provide and to protect.'[33] The man speaking is impossibly muscular and tanned and is walking bare chested and barefoot in the desert, holding hands with a beautiful, smiling, silent woman. His name is Brian Johnson, but to more than two million followers on Instagram he is 'Liver King', and he is striding across the desert with his Queen. Johnson is the bushy-bearded bodybuilder who has built a social media and fitness empire by promoting himself as the 'CEO of the ancestral lifestyle', and he is on a mission to restore weak, emasculated men to their strong prehistoric selves. Johnson, who used to work for his wife in her dental practice, is seen in his various Instagram videos walking shirtless, lifting weights and eating enormous amounts of organ meat, including bull testicles. He talks about himself in the third person and addresses his followers as 'primals'. In his palaeolithic fantasy world, men kill their prey, bring the food back to the tribe and protect their women, while today's men are 'submissive, subprimal and weak'.

While Tate appeals to men who want to get rich quick and Peterson to those in search of political discourse, Liver King is the wellness influencer who has turned men's anxiety about their bodies and their place in the world into his own money-making machine. His persona is highly constructed and not entirely serious: he apparently hired a brand consultant to create his caveman brand and empire.[34] And it really is an empire. In 2022, he told *GQ* he made $100 million through his various business ventures, which included Ancestral Supplements, a now defunct company that sold organ meat-based supplements for men who were hoping to achieve Liver King's physique.[35] Inevitably, this enterprise proved to be a scam, not just because he peddled nutritional misinformation to sell his supplements but also because he achieved his looks not by following his 'nine tenets for life' as he claimed but by consuming around $11,000 a month's worth of anabolic steroids. When outed as a fraud and forced to issue an apology on YouTube, he claimed all he wanted to do was to give direction to young men 'who are hurting'. [36]

Liver King is just one of a growing number of wellness influencers who are encouraging men to self-optimise in a society that wants to emasculate them, combining lifestyle advice with grave warnings about masculinity under attack and the need to return to an idealised past where real, healthy men could provide for their equally healthy, nurturing women. There are hundreds of them and they range in style from the *Übermensch* with a predilection for weightlifting and meat to those with a softer style who use New Age rhetoric and encourage men to rediscover their 'divine masculinity', and anything in between. Like the self-styled men's lifestyle coach (180,000 followers on Instagram) who is warning that 'feminists are destroying the family unit',[37] devoting countless videos to men's declining testosterone, while promoting his programme which promises to turn his clients into 'confident, testosterone-fuelled [men] who live [their] masculine purpose'.[38]

Matthew Remski is a cult survivor and the co-author of *Conspirituality* (2023), a book about wellness and conspiracy theories. He says wellness influencers are embracing a reactionary gender discourse which stems from 'anxious attempts at controlling and defining what bodies are and what they are for'. Remski sees the roots of wellness influencers' rhetoric in the mythopoetic movement, which emerged in the 1980s alongside the Men's Rights Movement and saw self-improvement and male initiation rituals as a way to rebuild masculinity against the background of the advances of second-wave feminism. The mythopoetic movement saw itself as a third way between men's feminist movements and the more overtly misogynistic Men's Rights Movement. It nevertheless subscribed – and still does – to essentialist beliefs about a 'deep masculine' nature which modern society is allegedly seeking to destroy, a belief which quickly lends itself to anti-feminist impulses.

Wellness and New Age influencers have their own red pill to offer men: waking up to the reality of men's deliberate emasculation by a toxic society. They point to declining male fertility and sperm count as evidence of plots against men. Male sperm count has indeed fallen almost 60 per cent since 1973,[39] a drop that is attributed to a range of factors including environmental causes which do genuinely deserve serious examination. However, they promote a similarly anxious discourse about plummeting testosterone levels, an issue on which there is no medical consensus and few studies have been conducted.

A politicised discourse around the male body, anxieties about emasculation and the desire to return to a mythical past of masculine grandeur is not entirely new. To a certain extent, it has been a feature of the brand of reactionary authoritarian politics that has emerged in recent years. During the 2016 US election campaign, Donald Trump had his testosterone levels read during a live show.[40] In 2022, former Fox News anchor Tucker Carlson released the documentary *The End of Men* in which he made alarming claims about men's fast disappearing testosterone, attributing the decline to corporate greed and a nebulous political agenda to destroy masculinity. To remedy the problem, Carlson advocates for red light therapy on testicles, promoting a company called Joov which manufactures red light devices.[41] Another political figure who has blended health misinformation and concerns about the decline of masculinity is former independent presidential candidate turned Trump ally Robert F. Kennedy Jr., who was nominated to be health secretary in the wake of Trump's re-election. A long-standing anti-vaxxer, Kennedy saw his political aura increase during the pandemic as he doubled down on his anti-vaccine rhetoric. He has claimed that chemicals in the water supply are encouraging 'sexual dysphoria' among boys and feminising men, a reference to studies showing that atrazine can lead frogs to change from male to female, something that also happens in the wild.[42]

This rhetoric exploits health anxieties alongside insecurities about gender norms. Recent years have seen a rise in body dysmorphia among men, with over half of British men, for instance, exhibiting signs of the condition.[43] More young men are actively trying to 'bulk up'. In the process they are turning to wellness influencers, bodybuilders and fitness instructors who have realised that an anxious discourse about emasculation and feminism is good for audience engagement and algorithmic amplification. The portrayal of the ideal male body in modern culture does little to reassure these men. The male bodies on screen are increasingly muscular, a phenomenon for which the Marvel movie franchise bears no small responsibility: witness Hugh Jackman's ever more defined muscles across the span of the *X-Men* and *Wolverine* films. The use of anabolic steroids has increased significantly in recent years in Western countries: around three to four million Americans use them for cosmetic or performance purposes,[44] with research bodies also reporting an increase in usage in the UK.[45]

## Restoring strong (white) men: the fascist foodies

'Ladies, delete your dating apps. They are full of soyboy simps. Go to the grocery store and look confused in the meat section instead. Full of meat eating men dying to help you decide between ribeye and New York strip.'[46] 'Carnivore Aurelius' is an anonymous wellness influencer who provides a mix of lifestyle and nutrition advice combined with male supremacist discourse and soft fascism, all propping up a business of dehydrated beef liver crisps and collagen supplements. Posts about different modern-day toxins go hand in hand with those about how contemporary society and feminism have destroyed men and women's life purpose, with token references to stoicism as a form of life hack (hence the name of the account and its use of a picture of a statue of Emperor Marcus Aurelius). Carnivore Aurelius has a lot to say to women. The account uses a mix of crude sexism and slut-shaming ('due to hoeflation, one good girl is now worth 5,000 b★tches'),[47] which it then counterbalances with posts praising the pure housewife in touch with her divine femininity, embodying health, fertility and modesty.

The account has a strong odour of the Proud Boys with its fetishisation of the housewife and soft white nationalist imagery, but it is Proud Boys-like rhetoric adapted for Instagram appeal. 'Men used to go to war for women; now they split the bill on their $41 first date,'[48] the account sadly intones, while multiple posts encourage men to rescue women from their 'soul sucking 9-to-5' jobs. Mothers are glorified: 'Mothers are literal superheros [*sic*]. Every birth is a glimpse into the divine,' say posts featuring stock images of blonde women dipping their toes in water or frolicking in fields surrounded by equally blonde children.[49] Carnivore Aurelius has an obsessive focus on female purity and sexuality and is relentless in his evangelising for the need to protect women from the depravity of a career and the toxicity of birth control. *Buzzfeed* investigated whether the ultra-macho influencer was secretly a woman, apparently considering that the account reflected women's fantasies of being courted by a warrior and protector – something that the person behind the keyboard disproved.[50]

Carnivore Aurelius is a representative of a new breed of semi-tongue-in-cheek male supremacist influencers who share a mix of nutritional and health pseudoscience and fascistic rhetoric about returning to a purer civilisation. He encourages the consumption of organ meat (perhaps unsurprisingly, given he also sells organ-based supplements) by men and women, to restore the former to past strength and to ensure the latter's fertility. He has a particular distaste for seed oils, which have become the centre of conspiracy theories promoted, among others, by male supremacists, the far-right and wellness communities, who all see them as toxic and like to compare them (deceptively) to 'engine lubricant'.[51] He also promotes other foods – including raw milk – which have become political signifiers for wellness enthusiasts, the far-right and traditional conservatives alike.[52]

Diets which are popular among these influencers are restrictive and tend to range from the fairly moderate paleo to the extreme carnivore diet. The prominent anti-feminist influencers have all made forays into diet-related commentary. Rogan, Peterson and Tate have all praised the carnivore diet. For the record, following a paleo diet, or any diet, does not make one a male supremacist or a far-right sympathiser. Food, which has always been political, has however become a tool for male supremacists to popularise their ideas, connect with the health-conscious and various other interest groups and hook men into a wider belief system about gender norms at a time of nutritional confusion, when headlines give the impression that we don't know if eggs are a 'superfood' or a silent killer. More and more research is showing that algorithms are taking us to more extreme diet-related content.[53]

Another similarity between Carnivore Aurelius and the Proud Boys is their common rejection of pornography and masturbation, which is also becoming a mainstream wellness trend. Semen retention has a long history, including in the practice of Hatha yoga (where it's called *vajroli mudra*). The NoFap movement, a movement of men who eschew masturbation, believing it to be harmful to men's health and depleting them of their energy, has grown in popularity. Early contemporary adopters of NoFap are the Proud Boys, who follow a regime of sexual frugality because it allegedly boosts testosterone levels.[54] More and more red pill influencers are also encouraging sexual abstinence as a form of masculine strength and an exercise in (self-)control. Reports have shown that NoFap communities have grown online, driven by men who increasingly feel dissatisfied with their sexual habits.[55] A 2022 peer-reviewed urology study found 'semen retention' to be the most popular search related to men's health.[56] In itself, the desire to quit pornography, given its predatory nature and the misogynistic scripts it promotes, can be considered laudable. The problem is what other discourse and groups men encounter when searching for tips on quitting porn.

## Gaming the 'sexual market': the dating coaches

'Are you a High-Value Man?' The duo asking the question are Walter Weekes and Myron Gaines, presenters of *Fresh&Fit*, a podcast that helps men navigate the 'three Fs' of 'females, fitness, and finances'. *Fresh&Fit* started out as a fitness podcast but grew rapidly when the hosts started branching out into dating advice. Then they realised that they could go viral by stating on air that 'a woman having an Instagram is 100 per cent cheating, especially if she has scantily clad photos of herself on the internet,' comparing having a girlfriend to owning a car and otherwise talking about women like objects for men's gratification who need to be coerced, disciplined and made to obey men's orders.[57]

Though demonetised by YouTube, their channel has 1.5 million followers and it has moved on to the alternative streaming platform Rumble. Co-host Gaines has a self-published book called *Why Women Deserve Less* (2023), which gives an overview of his sexual politics and in which he writes that 'the relationship between most men and women throughout all of history has been transactional. It has been prostitution. All men are Johns. All women are whores.'[58] If this sounds extreme, it is a belief which, in diluted form, has gained mainstream currency, as pseudoscientific ideas about socio-sexual hierarchies and crude ideas of sexual economics previously peddled by incels are entering collective discourse about dating and relationships.

Sexual Economics Theory, a notion popularised by social psychologist Roy Baumeister and marketing academic Kathleen Vohs to argue that heterosexual relationships function like a market, is also popular in the field of evolutionary psychology, which views human behaviour through the lens of evolutionary adaptation and whose findings male supremacists love to (mis)appropriate for their own worldview. Male supremacists' obsessive focus is on 'female mating strategy', particularly female 'hypergamy', the idea that women are biologically hard-wired to seek an alpha man. Academic studies have confirmed that this is largely nonsense and that male supremacist communities' use of evolutionary psychology mixes 'scientific theories and hypotheses with personal narratives, sexual double standards and misogynistic beliefs'.[59]

Sexual Market Value, one's desirability on the dating market, pervades male supremacist communities which have their made-up hierarchies, but it is an idea that can be capitalised upon in an age of growing insecurity where all of us have been encouraged by decades of neoliberalism to think of ourselves as brands. Male supremacists whip up these insecurities to sell their coaching but also use them to normalise the idea that women's sexuality needs to be controlled. Talk of the 'body count' (number of sexual partners one has had, specifically women's body count) has long pervaded male supremacist communities. Tate, for whom women are property, has stated that 'a lot of the world's problems could be fixed if women walked around with their body count on their foreheads' and that her body count is a measure of a woman's value (women should have a low body count but men are allowed to have as many sexual partners as they desire).[60] Discussion about the 'body count' verges on the obsessive on *Fresh&Fit* and features prominently in the discourse of red pill YouTubers. Vox pop videos asking people about the number of sexual partners they have had are reportedly gaining popularity on TikTok, as ideas previously peddled by fringe misogynistic groups become part of mainstream online conversation.[61]

In the contemporary sexual market where competition for good partners is rife, both men and women need to be 'high value', although what high value means depends on whom you ask. For *Fresh&Fit*, qualifying as a high-value man entails a variety of things, including earning at least $100,000 a year and engaging in coercive and controlling behaviour such as forbidding one's girlfriend from posting selfies online. The idea of the high-value man itself testifies to the rebranding and repackaging of male supremacist rhetoric as an aspirational lifestyle. The man who popularised the phrase was YouTuber and self-styled 'image consultant' Kevin Samuels, who died suddenly in 2022 just as his star was rising. Samuels, who dressed in slick tailored suits, was stylish and softly spoken. His work evolved from personal styling to dating advice geared towards Black men and women – which was more successful than his sartorial tips. Samuels used his YouTube channel to insult women, calling them 'fat' and 'lazy' and describing unmarried women over 35 as 'leftover': this led to a rapid increase in audience. Despite being called a 'plain-spoken, hypermasculine authority' by the *The New York Times* in his obituary,[62] what Samuels was, really, was a PUA. However, he replaced talk of being an alpha male with more aspirational language compatible with his corporate image.

It is not hard to see where beliefs in sexual economics lead us:[63] psychology researchers who made men watch videos promoting these views discovered they were quick, first, to agree with them and, second, to adopt 'adversarial views of heterosexual relationships' – in other words, to see women as an enemy that needs to be defeated.[64] The fact that many men lap up these narratives when exposed to them is because they sound scientifically plausible and offer a compelling explanation for their dating struggles. That need for control is something we all experience to a greater or lesser extent and explains, among many things, the long-standing popularity of the personality and dating quizzes which allow us to put ourselves in neat categories. Take as an example the 'green line test', a nonsensical theory based on pseudo-body language created in 2020 by male supremacist troll Rivelino.

Rivelino went viral on TikTok and received no less than 11.2 billion views by purporting to show who wields power in relationships by taking photos of celebrity couples, drawing a green line between them and analysing the angle at which partners lean towards each other. According to his flawless logic, alpha males stand tall, while men who lean towards their partners have a 'weak mindset' and are 'needy'. Emboldened by his success, Rivelino has made masculinity tests and associated shaming his online trademark, also coming up with other theories about the direction of men's crotches on photos and whether male celebrities are covering their genitalia (or whether they have 'cock confidence' or 'cock shame'). Trump and Putin, it will come as no surprise, are the sort of 'cock proud' leaders other men should emulate.[65]

This sort of viral game based on misogynistic pseudoscience provides quick gratification, but it also displays the fundamental need we have to find patterns and order in our lives. Apps like Tinder have turned dating into an actual marketplace, governed by algorithmic efficiency and a set-up of supply and demand which is difficult to escape. New words to describe online dating behaviours, many of them pointing to people's disposability and none of them good for one's self-esteem, have emerged: orbiting, ghosting and breadcrumbing, to name but a few.[66] Transactional views of dating inevitably leads to the idea that in a ruthless market everything is fair game. A man made headlines when he used ChatGPT to talk to 5,239 women on Tinder,[67] successfully meeting his wife at the end of it and presumably unbothered by the other 5,238 women who were deceived into believing they were interacting with a real person. New disturbing dating trends are emerging, including 'penny dating', a technique which entails encouraging men to treat women like a piggy bank and invest minimally in relationships.[68] It should come as no surprise that men who are taking their cues from the likes of *Fresh&Fit*'s Gaines, who has claimed that 'women deserve less' and that modern women have become entitled as a result of feminism, should have no qualms about using such tactics.

A 2022 Ipsos/King's College London poll of 20,000 men in 30 countries found that 33 per cent think that traditional masculinity is under threat and a fifth believe that feminism has led to economic, political and social power loss for men.[69] A 2023 study titled 'The state of American men' by Equimundo, an international organisation that focuses on involving men in gender equality, meanwhile, showed that 40 per cent of men polled across every age group 'trust one or more "men's rights", anti-feminist, or pro-violence voices from the manosphere'. This figure rose to nearly half for younger men.[70] The most trusted figures include Peterson, Tate and Paul Elam's A Voice for Men, a key reference for my friend Will.

Given the reach of these arguments, is it that surprising that I found a hardened MRA in my close circle? I knew Will for years and his connection to the MRA movement remained completely unknown to me until things suddenly began to escalate. That connection had gradually become stronger. There are many starting points for such journeys. They are sparked by a combination of online and offline influence. Will came to his ideas through personal experience, but online narratives provided the informational framework for him to be convinced. This discourse is now served by influencers to men who might be looking for advice on fitness, diet, politics or dating – or whose brothers happen to be experiencing a bitter custody battle. It is just one click away.

# 2

# Shadowy witch-hunts and the #MeToo backlash

It was a spring day in 1692, in a church in Salem, Massachusetts. The atmosphere in the little colonial town had changed of late. It had always been an unsettled, quarrelsome place, but something was new. A group of young women had begun acting strangely. Witchcraft was suspected. And suddenly, allegations began flying. And in the quiet of the church that Sunday morning, the voice of one of the chief accusers, Ann Putnam Jr, rang out:

'Look where Goodwife Cloyce sits on the beam suckling her yellow bird between her fingers!'[1]

Sarah Cloyce was interrogated and imprisoned shortly afterwards.

Women, it was believed in Puritan New England, were inherently more sinful than men. The two older sisters of Sarah Cloyce, Rebecca Nurse and Mary Eastey, had both been accused of witchcraft earlier. In a statement of solidarity with her imprisoned sister Rebecca, Sarah had previously made a dramatic exit from the Salem Village meeting house, slamming the door behind her after the pastor, Samuel Parris, announced his text for the day: John 6:70 – 'Have not I chosen you twelve, and one is a devil.'

Sarah Cloyce stood up for her sisters and was targeted for it. She was called out in church – a public space. Trials and interrogations took place in public, and alongside the official proceedings ran the mill of gossip, rumour and speculation of the fascinated onlookers.

Today, the Witch Trials of 1692 are famous: a tourism gold mine for the town of Salem. The witch-hunts of history, a misogynistic tool to punish women who did not conform to social norms, have become the metaphor of choice for powerful men wanting to avoid accountability for their own sexual misconduct and a host of other crimes and wrongdoings after #MeToo. In 2018, Donald Trump used the word 'witch-hunt' over 110 times in his tweets, including to refer to the investigation by special prosecutor Robert Mueller into possible collusion with Russian interference in the 2016 presidential election.[2]

The 'witch-hunt' metaphor itself encapsulates the male supremacist project: it aims to turn the dominant group into the victimised one and suck meaning out of language to better disguise the witch-hunts taking place today. We are living in an era of new shadowy witch-hunts against women. These witch-hunts, which largely play out online, are about shaping women's fate in the real world. They take many forms, but one in particular captured the attention of the world and serves as a powerful illustration of how male supremacists try to sway public opinion, undermine women's rights and shift the dial, sweeping us into their world.

## Pointing the finger

'Let's burn Amber!!!'

It was a private message that was destined to be seen by the world. Johnny Depp, one of the biggest film stars in Hollywood, texted his friend and fellow actor Paul Bettany in 2016. He was referring to his ex-wife, Amber Heard.

Bettany texted back with his own thoughts. 'Having thought about it I don't think we should burn Amber – she's delightful company and easy on the eye, plus I'm not sure she's a witch. We could of course do the English course of action in these predicaments – we do a drowning test. Thoughts? NB I have a pool', he wrote. 'Let's drown her before we burn her!!! I will f*** her burnt corpse afterwards to make sure she's dead' was Depp's reply. The exchanges, the actor later argued, were a Monty Python-inspired joke.

Jokes focused on violence against women would become a theme of *Depp v. Heard*, the nearly seven-week-long defamation trial that took place in Fairfax, Virginia, which saw Heard and

Depp pitted against one another in a court of law. 'I defended my truth and in doing so my life as I knew it was destroyed. The vilification I have faced on social media is an amplified version of the ways in which women are re-victimised when they come forward.'[3] With these words, published on her Instagram account on 19 December 2022, Heard settled one of the most followed and watched defamation lawsuits in history, putting an end to over three years of legal proceedings. The aim of the *Depp v. Heard* lawsuit was simple: to determine whether Heard had wrongfully accused her ex-husband, Hollywood star Johnny Depp, of domestic abuse, an experience she detailed in a 2018 *Washington Post* opinion piece wherein she described herself as a 'victim of domestic abuse', without explicitly naming Depp.[4] Depp claimed the op-ed affected his reputation and career. He sued for defamation and demanded $50 million in damages.

The world of Hollywood is no stranger to scandalous divorces or widely publicised lawsuits. What made the *Depp v. Heard* trial unique was its nature: over close to seven weeks, millions around the world tuned into the live-streamed celebrity trial on TV and online. Thousands of individuals took part in a collective humiliation exercise against Heard online. Major social media platforms, from YouTube to TikTok, descended into a torrent of misogynistic memes, 'ironic' hate-filled tweets and abuse towards Heard.

Some of the abuse borrowed directly from Depp's graphically violent repertoire as text messages by the actor resurfaced during the trial. Thousands of ordinary social media users painted Heard as a 'gold-digger', a 'whore' and a 'flappy fish market', using Depp's alleged words against her. Videos with the titles 'Johnny Depp calls Amber Turd a "FLAPPY FISH MARKET" LMAOOO' and 'Why is Amber Heard an abusive, narcissistic b★★★★?' were some of the most-watched on YouTube.[5] In June 2022, at the end of the trial, a jury ruled in favour of Depp and found that Heard had acted with 'malice' in describing herself as a victim of abuse. Millions of those who tuned into the trial online felt the same.

Though the scales of justice may have appeared balanced, outside the courtroom a parallel battle was taking place. *Depp v. Heard* was also being fought online, by different actors, for different reasons. And in the court of social media and public opinion, one side had a definite advantage. While the legal battle was unfolding in the courts, a large-scale influence campaign was taking place online to make the trial a referendum on the #MeToo movement. It was orchestrated by powerful political interests, facilitated by male supremacist networks and channels and capitalised upon by right-wing media and opportunistic brands. In the process it was hugely successful in sweeping up ordinary citizens who became complicit in the exercise.

On 5 October 2017, an investigative piece in *The New York Times* exposed widespread allegations of sexual assault against Hollywood producer Harvey Weinstein, paving the way for the development of the largest ever internet-led feminist protest movement under the hashtag #MeToo.[6] The hashtag, which connected millions of women across the world through a shared experience, exposed the failures of the legal system in holding perpetrators of sexual violence accountable. As results were not being achieved in the courts, calls for justice were transferred to the online world.

After years of impunity, #MeToo brought hope of accountability and seemed to lead to the downfall of a small handful of powerful abusers: Harvey Weinstein, Louis C.K. and Kevin Spacey. The consequences, of course, were only temporary: nine months after *The New York Times* published allegations of sexual abuse against Louis C.K., the comedian was back on stage, and many of the men who suffered consequences are working hard on their comeback.

The backlash against #MeToo was swift and started almost immediately. 'Has #MeToo gone too far?' asked a *New York Times* op-ed as early as January 2018.[7] An NPR–Ipsos poll the same year found that 40 per cent of Americans would answer yes to that question.[8] 'Women reveal why they hate #MeToo movement' ran a piece in the *Daily Mail*, among dozens of similar headlines.[9] A year after the *New York Times* investigation, University of Houston researchers found beliefs about false rape and harassment accusations – a key argument of male supremacist groups – to be widespread: 19 per cent of men said they were reluctant to hire attractive women and 27 per cent said they avoided meetings alone with female colleagues.[10]

Four years after #MeToo first trended, male supremacists saw an opportunity to turn the Depp–Heard trial into a referendum on the movement writ large and put a nail in the coffin of an ailing movement. When the trial began, many of us were hooked on social media updates. Very quickly, though, a few people noticed that something did not feel right. Daniel Maki, a former member of the Canadian intelligence community and now a director at a private investigation firm, was trying not to pay attention to the courtroom drama everyone else was eagerly following. Two years before the Virginia trial, a UK court had ruled in favour of *The Sun* against Depp, who had sued the tabloid over its use of the phrase 'wife beater' to describe him. The UK court ruled that Amber Heard provided enough evidence to show that that term was accurate.[11]

Maki is a survivor of sexual assault and abuse, hence his desire not to receive continual updates on the case. 'The #MeToo movement had given me the courage to confront my abuser; it was a turning-point in my life,' he says. On the first day of the trial, his timeline was flooded with posts supporting Johnny Depp, calling Amber Heard a liar and attacking the #MeToo movement. He clicked the 'not interested' button on Twitter (now X). It didn't work. He kept doing it but Twitter wasn't responding. More pro-Depp content just kept flooding in. 'Saying you don't want to see something is the strongest signal you can possibly give to a social media platform and its recommendation systems. And no matter what I did, it didn't work. That's when I understood that something was really off,' he adds.

Depp, like virtually every A-list celebrity, has his super-fans. At the time of his divorce, he was an Oscar-nominated actor who had appeared in some of Hollywood's highest grossing blockbusters. Before her marriage to him, Heard's career consisted of an eclectic mix of indie films, horror movies and supporting roles in action and comedy films. To anyone with an unhealthy interest in film stars, a stereotype built on misogynistic tropes isn't hard to construct: the wife as the gold-digger desperate to get her hands on the male genius's money, as the attention-seeker riding on the coat-tails of his fame.

On 23 May 2016, Heard filed for divorce from Depp and, four days later, obtained a temporary restraining order against him, claiming that he had physically abused her. She later withdrew her request for a domestic violence restraining order, and a $7 million settlement was reached out of court on 16 August 2016. Though the news cycle moved on, one group of people did not: male supremacists and their online networks. As the headlines died away, they continued to take an interest in the case, gathering on r/TheRedPill and on their various forums.

Male supremacist YouTubers and influencers started digging into the case, producing dozens of videos, among them 'ThatUmbrellaGuy'. His profile picture features a comic book-type character with a vintage hat and a tissue covering his face, giving him the air of a 1950s detective. On his YouTube channel, which has nearly 400,000 followers, ThatUmbrellaGuy has posted hundreds of videos focusing on the Depp–Heard relationship, an interest bordering on obsession. Each video picks up thousands of views. Another such influencer is 'ThatBrianFella', who runs a YouTube channel under the name 'Incredibly Outraged' and describes himself on his X account as a 'part-time investigator/journalist'.

While the rest of the world moved on to another celebrity split, these pseudo-journalists with affinities for male supremacist arguments and too much time on their hands dedicated many hours to sifting through old footage of the couple, running image searches and producing videos about their 'bombshell discoveries'. In January 2020 ThatBrianFella posted a choppy recording of an argument between Depp and Heard, allegedly taken before their divorce, on his YouTube channel.

By the time the trial opened in 2022, they were ready: after all, they knew the 'stakes of a trial like this on victim's and men's rights'.[12] They were ready to educate men that in this trial, things were 'not as they seemed'. Indeed, things were not as they seemed. As the trial started, thousands of Depp 'fan accounts' with pictures of Jack Sparrow and names like 'DeppieWarrior' and 'ILoveJohnny' started tweeting non-stop. The bots were out, and they swept onto our timelines in a deluge.

At the same time, plenty of regular individuals were tweeting about the trial. Maki likens the experience to watching a zombie film: 'People who are not zombies yet are walking among a crowd of zombies, and you're looking around, and you're not sure what is happening.' There were some zombies on Heard's side, but there was a veritable army of the undead behind Depp. Social media analytics firm Bot Sentinel said that anti-Heard tweets' 'intentional misspelling demonstrate[d] a calculated effort to manipulate hashtag trends' during March and April 2022, and close to a quarter of accounts posting about Heard had been created in the previous seven months.[13] Depp's supporters had 100 times more reach than Heard's, according to a study by tech analytics company Cyabra.[14] That is partly a reflection of an offline imbalance of power. Male supremacists benefit from misogynistic structures of power and belief, but they also benefit from social media platforms' curation and amplification mechanisms.

## What they do in the shadows

As Johnny Depp sat down in court in Fairfax County, Virginia, millions were watching on TV, on the *Law & Crime Network.* But hundreds of thousands more were logged into YouTube, where an unremarkable-looking white man in his 30s, wearing a red hoodie, was the master of ceremonies. His name: Nick Rekieta, a YouTuber who provided live commentary of the trial every day on Rekieta Law. Though the channel ostensibly provides popular legal commentary on big legal cases, its leanings are clear. Rekieta made a name for himself with live-streamed commentary on the trial of Kyle Rittenhouse, the 17-year-old who killed two men during Black Lives Matter protests (and was acquitted), and became a hero of the far-right.

The tone is a mix of pre-match banter, appreciative commentaries directed at Depp ('That's a nice tie, I like that tie') and misogynistic comments about Heard's cheekbones. Over the weeks of the trial, Rekieta produced a daily video on proceedings, a total of 24. Rekieta Law's videos, with its mix of 'investigation', banter and mocking commentary, proved a winning recipe for audience engagement.

In December 2017, an excerpt from the far-right and antisemitic website *The Daily Stormer* was leaked. It exposed a tactical playbook on how to spread antisemitism to the masses. One of the points that received the most attention was website founder Andrew Anglin's focus on humour. 'Most people are not comfortable with material that comes across as vitriolic, raging, non-ironic hatred. The unindoctrinated should not be able to tell if we are joking or not,' read the style guide.[15] Anglin himself is the perfect illustration of the crossovers between the far-right, misogyny and other types of hate. Among many similar quotes, he wrote that 'women deserve to be beaten, raped and locked in cages.'[16]

Offensive memes and 'naughty humour' all became part of the alt-right, far-right and male supremacist playbook in the years leading up to Trump's first presidential victory. The purpose is simple: spread a message while derailing online conversation and causing chaos. On the sixth day of the trial, Depp told the court that his ex-wife had soiled their bedsheets during their marriage as an act of revenge. YouTubers were jubilant. 'Let's make #MePoo trend,' Rekieta said on his live stream, calling on viewers to tweet actively with the hashtag.

We all like to believe we are independent thinkers, but we are easily led. It is why certain styles become inexplicably fashionable suddenly, why fringe political movements can explode into the mainstream and why a little settlement in Colonial New England can start believing themselves persecuted by witches. With changing online influence, we can all be dragged into shadowy witch-hunts. Male supremacists and bots may have steered the conversation, but thousands of ordinary social media users took part in the collective humiliation of Heard. This included people who described themselves as victims of abuse but who nevertheless felt certain their hero was wronged and were sucked into a social media game of abuse.

Renée DiResta, a writer and former research manager at Stanford Internet Observatory, has compared the movement of online mobs to the murmuration of starlings, as a representation of a network where each bird's movement affects the whole.[17] Social media platforms determine what we see (recommendation algorithms), how we congregate into online groups (connection mechanisms) and what incentives we are given to take part (bait). Carl Miller, a researcher at the think tank Demos, says we are all caught up in this 'whirling tangle of influence online' without understanding how it is happening or affecting us.

There are attempts to influence us, and whether it is advertising or AI deepfakes, it has become harder to spot how we are being manipulated in recent years. The Brexit referendum and US presidential election of 2016, with their concerns about 'fake news' and Russian interference, feel far away. Since the pandemic, while the nature of online influence has undergone major changes, simultaneously online disinformation has become a mainstream concern. Like Miller, my job is to identify and study online 'influence campaigns'. It's a growing profession: in 2020, the BBC appointed a specialist social media and disinformation correspondent. My job did not exist a decade ago, and it is one that reckons with the rapidly changing nature of what is happening online. 'We see all kinds of actors involved: states, for-profit actors, extremist groups and disaffected individuals, who all become connected fellow travellers and are almost impossible to delineate and tell them apart,' Miller adds.

As with scams, influence campaigns have become more professional and convincing. Clunky bots with poor grammar have died a death, replaced by slick cash-fuelled operations. Online influence has become a professionalised for-profit industry with PR firms, corporate briefs and key performance indicators. We are only now beginning to shine a light on this as examples of disinformation-for-hire emerge. A fake London PR firm, for instance, targeted European influencers and offered to pay them to smear Pfizer's COVID-19 vaccine.[18] Both sides of an ideological conflict can wage influence war via private companies: in the Central African Republic, pro-Russian and pro-French campaigns have used a range of deceptive tactics to battle each other.[19] And Ben Shapiro's *The Daily Wire* spent over $50,000 in paid advertising on Instagram and Facebook to promote stories about the *Depp v. Heard* trial with a bias against Heard.[20]

As researchers, we can only focus on the discourse – look at posts, tweets, online patterns – but the influence operations use plenty of unseen tactics, including bribes and intimidation, which are impossible to fully interrogate and understand, even with the best investigative resources. For Miller, these campaigns benefit 'the people who can access stagecraft, concentrations of money, concentrations of power and concentrations of willingness to subvert standards of how people can be influenced'. In other words, it benefits powerful people – and mostly powerful men – who are willing to play dirty. As Kamala Harris was poised to become the Democratic presidential nominee in the summer of 2024, researchers uncovered a group of influencers who were paid to spread misogynistic sexual rumours and racist narratives about the vice president. The unknown instigators of the campaign plotted the campaign on Zoom and over email where participants were able to stay anonymous: one such person reportedly earned $20,000 for their activities.[21]

The nature of influence campaigns has also changed. We often think of disinformation as lies designed to shape public discourse. Today's influence campaigns don't need to lie to people anymore, although they still do. Instead, they can flatter a worldview, capture a grievance and enhance it in a particular direction. In online influence, outrage activation has become the most powerful weapon, and there are plenty of online groups of Incredibly Outraged men ripe for plucking who are happy to nudge others along with a bit of algorithmic help.

Humour about and derision of Amber Heard flooded social media. When she cried in the courtroom while talking about her alleged rape, screenshots of her tear-filled face became a viral meme. On TikTok, videos instructed users on 'how to cover a bruise'. After Heard first took the stand, tweets started circulating claiming that she had 'directly' lifted parts of her testimony from the 1999 film *The Talented Mr. Ripley*.[22] A few days later, as she took a tissue to wipe tears off her face, Twitter was abuzz with claims that she was snorting cocaine in the court.[23] TikToks making claims like this received millions of views.

Many individuals spotted a chance to monetise a woman's humiliation. Among the groups who jumped on the misogynistic money-making digital bandwagon were lawyers. *Depp v. Heard* was good for the lawyers, but not just the lawyers in court. It provided an opportunity for real and self-styled legal commentators to promote themselves and monetise their commentary at the expense of accuracy and legal ethics. During the trial, ordinary social media users searching YouTube for updates about how the case was progressing were very likely to stumble upon Rekieta Law's content. Throughout the trial, his live-streamed videos included a 'Super Chat' donation system, allowing viewers to make donations. Rekieta may have earned over $130,000 during the trial by producing anti-Heard videos.[24]

Aside from Rekieta, Minneapolis-based defence lawyer Bruce Rivers made a series of videos about *Depp v. Heard* that he broadcast to his 800,000 followers, purporting to show how 'the more [Amber Heard] talks, the less she is believable.'[25] 'They couldn't bring this body language expert into trial to say that Heard is lying,' Rivers said in one of his videos, recognising that body language is not a valid form of analysis, 'but in the court of public opinion, we can say pretty much whatever we want. It's just entertainment.'[26]

The outcome of the trial was as messy as the relationship: Heard was found to have defamed Depp and he was awarded $10 million in compensatory damages, but Depp was likewise found to have defamed Heard and she was awarded $2 million. Both sides appealed before eventually bringing the whole saga to a close with a settlement in late 2022. But the result led to jubilation among male supremacists and their reactionary allies, who accurately felt they had deeply wounded #MeToo.

Fox News anchor Martha MacCallum rejoiced at the fact that it '[put] a bit of a stake in the heart of the notion that you believe all women'.[27] 'Johnny Depp defeated #MeToo', tweeted Steven Crowder.[28] They had won the influence battle. By doing so, the trial sent a message to all women who might want to speak up about domestic or sexual abuse. *Depp v. Heard* is a microcosm of the backlash against #MeToo, itself a microcosm of a greater backlash against women's rights. Heard was to be the example for every woman. Writing in *The New York Times* just after the jury verdict, Susan Faludi highlighted the inherent danger of celebrity feminism and making one person a representation of all women. 'If an individual embodies the principle, the principle can be disproved by dethroning the individual,' she wrote.[29] Or, as *New Yorker* writer Emily Nussbaum put it, 'When you're put on a pedestal, the whole world gets to upskirt you.'[30]

## Waving the pitchforks

The impact of the internet on political discourse has become obvious over the years as social media-facilitated mass protest movements, from the Arab Spring to Occupy and #SayHerName, have come and gone. Algorithms may have amplified #MeToo in the first place, but they also fed the backlash as organised male supremacists and their backers poured money into a campaign to destroy Heard, exploited social media platforms and mounted an outrage-activating campaign to convince thousands of digital passers-by that a woman recounting her alleged rape is worth making an ironic TikTok video about.

The male supremacist tactical playbook has changed dramatically in the last few years by learning how to subvert existing structures to its advantages. At this point it is impossible not to mention the significance of Gamergate, the 2014 harassment campaign started by a group of users of 4chan who spread rumours about video game developer Zoë Quinn. The incident was sparked by a blog post from Quinn's ex-boyfriend accusing them of sleeping with a gaming journalist to gain positive coverage of their new game, *Depression Quest*, which tackled issues of mental health inspired by Quinn's own struggle. The post was a lie – the favourable article did not exist – but it provided a conspiratorial narrative for those resentful of women's perceived encroachment into the male-dominated world of gaming.

In addition to Quinn, the harassment campaign targeted feminist critic Anita Sarkeesian, who had spoken in favour of more inclusive representations in gaming, gamer Brianna Wu and several people who supported them. Gamergate was not only unprecedented in scale for a social media campaign, it was the first large-scale manosphere-led campaign that was successful on a mainstream social media platform. It marked the point when male supremacy started moving from the backwaters of the internet out into the mainstream. Annie Kelly, who was studying the manosphere at the time, says:

> For a long time manosphere types did not think social media was for them. They thought Twitter (now X) was full of feminists. People who are part of the reactionary project are quite often envious of what they see as the progressive capture of culture, its popularity and the way it can mobilise instantly.

There had been previous failed attempts at anti-feminist campaigns with less inspiring slogans such as #FeministsAreUgly or the 4chan-inspired ‘Operation Freebleeding’, spoofing and impersonating feminists who are taking on the patriarchy by rejecting tampons.

Gamergate, however, succeeded because it combined long-term goals with small ones, encouraging a sense of participation, and experimented with different hashtags. It took off when actor Adam Baldwin shared a video using the hashtag and benefited from amplification by mainstream figures, including men’s rights influencers at a time when influencers were not the ubiquitous phenomenon they are today, conservative academics railing against political correctness and far-right figures. Academic Whitney Phillips wrote that Gamergate provided an opportunity for ‘chaos entrepreneurs’, charismatic influencers with murky motivations who stirred the pot in favour of the movement because they adhered to its message or because they sought personal gain.[31] Collusion between politicised harassment and self-interested personalities seeking to further their profile or make a profit was also a fixture of the *Depp v. Heard* trial.

The architects of Gamergate succeeded because they realised they could achieve success by borrowing and turning to their advantage the tactics of progressive movements, including the Arab Spring and Black Lives Matter. Media academics Liza Potts and Michael Trice found that Gamergate participants subverted social media platforms, tested which arguments worked best to influence online audiences and found news ways to recruit people to the cause. For example, Arab Spring pro-democracy activists used the fact that Twitter allowed ordinary people to write direct messages to verified accounts of celebrities, and what we were beginning to call ‘influencers’, and to call on the powerful online. The campaign participants realised they could turn this into a ‘dark pattern’ to direct abuse at Quinn and draw people in; some people became unwillingly targeted as the situation snowballed.[32] Gamergate disguised its true purpose by shape-shifting and reinventing itself in response to the fightback it encountered. When faced with accusations of misogyny, it framed itself as a debate about ‘ethics in journalism’. It ‘existed in a perpetual state of invention, spinning off argument after argument with no interest in selecting a consensus cause other than maintaining its amplified, aggressive, combative, and noisy existence’, as Potts and Trice write.[33]

Gamergate created a blueprint for subsequent reactionary campaigns, which usually combine some form of online recruitment, seek to blame a problem on an oppressed group, whip up broader culture wars rhetoric, deploy an expanding array of abusive online tactics (doxxing and rape threats, which featured prominently during Gamergate, have become sad fixtures of today's harassment campaigns), and allow platforms' amplification and networking mechanisms to work their magic. It was also a defining moment for the emergence of the alt-right and showed how men's anger could be weaponised for anti-feminist and reactionary political mobilisation. At the time, Trump's advisor Steve Bannon had just started working as the executive chairman of the far-right website Breitbart. He saw that an army of young men united by their resentment towards women could be turned into a political movement.

YouTuber Milo Yiannopoulos, who had described feminism as 'cancer' and made a name for himself by spouting an endless string of racist statements, was working for Bannon. He had previously described gamers as 'unemployed saddos living in their parents' basements', but having realised that gamers had coalesced around anti-feminism, did a quick U-turn and became one of the movement's loudest supporters, writing multiple columns in favour of gamers at the same time as he attacked feminist online campaigns like Emma Watson's #HeForShe. PUA Mike Cernovich,[34] who had written that '40% of women have a rape fantasy', offered his services to Quinn's ex-boyfriend.

The violent bullying impulses at the heart of Gamergate fuelled the trolling and meme-filled politics that became characteristic of Trump's first election campaign and his subsequent politics. These impulses did not go away when Trump's presidency ended. Aided by social media platforms' networking mechanisms, male supremacist communities have become structured and grown. They create what social media expert Stephanie Lamy calls an 'immersive experience in a highly hierarchical universe',[35] which facilitates men's understanding of themselves as a class whose rights are under attack and need to be protected. They have their own codes and language and create online spaces of solidarity based on anti-feminist conspiracy theories and a shared sense of grievance against women.

These groups of men can carry out harassment campaigns when they feel they are morally in the right. Media scholar Alice Marwick calls this 'morally motivated networked harassment'.[36] Once you manage to suck enough people into an organised movement based on grievances directed at the wrong target, you can get them to do anything you like. In a reminder that online mobs can turn into offline ones, aggrieved conspiratorial beliefs also led hundreds of citizens to storm the US Capitol on 6 January 2021, protesting what they believed was Joe Biden's fraudulent election win and asserting fascist and male supremacist power. The Capitol insurrection, in which extremist and militia groups breached the building for the first time in over two centuries, saw a display of vulgar misogynistic gestures.

House Speaker Nancy Pelosi's office was attacked with cries of 'Get Her Out', which echoed the chants of 'Lock Her Up' against Hillary Clinton during the 2016 election campaign. One of the rioters proudly put his feet up on Pelosi's desk,[37] in a show of masculine domination over one of the most powerful women in the country. Rioters also destroyed cabinets filled with books about women in politics,[38] and female insurrectionists sported scarves which said 'women belong in the kitchen'.[39]

## The war on language

Male supremacy is a reactionary project that aims to reassert men's dominance and control over women and actively undermine progress towards gender equality and accountability for violence, but it is doing a lot of work to present itself as a rights movement. Having appropriated the idea of widespread witch-hunts against men, male supremacist groups are now orchestrating witch-hunts of their own. Despite the common trope that angry feminists hate men, data has found that feminists have quite a positive view of men.[40] You wouldn't realise it from the story male supremacists tell. That story is important to the witch-hunts; it shapes public conversation, discourse and, they hope, behaviour and policies. In their mission to make their narrative sound plausible, it becomes necessary to be creative with language.

Academics Alice Marwick and Robyn Caplan have shown that the concept of misandry – the hatred of men as a systemic issue

– has been advanced by male supremacists as a way to rally men around common grievances, but it is also used to orchestrate backlash against feminism and achieve mainstream influence. Misandry is a concept coined by male supremacist movements to describe a largely non-existent problem. It is deployed in public conversation with a veneer of credibility but merely conveys old misogynistic tropes that feminists hate men and the unfounded idea that men are systematically oppressed. Misandry, once a term no one had heard of, is now making appearances in the columns of right-wing media.[41] It suddenly turns a manufactured problem into an issue by virtue of it being referred to and establishes false equivalences between systemic patterns of dominance and individual inequities.

Male supremacists have created a linguistic mirror world, stealing language used by the feminist movement to make sense of women's reality under the patriarchy to act as a shield for their true project and give legitimacy to their demands. British Conservative MP Christopher Chope, for instance, described investigations of sexual harassment as a form of 'institutional misandry', mirroring the concept of 'institutional misogyny'.[42] Attempts to make misogyny a hate crime in the UK have been met with a counter-push by MRA groups like Fathers4Justice to make misandry a hate crime. International Women's Day is met with the manosphere-led attempt to create and get brands on board with International Men's Day, in a clear sign that despite every other day of the year being a man's day, male supremacists cannot let women have 24 hours to bring attention to gender equality.

A measure such as making misandry a hate crime is unlikely to pass, but the aim is to momentarily capture attention in an age where public attention is a hotly contested resource. The logic behind some instances of both-sidesing is more or less convoluted. Incels who think women are unfairly denying them sex are calling women's lack of desire to sleep with them 'reverse rape' and have asked for no less than their own #MeToo movement.[43]

The colonisation of the language of liberation movements and human rights is central not just to the male supremacist project but also to the new breed of conspiratorial movements that have thrived since the pandemic, as Naomi Klein details in *Doppelganger* (2023). Klein argues that the appropriation of this language, itself the result of a broader cheapening of words in public discourse, is weakening radical and progressive movements, making a mockery of the real violence taking place around us.[44] The pro-police 'Blue Lives Matter' emerged in 2014 alongside Black Lives Matter to distract attention from systemic racism in the police against African Americans and turn the police into the victimised group. Its underlying hypocrisy became more evident when protesters carrying 'Blue Lives Matter' signs stormed the Capitol and brutalised law enforcement, showing the scant regard they really had for officers' lives. Anti-vaccine movements calling vaccination 'forced penetration' are further examples of the twisting of language.[45] Popular feminist slogans seem to be popular targets for groups of every stripe. 'My Body My Choice' has proved popular among far-right movements, anti-vaccine groups and male supremacists alike.

## Social media: the new town square

Male supremacy as a project has the backing of patriarchal norms and misogynistic social structures, but it also benefits from social media platforms' commercial interests and increasingly politicised CEOs. X CEO Elon Musk, who a decade ago described himself as 'half Democrat, half Republican',[46] has used his wealth and power to boost Trump's re-election campaign, and joined his government. He has reinstated a host of banned influencers on the platform, including Andrew Tate, former English Defence League leader Tommy Robinson and Andrew Anglin.[47] Misogynistic hate speech increased sharply after Musk's takeover of Twitter,[48] making a platform already hostile to women and minorities even more so.

Women have to do more work to exist online, and they face more scrutiny over any real or manufactured controversy. In a world where visibility is currency, attempts to silence women by driving them off social media platforms are a way to reduce their political agency and to exert economic punishment: as our professional lives are increasingly dependent on our ability to exist online, women who are driven off social media platforms pay a professional and financial price. Male supremacists also receive a high return on investment online and get disruptive results out of 'quick and easy' activities, including those known as slacktivism (for example sharing a post or signing a petition). They also show a predilection for Trojan horse tactics such as creating feminist parody accounts, a practice Lamy calls 'Fem Spoofing', which originates in early 4chan hoax campaigns. In more mainstream public discourse, spoofing remains a popular tool to mock feminists and the 'woke', as the parody account Titania McGrath shows.

That isn't to say they are not putting work into honing their messages or producing content; as Marwick and Caplan note, discussion about misandry built up over years on websites and was the result of a carefully crafted strategy before it received mainstream amplification. Old hashtags including #NotAllMen keep resurfacing regularly, for example following the rape and murder of 33-year-old Sarah Everard in South London in March 2021.

In the last decade, social media platforms have come a long way in creating anti-harassment tools, but misogynists have found ways to subvert these too and are now using them against women. Male supremacists are using tools initially conceived to reduce online abuse – including the option to 'report' users to tech companies – to shut down women's social media accounts. While much influence remains hidden from view, sometimes it is out in the open, like MRA-friendly YouTubers telling their followers to make #MePoo trend and influencers shamelessly monetising misogynistic mockery. During France's 2022 presidential election, the far-right party Reconquête did not try hard to hide the fact that it was using astroturfing to artificially generate support, creating and amplifying petitions in favour of their candidate Éric Zemmour[49] – the same Zemmour who came into prominence by writing *The First Sex* (*Le Premier Sexe*, untranslated, 2006), a male supremacist manifesto about the alleged feminist assault on men.

## A misogynist's dreamland

As a French-born woman, I swear by a good cooking pan. Le Creuset is a favourite of mine. Taylor Swift also likes Le Creuset apparently, and this is sadly where the similarities between the uber-glamorous pop star and me end. 'Hey y'all, it's Taylor Swift here. Due to a packaging error, we can't sell 3,000 Le Creuset cookware sets. So I'm giving them away to my loyal fans for free,' Swift said in a video – except she didn't. The video of Swift giving away cookware was a deepfake, an artificially generated video impersonating the singer's voice and features, used by scammers online to encourage people to pay shipping fees for the non-existent giveaway. The video was convincing enough for a few Swift uber-fans, or 'Swifties', to fall for it.[50] A few days later, AI-generated pornographic images of the singer, which originated on 4chan, spread rapidly on X for the best part of a whole day. One image was seen 47 million times before it was deleted.[51]

No one embodies women's power more than Swift, who has reached dizzying levels of celebrity and wealth and whose stardom has been matched by an equally unprecedented amount of scrutiny, obsession and projection. Her self-declared feminism has been the subject of intense analysis and criticism (from different political sides) for the last decade.[52] Before #MeToo became a mass movement, she won a sexual assault lawsuit against DJ David Mueller.[53] Her songs have not spared the manosphere. In her song 'The Man' and the accompanying music video, Swift assumes the role of a man, playing the PUA, the 'good dad' and the casual misogynist and idiot.

The two deepfaking incidents concerning Swift reflect a telling reality. While the deepfakes that make the headlines and trend on social media are often offbeat and entertaining – the Pope wearing a white puffer jacket or Kit Harrington as Jon Snow apologising for an underwhelming last series of *Game of Thrones*[54] – the vast majority are pornographic and overwhelmingly feature women. When I speak to Sophie Maddocks, a researcher in cybersecurity at the University of Pennsylvania, she shares some staggering figures with me. Dozens of deepfake porn apps and web services are launching every month. The year 2023 alone saw a higher number of deepfakes than the six previous years *combined*.

Early deepfakes looked clunky and unconvincing, but the new wave is highly convincing and the tools available to create them, especially pornographic ones, are becoming more democratic. 'You no longer have to fantasize over the picture of your favourite girl, TV girl, workmate, neighbour or whoever you want to see nude,' gushes a technology website in an article reviewing its top pick of 'nudifying apps', apps which allow users to virtually undress any woman or transpose a woman into pornography, promising to produce very realistic results.[55] 'Deepfakes are becoming the new normal; they're a form of entertainment,' Maddocks tells me. The AI investigation firm Sensity found a network of bot accounts on Telegram that automated the creation of pornographic deepfakes, producing non-consensual nude images of over 100,000 women.[56] The technology is becoming cheaper, more accessible and realistic, although how realistic it is has no bearing on how hard it hits those affected, as Agnes Venema, an academic expert on deepfakes says: 'Just because a deepfake is not of great quality doesn't mean the harm is less. This is a common misconception.'

In January 2022, a 17-year-old Egyptian girl killed herself after being blackmailed with deepfake images after she refused to go on a date with a boy.[57] Teenage girls can be affected in the same way as women in politics or with a public profile. Like other forms of image-based abuse, it is a sexual violation with devastating consequences which can cause intense distress and have life-changing consequences.[58] Deepfake pornography has also become a backlash instrument. Women who speak up and represent freedom, success and agency or who try to hold powerful institutions to account are prime targets for deepfakes. In 2018, Indian journalist Rana Ayyub was the target of a politically motivated deepfake campaign after reporting on the rape of a Kashmiri girl, and the ruling Bharatiya Janata Party (BJP) came out in support of the men accused of rape. She ended up in hospital with extreme anxiety. 'You can call yourself a journalist, you can call yourself a feminist, but in that moment I just couldn't see through the humiliation,' she wrote in the *Huffington Post*.[59]

Deepfakes and other generative AI images and videos are a 'misogynist's dreamland', Maki says. To conduct their campaigns, the men who hate women no longer need large amounts of paid-for people sitting somewhere in a troll farm. AI can automate it for them and produce unprecedented volumes of smear or sexualised material within minutes and spread it widely into the world. ChatGPT, OpenAI's chatbot, launched in November 2022 to much fanfare, has been very good at producing convincing and highly misogynistic conspiratorial narratives.[60] 'We are always playing whack-a-mole with bad actors, but with generative AI we are now in the middle of an industrial revolution in online influence. We're moving from the farm to the factory. What this means for women is terrifying,' Maki adds.

Trust-based structures, from financial institutions to elections, are already under pressure. An investigation by the US company Graphika found a Chinese-state-backed influence campaign that used AI videos.[61] In January 2023, videos of AI-generated characters expressed support for the junta responsible for a military coup in Burkina Faso.[62] From Slovakia to Bangladesh,[63] deepfake videos are already wreaking havoc on election campaigns. It only took a few weeks for an online influence campaign to wound the #MeToo movement. What an anti-feminist campaign built on deepfakes and other generative AI technology could achieve remains an unknown horizon.

## Crying witch: old and new abuse campaigns

Despite utopian talk of an internet without abuse, researchers were alerting people to the widespread misogyny on online forums as early as the 1990s. In recent years, violently misogynistic abuse and harassment are not just affecting women and girls around the world, they are also used to silence women who want to speak up and take part in political life and public debate. Virtually every election campaign across the world is marked by intense vitriol targeting women. This reflects an offline reality: women running for office have been attacked by violent mobs in India and cartels in Mexico.[64] Candidates across the world have also been faced with a deluge of image-based sexualised abuse.[65] The offline ramifications of hateful extremism and radicalisation have become only clearer. The 2016 murder of British MP Jo Cox by a violent neo-Nazi was one of the first shocking examples of how women's lives are at stake. In October 2020, four members of the far-right militia group Wolverine Watchmen were arrested over plots to kidnap Gretchen Whitmer, then a Michigan Democratic gubernatorial nominee, as retaliation for her policies to limit the spread of COVID-19.[66] In July 2024, a 37-year-old British man was arrested for plotting to kidnap, rape and murder British TV presenter Holly Willoughby; he had used the anonymous messaging app Kik to share violent fantasies and misogynistic and sexualised comments about the presenter and had posted in a public group called 'Abduct Lovers'.[67]

Gender equality advocate Lucina Di Meco is the co-founder of #ShePersisted, a movement which works to end gender-based abuse and disinformation against women in public life. She has spent years interviewing journalists and politicians and observing how patterns of abuse have shifted. She says that women who advance policies towards greater equality are particular targets.[68] It's true that male politicians also face violent abuse, but the abuse levelled at women is often different. Research on the topic has shown that while male candidates face generic insults,[69] the abuse that women receive is strongly sexualised and aimed at discrediting them, a reflection both of the persistence of misogynistic tropes and of how they can be deployed to undermine women.

When it comes to elections, Di Meco summarises how abusive campaigns try to depict women: as untrustworthy, unqualified, unintelligent and unlikeable – in other words, unfit for leadership. Establishing themselves as credible for political leadership has been the central battle of women's struggle to become involved in politics. 'Likeability' is an ill-defined concept which women are particularly held to and, as Di Meco notes, can be the 'death knell of their campaign'.[70] This became Hillary Clinton's 'woman problem' in the 2016 US presidential campaign: multiple newspapers columns were devoted to analysing why men and women did not like her, a comment that Trump repeated, while also stating she did not have a 'presidential look'.[71]

Hillary Clinton's 2016 campaign showed a clear backlash pattern. The use of crass misogynistic language by (mostly) right-wing commentators and Republicans was the mainstream and socially sanctioned manifestation of the kind of rage that simmered on r/TheRedPill, where young men with a dislike of feminists and social justice warriors cheered on their candidate. Clinton's former aide said the torrent of abuse she received was so relentless that the campaign team had 'no idea' how to deal with it.[72] Kamala Harris has faced similar treatment and has been the target of racist and misogynistic conspiracy theories since her nomination as vice-presidential candidate in 2020. Trump, who did not try to keep a lid on crude misogynist remarks, called Harris 'very low IQ' during his campaign appearance on Joe Rogan's podcast.

Researcher Nina Jankowicz has spoken of the 'malign creativity' of abusers,[73] who are increasingly diversifying their formats, using memes, photoshopped images and now AI-generated creations. While the format looks modern, the content is not. From images of Hillary Clinton riding a broom and cackling maliciously during the 2016 campaign to Nancy Pelosi in a black pointy hat,[74] depicting middle-aged women as hags is still as popular as ever. Images and memes depicting Amber Heard, who is openly bisexual, as a witch circulated widely during the *Depp v. Heard* trial, playing into tropes of powerful women with sexual agency. As a growing body of research has shown, this abuse is magnified for women of colour and with intersecting identities. The Center for Democracy & Technology found that women from ethnic minority backgrounds were twice as likely as others to be targeted with disinformation aimed at discrediting them during the 2022 midterms.[75] A report by anti-abuse charity Glitch in the UK has shone a light on the extent of online misogynoir and 'the continued, unchecked, and often violent dehumanisation of Black women on social media'.[76]

Attempts to erase women from public life increasingly take the form of gendered misinformation, particularly narratives centred on women's sexuality. Conspiracy theories which emphasise women's sexual autonomy have propped up backlashes against women throughout history. They remain a very effective tool in today's online witch-hunts, and still the easiest way for trying to bring a woman down. After the death of Russian political opponent Alexei Navalny in February 2024, a Kremlin-linked disinformation campaign against his widow, Yulia Navalnaya, claimed that she had multiple affairs and abortions, just as hopes emerged that she could be a new face of Russian opposition.[77] During the 2024 US presidential campaign, crude misogynistic claims that Kamala Harris 'slept her way to the top' were at the centre of the online campaigns against her, alongside racist insinuations about her eligibility.[78] Meanwhile, Elon Musk's retweet of a deepfake video of Kamala Harris, which showed her saying 'I was selected because I am the ultimate diversity hire,' offered further proof of how powerful men and interests sanction attempts at undermining women. The same Musk suggested in a tweet that he would impregnate Taylor Swift after she endorsed Harris for president, comments which plainly reflect powerful right-wing men's intention of coercing and restoring control over women's bodies.[79]

During the 2016 election campaign, Trump said of Clinton: 'She doesn't quit. She doesn't give up.' Plenty of women are quitting, and online and offline abuse is playing a part. In the UK, female MPs and government ministers have said they no longer take the Tube for fear of encountering physical abuse and intimidation. They are reporting more death threats to the police and are choosing not to stand in elections again.[80] While not directly referencing misogyny, female leaders who stepped down from politics in recent years have spoken of the mental toll of leadership. The prime minister of New Zealand Jacinda Ardern resigned in January 2023 saying she 'no longer [had] enough in the tank to do [the job] justice', and other political figures cited relentless abuse as a contributing factor for their retreat from public life.[81]

New abuse campaigns don't just take place in the shadows, they also use shadowy evidence. In mediaeval times, women tried for witchcraft were frequently indicted on 'spectral evidence', unreliable testimonies in which witnesses claimed they'd had a vision of the accused perpetrating a crime in a vision or dream. The 1692 Salem Witch Trials used such forms of evidence. Today's witch-hunts use new forms of spectral evidence. As legal scholar Brie D. Sherwin has noted, multiple legal cases in recent years have used dubious evidence, unsubstantiated claims and reactionary dog whistles to support socially regressive policies.[82] As Sherwin shows in her analysis, US states' decision to curtail education which includes considerations of Black history and LGBT+ populations was done on the basis of spectral evidence and concocted fears about Critical Race Theory (CRT). CRT, a form of legal scholarship that focuses on racism in US law, has been appropriated by a reactionary movement to undermine attempts at diversifying education curricula and attack the Black Lives Matter movement.[83] Similarly, in April 2023, a Texas judge ruled to suspend the Food and Drug Administration's approval of mifepristone, a drug used for abortion, on the basis of unfounded medical claims. It prompted the American Medical Association to condemn the court's 'disregard for well-established scientific facts in favour of speculative allegations and ideological assertions'.[84] And what to call the wild rumours which circulated online during the Depp–Heard trial?

When he couldn't seem to turn off social media updates about the *Depp v. Heard* trial, Daniel Maki shared his suspicions with Alexi Mostrous, an investigative journalist at Tortoise Media. Over two years, Mostrous and his team analysed millions of anti-Heard tweets produced during the trial and found that half were 'inauthentic': they were either bots or accounts belonging to individuals who were being paid to attack the actress. Their investigation found that many of these bots were linked to Saudi Arabia and praised Saudi Crown Prince Mohammed bin Salman, or MBS as he is sometimes called.[85] While they stopped short of proving that the smear campaign against Heard was orchestrated by bin Salman himself, the investigation demonstrated strong links to Saudi interests.

Maki summarises it like this: 'There was a large-scale coordinated paid-for operation to smear Heard.' While the MRAs were riling up aggrieved men online and seeking to convince all of us that #MeToo had gone too far, someone more powerful than any of them was funding and sitting atop the influence pyramid, although it's impossible to fully prove who. In February 2024, a piece in *Vanity Fair* reported on Depp's newfound 'bromance' with MBS.[86]

The 2018 assassination of journalist Jamal Khashoggi by the Saudi state cost the Crown Prince a lot of political capital and he has embarked on a serious rehabilitation mission since then. *Vogue* reported that Johnny Depp was reportedly contacted by bin Salman's team while he was shooting his first post-trial film *Jeanne Du Barry* in an attempt to re-establish his reputation; Saudi Arabia also happened to be a key funder of the film.[87] Since then, Depp has spent weeks in Saudi Arabia's royal palaces and become not only the prince's friend but a possible ally in MBS's plan to improve the country's image abroad, as media outlets reported.

Women are victims of new witch-hunts, but there are still old ones going on. In Ghana, marginalised and unwanted women are sent to witch camps. ISIS executed women for witchcraft,[88] as did Saudi Arabia in recent years, one of the last few countries to do so.[89] It should perhaps come as no surprise, then, that while seeking to rebrand itself as respectful of women, Saudi Arabia continues to kidnap, imprison and harass women who ask for basic rights at home or that it also had something to do with a large-scale witch-hunt that was about sending a message to the greater world.

# 3

# Barbie and me: women's bodies and the backlash

In the spring of 2023, images swept across the internet of a hot couple in hot pink; two of Hollywood's major stars looking like plastic perfection in 1980s Lycra and dayglo roller-skates. They were Margot Robbie and Ryan Gosling in character as Barbie and Ken promoting the *Barbie* movie. Despite its tongue-in-cheek tone and source material of an improbably proportioned child's toy, this film promised to be a feminist statement. With director Greta Gerwig at the helm, *Barbie*'s posters introduced a far wider cast than just Robbie and Gosling as the title character and her boyfriend. 'This Barbie is President' the posters proclaimed of Issa Rae's character. There were plenty more in the diverse cast of women: Sharon Rooney: 'This Barbie is a lawyer'; Ritu Arya: 'This Barbie has a Pulitzer'; Hari Nef: 'This Barbie is a doctor.' All the actors playing Ken, meanwhile, were 'Just Ken'.

Thanks to the marketing department at Warner Bros, not only did the promotional images sweep the internet but millions visited a Barbie Selfie Generator and put themselves in a 'This Barbie is…' poster of their own. For one particular Barbie, the opportunity was too good to pass up. And her selfie's message to her 14,000 followers read: 'This Barbie is pro-life.'

At first glance, the Instagram account of @prolifebarbie looks like that of countless millennials, with its selection of carefully curated selfies, beach holidays and sunsets. Amid this wholesome content, a post with a light pink background and an inspirational quote-type font describes abortion as 'satanic'. Another states that 'real feminists love masculinity'. @prolifebarbie is an anti-abortion activist for the millennial age, mixing pop feminist aesthetics (one image shows her holding a sign with the words 'post-Roe feminist') with a long school of anti-abortion rhetoric, comparing the procedure to murder. One post is of Robbie's Barbie in her pink car with the caption: 'Get in girl! We're abolishing abortion!' Another has a picture of a firearm crossed with a baby's arms. The text reads: 'The NRA [National Rifle Association] doesn't sell arms … Planned Parenthood does,' suggesting that one of the oldest sexual health organisations in the US sells babies' body parts.

The overturning of *Roe v. Wade* was a seismic moment in American politics and a shocking regression for women's rights. On 2 May 2022, *POLITICO* magazine published a leaked document from the US Supreme Court showing plans to reverse the landmark 1973 decision that established a constitutional right to abortion.[1] Weeks later, the decision became official as the American court ruled on *Dobbs v. Jackson Women's Health Organization*. The decision, the culmination of years of anti-abortion activism in the US, was much feared but not entirely surprising. When it happened, 22 states in the US had restrictive abortion laws in place. Ultra-conservatives and evangelical Christians like @prolifebarbie were jubilant and celebrated boisterously in their communities.

But elsewhere, a holistic sex coach had a rather different opinion.

'*Roe vs. Wade*. Do I Give a Shit? Whenever I see women begging for the right to use and govern their own bodies – especially those who identify as "feminists" – I have to refrain from rolling my eyes.' So Kim Anami said to her 150,000 followers in an Instagram Live the day before the Supreme Court overturned *Roe v. Wade*.

'For any woman who knows her own body and how it works, the whims of a bunch of Sith Lords in cult Halloween costumes is irrelevant to her. Who is in control of you and your fertility? If the answer is anyone else other than you, let me school you,' Anami continued, chastising women who took to the streets to protest.[2] The self-styled 'Holistic sex + relationship expert' runs a sex coaching business which she claims is inspired by tantra and 'a host of quantum growth-accelerating practices' and promises to transform those who come to her into 'well f★cked' women. She also made international headlines by lifting weights with her vagina. @prolifebarbie, firmly from the abstinence before marriage school of Christianity, probably wouldn't think much of her, but despite their differences in lifestyle and attitude to *Roe v. Wade*, they share something in common: they are two faces of today's assault on women's health and sexual and reproductive autonomy.

There is another.

Days after Anami's Instagram Live, the Proud Boys created a channel on the encrypted messaging app Telegram to discuss the Supreme Court decision. 'Well whores and sluts the game is over', the first message read. As the news spread, the channel was flooded with hundreds of anti-abortion messages and violently misogynistic comments. A meme of the 'woman with glowing red eyes' comes with the caption 'Say goodbye to your abortions whores!!!' In the chat, a member starts a poll about 'what should be done to women who have had an abortion?', offering responses such as 'Jail them until they are sterilized' and 'Try them and execute them by firing squad'. Further down, another member shares an article from Bloomberg about upcoming protests against the Supreme Court's decision, calling for the group to 'show up with mobile training units for these degenerate sluts'. In the following weeks, the Proud Boys and various militia groups appeared in anti-abortion demonstrations outside abortion and sexual health clinics, armed with assault rifles.[3]

A tantric sex coach, a Christian evangelist and the Proud Boys look like an unlikely set of bedfellows. Yet they represent a new unholy alliance of far-right ideology, faux-feminist New Age libertarianism and millennial-friendly reactionary activism which all make women's reproductive and sexual autonomy the centre of a battle for control.

## The fight for information

The overturning of *Roe v. Wade* is neither the beginning nor the end for women's abortion rights in the US. Years of litigation lie ahead and online conversations will shape real-life legislation. 'Just the beginning' is how the overturning of *Roe* is described in Project 2025, the report published by the right-wing Heritage Foundation think tank to shape Donald Trump's campaign promises for the 2024 elections and future conservative politics in the country. Anti-abortion groups with decades of activism behind them were well aware of that fact as they churned out anti-abortion memes and TikTok infographics in the weeks after *Dobbs*. @prolifebarbie was one among many anti-abortion activists who used their Instagram to give women the phone number of '24/7 pregnancy helplines' – in reality, anti-abortion centres disguised as pregnancy advice services – and advertising 'abortion pill reversal', a procedure which involves taking progesterone to reverse an abortion and which the American College of Obstetricians and Gynecologists has described as 'unproven and unethical'.[4]

One of the people following the onslaught was public health researcher Jenna Sherman. She grew up in the Deep South, steeped in evangelical Christian messages about sexual purity and the sanctity of life. She rebelled against her upbringing, studied at Harvard, where she developed a passion for maternal health, and became a doula, someone who provides support to women during pregnancy and childbirth. She recalls the fear that gripped the country in the wake of the *Dobbs* decision and the horrifying events that followed, including news that a ten-year-old rape victim from Ohio had to travel to Indiana for an abortion.[5]

Some people had answers amid the panic. They urged women to keep calm and take some herbs. Videos of 'herbal abortions' went viral on TikTok. Alternative health influencers who usually dispensed dubious advice about gut health now had opinions on abortion. If women with unwanted pregnancies could not access medical abortion, they could take mugwort, pennyroyal and blue cohosh to induce one.[6] 'Every uterus owner should know emmenagogues, herbs for the stimulation of menses,' proclaimed one widely shared video on TikTok, posted by a 'herbalist' who also urged women to 'take charge of [their] body'. 'You do not need big pharma's drugs or archaic practices nor the government's approval to take control of your fertility,' another TikToker asserted,[7] mixing soft conspiratorial language with that of reproductive autonomy.

Ineffective at best and dangerous at worst, this type of alt-health talk betrays the same underlying libertarian individualistic ethos Anami shares: who needs abortion rights when you can take charge of your own body? Just buy our herbs, or maybe attend a workshop on how to become a well f*cked woman.

While some were encouraging 'natural' abortions, others earnestly warned about the dangers of 'chemical' ones. Sherman, who studied hundreds of social media posts before and after *Dobbs*, said that misleading talk of 'chemical' abortions, with its connotations of impurity and poisoning, dominated social media conversation, preying on the distrust of medical institutions that the pandemic had awakened. By using the word 'chemical', anti-abortion groups spoke to the clean-eating smoothie-drinking millennial women who might be tempted by an abortion but would think twice if confronted with the thought of swallowing toxic pills.

In the weeks after *Dobbs*, I set up accounts on social media platforms and arranged the settings to put myself in the shoes of a 25-year-old woman living in the US. On YouTube and TikTok, I typed the neutral term 'abortion' in the search bar and watched the first ten videos recommended to me. Within minutes, I was being recommended YouTube videos showing graphic footage of full-term foetuses being dismembered in the womb by a 'surgical abortion'. On Instagram, I encounter posts saying 'what is abortion pill reversal?', which redirect me to pro-life clinics, and ones telling me that 'all forms of hormonal birth control raise the risk of breast cancer' and are 'deadly to children'.

The backlash to abortion and reproductive rights always begins as soon as, if not before, they become law. These rights were hard won by feminists, but their opponents are just as implacably determined. They have been fighting back for decades, refining their communication tactics and playing the long game. In *Backlash*, Susan Faludi described how Reagan-era anti-abortion groups embraced pseudo-feminist language and pseudoscience to win over the public. Jack and Barbara Willke's *Handbook on Abortion*, first published in 1971, was a prime example of a shift from traditional anti-abortion arguments focused on the sanctity of life towards health misinformation and the side effects of abortions.

Anti-abortion movements have learned lessons over time. For starters: tone down the religious preaching. Large sections of the anti-abortion movement are religious, but they have realised they can achieve more wins in increasingly secular countries by using the language of individual autonomy – and by stoking fears of

Big Pharma – than by attempting to put the literal fear of God into people.

Take the example of Live Action, an anti-abortion organisation founded by millennial activist Lila Rose when she was 15, which counts over half a million followers on some of its social media channels. It made a name for itself by sending actors impersonating pimps and pregnant under-age girls seeking abortions to Planned Parenthood facilities in order to expose alleged malpractice. While it did uncover some cases of illegal practice, Live Action also faced criticism for manipulating recordings to falsely indict Planned Parenthood.

Live Action is not short of social media experts: its website is slick and its online communication impeccable. It has both long-term vision ('Tell Congress to pass legislation to end abortion') and short-term campaigns ('Send a box of diapers to a mom in need!'). Not one to pass up an opportunity to fundraise, it sells a range of paraphernalia and has a series of explainer videos on 'how to reply to pro-choice arguments', its own version of a digital literacy guide.[8] It uses anti-abortion memes and TikTok infographics expertly.

Anti-abortion influencers and groups also talk to women and communities who have plenty of good reasons to be wary of healthcare and political institutions. 'Planned Parenthood kills more people in a day than the KKK [Ku Klux Klan] lynched in a century,' read a widely shared post by a Christian influencer after the ruling. One of the most viewed YouTube short videos post-*Roe* showed conservative pundit Ben Shapiro comparing anti-abortion activists to abolitionists (it received 16 million views). Two years after the Black Lives Matter movement, anti-abortion groups hijacked the language of racial justice and the fight against structural racial violence by using the hashtag #UnbornLivesMatter.[9] One-time presidential candidate Ben Carson told Fox News that Planned Parenthood places the majority of its clinics in Black neighbourhoods, thereby engaging in a form of racist population control,[10] while Rush Limbaugh declared that the goal of the organisation was to 'abort various minorities out of existence'.[11] Anti-abortion campaigners could count on tech giants' inaction. Only YouTube updated its policies on abortion after the ruling.[12]

Anti-abortionists across the globe are doing the same things. Take France, where religious belief and the power of Catholicism have decreased. Abortion was legalised in France in 1974, and growing up there in the 1990s, the messages I heard were far from what Sherman experienced. Sex education was limited but purity pledges, contraception shaming and anti-abortion messages were mostly unheard of.[13] As in the US, the French anti-abortion movement kept plugging away after legalisation passed. It organised 'commando operations' by blocking hospitals, finding inspiration from the US group Operation Save America, but despite the sometimes violent tactics, it looked performative, the work of an ultra-religious minority.

In recent years, French anti-abortionists have learned about PR and toned down the kind of discourse about the 'sanctity of life' that convinces few in secular France. The group Les Survivants (The Survivors) is a prime example of that shift. It is run by Émile Duport, a Parisian communication and branding consultant, who is personally low-key on social media but is considered something of a social media guru among the French anti-abortion movement.

Duport, who has a Christian pop-rock band, has led some of the most notable anti-abortion campaigns in the country. In 2017, he was behind the creation of a portrait of Simone Veil, the politician who was behind the legalisation of abortion in France. It was modelled on the work of Shepard Fairey (creator of the Obama HOPE image), went viral on Facebook and was sent to media outlets to use free of licence. The artwork directed whoever clicked on it to a website featuring a documentary falsely claiming that the architect of the abortion bill had changed her mind in later life. The website still exists and hails Simone Veil as a 'feminist icon' whose ideas have been betrayed,[14] although Veil's surviving family went to court to recover the original domain name used by the group.

Duport runs a branding and communications agency deceptively called Progressif Media, which goes to great lengths to describe itself as an ethical and mission-oriented consultancy. The website resembles that of countless Parisian communication start-ups with its slick animated reels and use of *franglais*. The company's true missions are barely perceptible behind the corporate-speak. Look closer and they become a bit clearer.

Progressif Media promises to help businesses on their mission 'freeing us up from overconsumption and greed', 'responding to young people's anxieties' and 'restoring family', also hoping to become 'the digital advertising agency at the service of those who work for the virtuous progress of the world'.[15] Among the many clients who match the company's apparently virtuous mission are Thierry Casasnovas, a prominent alternative health YouTuber who promotes raw diets to cure cancer, is a convicted fraudster and has faced accusations of coercing women. Duport's clients also include the French branch of Generation Identity, a far-right European movement dedicated to restoring Europe's 'ethno-cultural identity' and banned as a hateful extremist group by the French government in 2021.[16] In 2022, reactionary French media mogul Vincent Bolloré bought 8.5 per cent of the company and tasked it with designing influence campaigns aligned with his views.[17] He also owns the TV channel CNews, where male supremacist Éric Zemmour hosted a daily talk show between 2019 and 2021, giving him a megaphone into French households to spread into the mainstream a relatively fringe idea which is increasingly at the heart of the backlash against women's rights: the idea of the 'Great Replacement'.

## Putting women back in chains

President Donald Trump sits in the Oval Office, his lips half-pursed in concentration as, pen in hand, he scratches his unmistakable spiky signature on an official document. The evangelical Christian vice president Mike Pence stands behind him, peering over his shoulder as if to make sure the pen goes to paper. Off to one side is a gaggle of onlookers, all men. Most of their expressions are neutral, though one face bears the ghost of a smile: that of Steve Bannon, chief strategist to the president.

The photo, taken in January 2017, went viral, because it was Trump's first day in office and because the official document was an executive order banning NGOs from offering information about abortions if they receive US funding. The measure, known as Mexico City Policy or the 'global gag rule', first came into place during Ronald Reagan's presidency and was successively cancelled by Democratic presidents and reinstated by Republicans. The image gained much traction because it acted as a visual reminder of a fact that is both historical and acutely relevant in the present: that most lawmakers ruling on women's reproductive rights are men, some of them with sketchy records with regard to respect for women. The justices who overturned *Roe v. Wade*, after all, included Brett Kavanaugh, who had himself faced accusations of sexual assault.

Justice Samuel Alito wrote in overturning *Roe* that 'a right to abortion is not deeply rooted in the Nation's history and traditions.' Historians quickly pointed to America's long tradition of allowing abortions until late into a pregnancy; historian Sarah Churchwell noted that restrictive laws only came in the late 1800s and stemmed not just from moral and religious beliefs about the beginning of life but from cultural anxiety that followed the end of the Civil War and early fears of 'racial replacement' and perceived threats to white people's domination.[18]

In 1973, the same year that *Roe* was decided, an obscure French writer called Jean Raspail published *The Camp of Saints*, a dystopian novel about waves of Indian migrants invading France's southern coast, resulting in the collapse of Western governments and culture. While long forgotten in France, it became a key text of white supremacist groups in the US, playing on those same anxieties about racial replacement, and was an early precursor to the Great Replacement, a racist conspiracy theory developed by another Frenchman, Renaud Camus, who argued that there is a concerted plot by elites to replace Christian white European populations with Muslim immigrants through mass migration and falling birth rates.

Once a fringe conspiracy theory, the Great Replacement has inspired a wave of terrorist attacks, starting with the Christchurch attack in New Zealand in March 2019, followed by El Paso in August 2019 and many others since, targeting religious and ethnic minorities. It has also entered mainstream reactionary conversation. During his time at Fox News, Tucker Carlson mentioned the Great Replacement over 400 times.[19] Zemmour ran in the 2022 French presidential elections on a platform primarily focused on this conspiracy theory, achieving 7 per cent of the vote. In the US, former Republican presidential hopeful

Vivek Ramaswamy, born to Indian Hindu immigrants, also embraced the theory – without irony.[20]

The Great Replacement theory goes hand in hand with a notion of what white women's bodies are for: producing white babies. Reproductive autonomy, in the form of abortion and contraception, is seen as a leading cause of declining birth rates among white populations among proponents of the theory. At the most extreme, extremist groups have advocated for extreme violence to increase white populations. In July 2022, weeks after *Roe* was overturned, *Rolling Stone* reported that a former Marine who self-identified as the leader of the neo-Nazi group Rapekrieg had been arrested after plotting the mass murder of ethnic minority Americans and the rape of 'white women to increase the production of white children'.[21] The white supremacist Telegram channel Rapewaffen Division is primarily dedicated to promoting rape as part of a racial war.[22] White supremacist and neo-Nazi groups have become a familiar presence in anti-abortion marches.[23] Holocaust denier and leader of the Groypers (a group of white nationalist trolls) Nick Fuentes celebrated the overturning of *Roe v. Wade* with this message to women on his Telegram channel: 'Hey women we are gonna put y'all back in chains.'[24]

These are extreme examples, but the association between the overturning of *Roe* and racial conspiracy theories also appeared in the pro-Trump wing of the Republican party. Congresswoman Mary Miller called the overturning of *Roe* a 'historic victory for white life', later claiming that it was a slip of the tongue (certainly a revealing one).[25] Senator Steve Erdman blamed abortion for the decline of Nebraska's population, saying: 'Our state population has not grown except by those foreigners who have moved here or refugees who have been placed here.' He further stated that if abortion had been banned earlier, more people (read: white people) 'could be working and filling some of those positions that we have vacancies'.[26] The irony is that women from ethnic minority backgrounds are more likely to seek abortion than white women, a circle which some anti-abortionists have sought to square by advocating banning abortion for white women but allowing it for women of colour.[27]

While believers in the Great Replacement see abortion as a plot to reduce white birth rates, history shows that attacks on women's reproductive autonomy overwhelmingly affect Black women and are not limited to abortion. Black feminists who have conceptualised notions of reproductive justice have shown that legal access to abortion is just one manifestation of reproductive rights. A long history of slavery, segregation and institutional racism looms over Black women's reproductive autonomy and includes brutal waves of forced sterilisations of Latino, African American and Native American women over decades.[28]

These crimes explain why some of the lies that spread after the overturning of *Roe* may have struck a chord. Posts targeting African American and Latino communities and describing abortion as a plan by white people to exterminate ethnic minority Americans are disingenuous ploys to roll back women's rights but are rooted in a history of racism and systemic inequity. 'Why the Most Dangerous Place for African Americans Is the Womb', was the title of one of the most viral YouTube videos post-*Roe*, while others likened abortion to 'Black genocide' and claimed it '[Kills] More Blacks Than the Police'. They were embraced by mainstream figures: rapper Ye (formerly Kayne West) said that Planned Parenthood clinics 'have been placed inside cities by white supremacists to do the Devil's work', echoing long-standing arguments used by anti-abortion activists that link historical figures within the abortion movement, often accurately, to the eugenics movement.

The general framing of abortion as a form of modern-day eugenics has grown among anti-abortion activists to recruit diverse communities. Justice Clarence Thomas wrote in 2019 that 'abortion is an act rife with the potential for eugenic manipulation.'[29] adding that 'from the beginning, birth control and abortion were promoted as a means of effectuating eugenics,' a statement that multiple legal experts and historians have described as an ideologically motivated misreading of history to justify curtailing fundamental rights.[30]

While anti-abortion activism has draped itself in feminist and social justice rhetoric, anti-abortion policies are driven by political parties, interest groups and men not known for their feminist credentials. The crude Proud Boys-style sexism at the heart of the anti-abortion project is clear: Republican Congressman for Florida Matt Gaetz, briefly nominated by Trump to be attorney general following his re-election, told a right-wing student conference that 'disgusting' women 'who look like a thumb' should not concern themselves with abortion, also pondering how many women who demonstrated against the overturning of *Roe v. Wade* are 'over-educated, under-loved millennials who sadly return from protests to a lonely microwave dinner with their cats, and no Bumble matches'.[31]

Claims to ownership of women's bodies by the state have been a central element of fascist and extremist ideologies as well as authoritarian governments. Hungarian prime minister Viktor Orbán, who has made flouting democratic principles a matter of pride, has encouraged Hungarian women to have as many children as possible and hosts bi-annual 'Demographic Summits' in Budapest which have become a who's who of far-right, reactionary and male supremacist figures.[32] Vladimir Putin has urged women to have 'eight or more babies' amid heavy casualties in his war on Ukraine.[33]

Even when abortion remains legal, there are many ways to make it inaccessible. Russia has put pressure on private clinics to stop performing abortions, circulating guidelines to doctors to discourage women and restricting the sale of abortive medication.[34] In 2022, Orbán's Hungary introduced a law which forces women to listen to their foetus's heartbeat before having an abortion.[35] In Italy, Giorgia Meloni's government has reinstated a 1978 law which allows anti-abortion activists to enter family counselling centres to dissuade women from seeking abortion.[36] Even in the UK, the British Pregnancy Advisory Service has stated that police are increasingly demanding women's medical records from abortion providers, with such requests rising to about one a month from September 2023.[37] Meanwhile, post-*Roe* America shows what can happen when considerations about equity are sidelined as corporations started offering to pay for abortion-related costs as part of their employee benefit programmes, supporting the people least likely to need it. Meanwhile, as many US states legislation on abortion rights, the impact of the overturning of *Roe v. Wade* and the country's uncertain legislative landscape have become all too clear: in September 2024, Amber Thurman, a Black 28-year-old mother, died of abortion-related complications, after being denied care in Atlanta for an infection she contracted after taking abortion pills, weeks after Georgia's abortion ban came into effect.[38]

## First they came for abortion

The overturning of *Roe v. Wade* is one step in the male supremacist fantasy of 'putting women back in chains'. The aftermath of the *Dobbs* decision gave a chilling view of the future that may await American women. In April 2023, Idaho restricted out-of-state travel for abortions for minors.[39] Days after the Supreme Court decision, a Texan man using Senate Bill 8 – also known as the 'bounty hunter law', which gives financial rewards to anyone who successfully sues someone who has helped a person get an illegal abortion – sued three of his ex-wife's friends for $1 million each for helping her undergo an abortion.[40] On almost the same day, a 32-year-old pregnant woman became an international sensation after arguing that she should not be fined for parking in a high-occupancy vehicle lane because her unborn child counts as a person.[41]

Beyond the headlines, these cases are indicative of the next frontier of the anti-abortion movement. Several US states have launched proposals aimed at giving a foetus personhood status, a decision with significant implications for women's rights well beyond abortion, potentially limiting a woman's ability to make healthcare decisions during pregnancy or even making them criminally liable for certain behaviours (e.g. smoking during pregnancy), something that lawmakers in the UK, for instance, have refused to do.[42]

The backlash frontier has moved on to new areas of reproductive health and autonomy, including assisted reproductive techniques and contraception. Alease Barnes is an embryologist based in North Carolina. Every day, she helps her patients with fertility treatments, including in vitro fertilisation (IVF). She also has an active TikTok account, which she uses to address misinformation about fertility and assisted reproductive technology. She tells me that health disinformation and mischaracterisations of abortion are now used to target her and undermine her work. After *Roe v. Wade*, anti-abortion movements are increasingly turning their attention to new topics like IVF and are spreading falsehoods about the procedure, which affect patients' access to care. 'They are likening IVF to killing embryos; a lot of it uses misconceptions about where conception begins,' she says. The same goes for contraception such as Plan B, or the 'morning after pill', and intrauterine devices, which are wrongly depicted as having an abortive effect. While Trump stated that he wanted to be a 'leader on IVF', Republicans in several states have made concessions to anti-abortion lobbyists on IVF, and Senate Republicans blocked a June 2024 bill which sought to make access to the procedure a federal right.

This trickles into public discourse and policy. The conversations about reducing access to or banning contraception are underway. A Michigan state House candidate endorsed by Donald Trump has said birth control 'should not be legal'.[43] Banning birth control, once seen as a far-fetched idea, has become a suggestion several prominent Republicans and conservatives are making. Is it likely? A complete ban seems inconceivable but new restrictions on contraception access seem nothing but. Project 2025 includes unprecedented recommendations to roll back abortion and reproductive rights by prosecuting people who send abortion pills through the post and cutting funding for abortion and contraceptive pills.

The resistance to reproductive rights in North America, Europe and beyond is not just a manifestation of traditional values or reactionary politics. It represents a deliberate international effort to reinstate traditional gender roles and curtail women's and LGBT+ rights. At the heart of the contemporary anti-abortion movement is a transnational web of reactionary and ultra-religious think tanks, NGOs and foundations dedicated to protecting 'traditional' families and Western Christian civilisation and gravitating around the World Congress of Families (WCF), which acts as a hub of sorts. One of the WCF's key missions is implementing 'Agenda Europe', a fundamentalist campaign kick-started in 2013 by a group of activists based in the US and Europe. Today, the 'Agenda Europe' campaign counts at least 100 organisations across Europe and has clear policy goals. It seeks to overturn existing legislation on fundamental human rights, including women's access to contraception and the right to divorce. Its goals have been articulated in a policy manifesto called 'Agenda Europe: Restoring the Natural Order', which aims to be a coherent policy strategy and values statement.[44]

Despite being rooted in religious beliefs, the proponents of Agenda Europe couch their goals not in religion but in essentialist beliefs about sex, gender and the body, the so-called 'natural order', thereby divorcing reactionary policies from religion and turning them into a philosophical belief. The move from religious-based to this sort of essentialist language is a clearly thought out strategic realignment, aimed at achieving mainstream impact and influencing policy makers. The founding document of Agenda Europe outlines four key tactics for achieving mainstreaming influence. First, 'use the weapons of our opponents and turn them against them'. Second, colonise the language of human rights, such as framing opposition to inclusive sex education in school as 'the right of children to receive correct information'. Third, discredit opponents by seeking examples of shortcomings and trying to cut off their funding. Fourth, gain a foothold in and funding from international institutions like the UN and EU, a goal which naturally derives from other attempts at muddying the waters about what the group stands for. The most comprehensive investigation of its opaque funding, impossible to quantify but certainly substantial, shows it comes from US-based evangelical and right-wing foundations, climate denying billionaires and Russian Christian Orthodox oligarchs. These movements have a long-term view: their aim is to redraw gender norms and overthrow reproductive rights over years, if not decades. Their work to overturn *Roe v. Wade* was decades in the making, and they know their efforts go beyond one administration or presidential term.[45]

## My rabbit hole: how influencers lure us in

Weeks after giving birth to my son in early 2022, I found a breast lump. I went for an ultrasound, which I hoped would give me the all-clear, only to find that the lump was deemed suspicious and required a biopsy. With a family history of breast cancer, the two-week wait for the results was a deeply frightening experience. But for me, the horror didn't end when the lump was found to be benign. In the months that followed, I descended into a spiral of health anxiety. I cut out food groups one by one. I became obsessed with 'toxins' and may have said too many times that conspiracy theorists have a point about 'Big Pharma', much to my partner's dismay. An eating disorder I had battled as a teenager returned as my body felt again like something that needed to be tamed. The pressures of new parenthood may have triggered my anxiety, but it was made much worse because at the same time as this was going on, I had been receiving months of drip-drip content telling me all about 'cancer causing toxins' on my timeline. I had been researching conspirituality.

I remember when I first realised how much of a phenomenon conspirituality – the combination of New Age spirituality and conspiracy theories – was. It was 2020, I was locked down and on furlough and I spent too much time online. It came to me in the form of posts that claimed COVID-19 vaccines caused infertility. As the world was experiencing lockdowns, I was tracking emerging misinformation about the new virus, and soon, the vaccine. In addition to my day job, I had a long-standing yoga practice and, like too many students of yoga, had managed to be convinced to do yoga teacher training, becoming one more cog in the sprawling yoga industry. Soon the disinformation I was observing in my work started to appear in my personal timeline. My mentors were stoking fears about the vaccine on Instagram and urging followers to trust their bodies' inner ability to heal. One of the characters who eventually slid onto my feed was a woman by the name of @selfhealingmama.

@selfhealingmama (real name Chloe Angeline) has an Instagram account dedicated to motherhood, homoeopathy and 'living off-grid'. During the pandemic Angeline dedicated herself to creating videos validating fears about vaccination and stating that women were reporting menstrual abnormalities after coming into contact with vaccinated people, the nonsensical theory known as 'vaccine shedding'.[46] The offbeat claims I had been accustomed to hearing from a certain brand of yoga influencer were becoming more political: that the vaccine was a plan by elites for population control. QAnon, the pro-Trump conspiracy theory, had moved from 4chan and 8chan straight into my yoga class. Canadian researcher Marc-André Argentino coined the term 'Pastel QAnon' to refer to the palatable Instagram-friendly version of the conspiracy that gripped many parts of the world.[47] While QAnon had emerged on male-dominated forums characterised by their dark humour and violence, it spread like wildfire when it reached new communities of young mothers, wellness enthusiasts and New Age followers of love and light, with some light pink packaging for Instagram.

Despite its decline, QAnon has provided a blueprint for the kind of 'broad tent' conspiracy theories which have thrived since the pandemic faded away,[48] notably the 'Great Reset', a conspiracy theory which posits that there is a sinister plan by elites to impose health measures, lockdowns and mass surveillance for nefarious purposes.[49] This conspiracy theory lends itself to a plethora of interpretations and can be endlessly reinvented and projected onto new policies. Governments are thinking about introducing measures to make the city more walkable (15 minute cities)? It's called 'climate lockdown'. Wildfires are happening? It's arson deliberately orchestrated by elites to cow you into compliance. Scientists are warning about the impact of meat and dairy consumption on carbon emissions? Elites want you to eat bugs to make you stupid.[50]

Sections of the wellness community have become fully immersed in this type of rhetoric. The 'woo to fascism pipeline' is actually a logical progression for New Age and wellness culture, which has built itself on libertarian ideas of individual self-realisation, autonomy and purity. The view of contemporary yoga as a progressive countercultural practice, epitomised by yoga gurus joining Woodstock in 1969,[51] has obscured the fact that early 20th-century fascists were fond of yoga and New Age spiritual practices. Nazi Germany saw increased interest in astrology and alternative medicine, and in Britain, Francis Yeats-Brown, who popularised yoga and wrote books on the topic in the 1930s, was a leading fascist sympathiser.

Yoga was seen as a masculine discipline that could provide inspiration for authoritarian political leadership. More recently, Indian prime minister Narendra Modi and his nationalist BJP party have used yoga as a form of soft diplomacy while they downplay the repression of ethnic minorities, engaging in what writer Sheena Sood calls 'om-washing'.[52] Early wellness and yoga gurus in the West were men, and many were later accused of sexual assault, including Yogi Bhajan, the founder of Kundalini yoga in the West and the ubiquitous Yogi Tea brand,

and Bikram Choudhury, founder of the brand of hot yoga that bears his name.

It's not surprising that conspirituality has bloomed into a phenomenon. The pandemic was a turning point for the prioritisation of self-care over collective solidarity and individual focus on one's optimisation. The international vaccine roll-out programme and lockdowns, both public health policies implemented to protect the most vulnerable and to benefit the wider community, gave this hyper-individualistic community a reference to rally against and came to be interpreted as a form of infringement on individual sovereignty and pure, optimised bodies, whose interests trump those of the community and the most vulnerable.

Over the last few years, I have followed conspirituality closely, immersing myself every day in conspiratorial wellness communities and observing their broader shift rightward. Social media pushes holistic health coaches, crystal healers, womb-warming advisors and 'off-grid' anti-vaxx mothers my way.[53] Every day, I log into my account and scroll through hundreds of posts. I follow the algorithm wherever it takes me. I have become familiar with the new health panics that imbue these communities, from sun cream and seed oils to sunglasses. During the pandemic, I'd debunk claims that the vaccine caused infertility by day and log into a parallel online bubble where it did in the evening.

I thought that by following communities where QAnon meets crystal healing, I was seeing how 'the other half' thinks. In reality, as Naomi Klein showed in *Doppelganger* (2023), conspiracy theories offer a distorted image of inequities and hold a mirror to our own failings. While its fascistic implications are sinister and not hard to see, conspirituality is a monstrous but not entirely surprising reaction to the feeling that current structures are badly equipped to sustain us. The pandemic made what was true before – that we are not all treated equally and that our neoliberal societies care little about many people and communities' lives – even more clear: as the virus spread, Harley Street Clinic in London marketed immune-boosting intravenous drips for £350,[54] while the virus disproportionately killed those from ethnic minority and poorer communities.[55]

Because of their focus on purity and health, alt-health influencers articulate real problems, particularly about environmental damage and the shortcomings of medical institutions towards women and minorities. Recent years have seen a mainstream reckoning with this misogyny. From genital mutilations to sexual violence and the prescription of addictive drugs, the history of neglect towards women by doctors and medical institutions is damning. That misogyny continues to this day. Women's pain continues to be dismissed, as a series of memoirs in recent years, from Lynn Enright's *Vagina* (2019) to Emma Barnett's *Period* (2019) have shown. The 'gender data gap' that Caroline Criado-Perez has detailed in *Invisible Women* (2019) runs the full gamut of research, prevention and treatment.

Into this injustice have stepped predatory wellness influencers who are positioning themselves as pro-empowerment figures helping women reclaim their health and intuition against a misogynistic medical establishment and promising them that they can thrive and be well if only their take their own red pill.[56] This pill involves rejecting conventional medicine, embracing their divine femininity and natural womanhood (which includes no hormonal birth control, unmedicated birth and natural parenting) and embarking on a long journey of self-healing and self-responsibility, presented as an act of feminist defiance against a misogynistic 'medical-industrial complex'.[57]

Following these communities made me realise a few things, mostly that I am susceptible to this form of red-pilling and that I can be gripped by fear and tempted by illusory promises of self-optimisation which steal away my time to do more socially valuable work. Being aware of one's unpleasant impulses is important in order to pull back from them. I have also come to believe that libertarian wellness is the underestimated Trojan horse of regressive gender norms and male supremacist agendas, because they disguise themselves convincingly in feminist rhetoric and are the default option many of us turn to when we're vulnerable. Abortion herbs become attractive amid panic and limited options. In an age of climate emergency and associated deteriorating health, the temptation to retreat into self-protection can be strong.

After several months of intense health anxiety and sometimes taking my cues from dubious New Age influencers peddling

Satanic panics, I decided I'd had enough and would address my eating disorder with the help of medical professionals. Of course, I was always able to rationally understand these influencers were harmful scammers, but the kernel of truth they shared was compelling. Some wellness influencers speak convincingly – though often superficially and to serve their own financial interests – about harmful corporate interests, and they are not wrong: look no further than how companies like Monsanto lobby to continue distributing glyphosate.[58] Fossil fuel companies and car manufacturers spent decades trying to conceal their knowledge of man-made climate change.[59] It is only a short step to seeing plots hatched by every institution, including public interest institutions, all of which are inevitably flawed.

## Everybody hates the pill

I have not beaten my anxiety. Cancer headlines, bogus wellness claims and stories about pollution elicit a familiar panic reflex. I regularly Google aches and pains against my better judgement and inevitably find some horrific condition they are connected to. Perfectly ordinary spots and blemishes spark days of worry. I go to the doctor and walk back home concerned they have missed something. I'm not alone in this. Studies have shown that women are more likely to be health anxious,[60] which is why wellness influencers are not short of an audience. They target poorly understood conditions disproportionately affecting women, from hormonal conditions like polycystic ovary syndrome (PCOS) and endometriosis, which affect around 10 per cent of women in developed countries,[61] to auto-immune conditions including Hashimoto and lupus.

As I'm writing, there are over four million mentions of #PCOS on Instagram, over five billion on TikTok, and the subreddit channel r/PCOS has over 125,000 members. Over two million posts on Instagram include the hashtag #endometriosis. A study of the most widely followed influencers communicating about PCOS on X (then Twitter) reveals a mix of medically trained doctors, naturopaths, dieticians, and people writing about their experience of having the condition and seeking to increase knowledge among their followers, an eclectic crowd with well-intentioned though not medically qualified people among them.[62]

In the world of wellness influencers one thing seems to be universally maligned: hormonal birth control. Canadian obstetrician and gynaecologist Dr Jen Gunter is one of the most vocal women's health educators in the public eye today, and she uses her public profile to respond to common myths and misconceptions about the pill with the latest scientific evidence.[63] Her efforts, and that of other experts, to bring some sanity to the debate about hormonal birth control risk falling on many deaf ears as young women flock to 'Birth Control TikTok' for information.[64]

The hate for the pill captures perfectly the dynamics of the anti-feminist backlash. Curtailing access to contraception is at the heart of projects like Agenda Europe and the long-term plan of reactionaries and authoritarians. In public and online, a broad range of different actors are loudly sharing their dislike of the pill for their own ideological aims and know they will have a receptive audience: from the self-described 'anti-feminist' wellness influencer who describes the pill as 'literal poison' to anti-abortion groups such as Live Action who like to repeat the (simplified) claim that the pill is a 'Class 1 carcinogen' and, parroting the language of informed consent and patient empowerment, that 'women deserve to know what they're putting in their bodies.'[65]

Reactionary conservatives ranging from Ben Shapiro to conservative podcaster (and member of the pro-Trump conservative youth movement Turning Point USA) Alex Clark have stoked fears of side effects.[66] Jordan Peterson has devoted videos to explaining that the pill makes women attracted to less masculine men,[67] repeating contested claims gathered from selected evolutionary psychology research and warning that birth control has led to a decline in birth rates 'below replacement levels':[68] a claim which makes sense given that Peterson has been a speaker at Orbán's Budapest Demographic Summit where speakers are stoking Great Replacement fears.[69] Far-right figures and movements don't like the pill either, in case you wondered. 'Get rid of all voluntary birth control,' alt-right figure Greg Johnson told undercover researcher Patrik Hermansson.[70]

The development of the pill was a central element of the sexual revolution and first-wave feminist efforts for greater social liberation of women. The pill has had a deeply transformative effect on contemporary societies, including freeing women (to a large extent) from unwanted pregnancies and giving them greater autonomy. The backlash against the pill today is a tool of the anti-feminist backlash because the two are interlinked. This is somewhat complicated by the fact the contraceptive pill has its own dark history of racism and misogyny. The first birth control pill, developed in the US in the 1950s, was tested on Puerto Rican women without informed consent; many of these women experienced severe side effects and some died.[71] Plans to develop a pill for men were dropped over concerns of side effects, as its architects thought that side effects were something all women could bear the brunt of and women from ethnic minority backgrounds serve as guinea-pigs for.[72]

Given this, and many women's personal experience of side effects, we can be forgiven for wondering if the pill is 'literally poison', as some wellness influencers might say. There are signs that more and more young women in some Western countries are giving up hormonal birth control, a move driven partly by the wellness industry's maligning of the pill but also rooted in lived experiences of the side effects and increasingly politically motivated messaging.[73] In early 2024, *The Washington Post* reported that more and more women of reproductive age in the US are shunning hormonal birth control because of a surge in medical misinformation driven by wellness influencers,[74] amid limited abortion options and a conservative push in some states to reduce access to birth control.[75]

From some women's magazines' nuanced coverage of the side effects of hormonal contraception to documentaries shining a light on the same issue, there has been a parallel mainstream reckoning with the problems that come with hormonal contraception. These legitimate debates can be weaponised by anti-feminists, but it doesn't mean they shouldn't happen. One would argue that they are especially important because there is a danger that reactionaries, boosted by algorithms and outrage, will dominate online and public conversation about contraception, and will manage to implement policies which restrict access to it.

Better contraception and better treatment options for hormonal conditions for which the pill remains the first line of treatment are a feminist imperative. For many women, hormonal birth control is a less than ideal solution; for others, it is (perhaps unfortunately) still the best available option and a necessary aid in managing complex conditions. Women are bearing the burden of contraception, something reactionaries with a natural aversion to contraception and women's autonomy have rightly identified. These people do not want women to have access to better contraception methods. They want them to use the cycle tracking apps they are sharing discount codes for. A male contraceptive pill might be on the horizon,[76] though it's doubtful that the men who are buried deep in their misogynistic rabbit holes and in their own concerns about purity will be likely to adopt it. None of these conversations about health, equity and autonomy are best served by QAnon-adjacent wellness influencers selling 'hormone-balancing' powders and anti-feminist activists who believe in restoring a natural order.

## Anti-feminist empowerment

Conspirituality is easy to fall into because wellness culture is so ubiquitous. In the 2010s, Gwyneth Paltrow and Dr Oz turned wellness into a mainstream obsession. We are all conned a little bit by the ever-expanding wellness industry, which sells us bubble baths and expensive vitamins we don't need. Most of this is pretty innocuous, but it can veer into something darker. In recent years, the wellness industry has exhibited shocking levels of predatory behaviour. There are extreme cases – for instance, Belle Gibson, an Australian influencer who gathered hundreds of thousands of followers by faking terminal cancer, which she claimed to have cured with supplements and diet.[77] Wellness influencers have an endless supply of dubious remedies for our ills: vitamins, powders and cleanses as well as courses and workshops. This can be a personal and public health danger, from individuals refusing conventional treatments for life-threatening illnesses to parents treating their children for complex conditions with unproven and potentially harmful remedies.

While the wellness movement has lurched to the right since the pandemic, early New Age movements seemed to want to offer some feminist promises. The natural birth movement, for instance, emerged in the 1980s as a reaction to a male-dominated medicalised birth process which had become the norm across much of the industrialised world in the 1960s and 1970s and came with its fair share of horrors. Natural birth and motherhood became touted as a feminist reclaiming of women's bodies. Ina May Gaskin, one of the key figures in the contemporary natural birth movement, founded a home-birth centre on The Farm, the commune she created in 1971 in Tennessee with her husband, Stephen, a known figure in the San Francisco hippie movement, eventually attracting a clientele of middle-class white women and interest from celebrities, reaching its natural neoliberal endgame. The conservative roots of the movement are clear though. Grantly Dick-Read, the British obstetrician who founded his own private clinic at Harley Street and popularised 'natural childbirth', was a devout Christian. William Sears, the founder of 'attachment parenting', was an evangelical Christian with a clear notion of what women's natural calling was: 'Woman fails when she ceases to desire the children for which she was primarily made.'[78]

Today's new libertarian self-realisation also posits itself as a reclaiming of women's bodies, at least rhetorically. What it has in common with reactionary conservatism is the belief in essentialist, primal and biologised notions of the body, feminine and masculine, and a dislike of state intervention and collective policies that could infringe on it, even if these interventions are about guaranteeing basic rights and protection for others. This goes hand in hand with a sacralisation of the complementary gender binary, the divine feminine and masculine, the yin and the yang, which wellness-oriented manosphere influencers and QAnon self-healing mothers subscribe to, like the reactionaries shaping their policy manifestos for the future behind closed doors. It is not surprising that someone like @selfhealingmama believes both in her divine feminine nature and self-healing intuition and in the need for a primal man in touch with his masculinity and 'who doesn't bend over for the government'. 'We need the Strong men to rise up now more than ever,' she writes. 'My husband is deeply connected to his primal instincts and ancestors. Oddly enough, the system has done everything in its power to label this type of man as toxic.'[79]

Anti-abortion influencers offering tips on gut health and sourdough baking on Instagram look as far away as possible from tantric sex coaches who run orgasmic enlightenment workshops, yet both believe in a form of anti-feminist self-realisation steeped in women's innate wisdom. While the former advocate for sexual restraint, the latter offer a shallow, and narrowly scripted, discourse about sexual fulfilment and empowerment which acts as a smokescreen for a regressive gender discourse and for the fact that, for all their talk about corrupt Big Pharma, they are the ones who benefit financially when women give up their medication in favour of a self-healing workshop.

This strand of New Age anti-feminist empowerment is gaining ground, exemplified by figures like Anami as well as Kelly Brogan, the self-described 'holistic psychiatrist' who was named in early 2021 in a report by the Center for Countering Digital Hate as one of the 'dirty dozen', the 12 influencers who contributed to the circulation of two thirds of anti-vaccine content during that period.[80] While Brogan made a name for herself mostly through her anti-vaccine activism and her opposition to anti-depressants to treat mental health conditions, she has recently embraced overt anti-feminist discourse while selling her own brand of empowerment, which she calls 'reclaimed womanhood' and which comes with online courses, a private community (or 'inner circle') and a book.[81] 'Feminism has promised women empowerment and freedom, but at what cost? Feminism encourages us to fight against men, but real empowerment lies in embracing our natural strengths and roles,'[82] writes Brogan, who also tells women that every time they say no to conventional medicine, they are freeing themselves of an oppressive system,[83] and every time they refuse to take the pill, they 'say yes to the wisdom of [their] biology'.[84]

Next to the immediate impact on individuals in need of treatment for various conditions, one of the most pernicious dangers of libertarian self-improvement sold as a feminist promise is that it makes one believe one does not need collective policies that benefit everyone and cuts one off from any understanding of oneself as part of a community with a responsibility to others. The more access to care is restricted, the more individuals will turn to Google and try to manage their conditions on their own.[85]

Legislative restrictions of abortion rights pre-*Dobbs* correlated with increased searches on self-managing abortions.[86] The more structures of support are dismantled, the more women are likely to stumble upon an online influencer telling them they need not worry about their reproductive rights because they can be well f*cked.

Upon its release in July 2023 *Barbie* would form an unlikely pairing with *Oppenheimer* to become one of the summer's smash hits. Inevitably, it divided opinion. The manosphere hated it. After all, Ken's narrative arc showed him becoming red-pilled, played for laughs. Progressives too had mixed reactions to the film. Some enjoyed its witty message; many observed that Barbie's owner Mattel was the true beneficiary of the film.

Still, the film had much to recommend it, not least the last line: 'I'm here to see my gynaecologist.' Director Greta Gerwig explained its meaning beyond its use as a mic drop joke.

> When I was a teenage girl, I remember growing up and being embarrassed about my body, and just feeling ashamed in a way that I couldn't even describe. It felt like everything had to be hidden … and then to see Margot as Barbie, with this big old smile on her face, saying what she says at the end with such happiness and joy. I was like, if I can give girls that feeling of, 'Barbie does it, too' – that's both funny and emotional.[87]

Thanks to wellness influencers selling their own brand of empowerment and cuts to healthcare services, more and more women might be giving a visit to the gynaecologist a pass.

# 4

# Apron-clad armies: women for male supremacy

A woman wearing a light blue flare dress stands on a country road, her faithful dog gazing up at her. Sunlight streams through the trees in the background, casting an ethereal halo around her flowing brown hair.[1] She's turned away from the camera, making the idyllic rural setting a universal one, inviting the viewer into her world. Elsewhere on this Instagram account are pictures of mountain hikes, campfire cooking and a rural homestead somewhere in America, alternating with photos of vintage dresses and sewing magazines.

But in each one that features the woman, her face is hidden, sometimes masked by her long hair, sometimes artistically cropped out of frame, but sometimes crudely scrubbed out with a Paint tool. Pictures come with a block of hashtags: #countryliving, #vintagefashion, #escapesociety and #femininenotfeminist, among others. The woman behind the account is a tradwife, part of an international online community of women who promote traditional gender roles, submission to one's husband and a life centred around homemaking and childrearing. Tradwives also advocate for meek behaviour and modest attire. And they are anti-feminist.

In early 2020, as countries went into lockdown and half the world suddenly started learning how to make sourdough, a collective dream sprang up. Much of the conversation focused on how COVID-19 had forced us to slow down, appreciate what is truly important: family, a garden, really great bread. The internet trend of 'cottagecore' arose, an idealised picture of rural life featuring cottages with well-tended gardens, vintage furniture and peaceful surroundings and offering the glimpse to a better, simpler life – the kind of life that feels out of reach for many millennials and Gen Zers. Cottagecore itself is a progressive aesthetic which has a following among lesbian women and pro-Black Lives Matter communities.

But it overlaps with the tradwife aesthetic, which grew alongside it on those social media platforms that favour idealised representations of one's lives. The #tradwife hashtag on Instagram and TikTok spews out endless images of domestic bliss, lattice crust apple pies and well-tended roses interlaced with stern messages telling women that feminism is a scam. Google searches for tradwives have increased dramatically in recent years, particularly since early 2024.[2]

At first glance, nothing distinguishes Caitlin Huber, or Mrs Midwest as she is known to her over 50,000 followers on Instagram, from countless other lifestyle, beauty and parenting millennial bloggers who populate the platform. Selfies show Huber advertising her favourite makeup brand with discount codes. She looks like a woman who has perfectly mastered the art of Instagram life blogging. So too does Alena Kate Pettitt, a British woman who across the Atlantic runs The Darling Academy, a self-described 'lifestyle website for housewives, homemakers, traditionalists & anglophiles'. Their online branding is very different. While Huber caters to hip millennial women, Pettitt's Instagram account harks back to 1950s Britain, offering the image of a life where days are all about high tea. Estee Williams, a TikTok influencer and one of the most followed tradwives online, cultivates a Marilyn Monroe bob and a 1950s pin-up look.

Tradwives as an organised online movement emerged on Reddit in 2013 with a group called r/RedPillWomen (60,000+ members today),[3] a counterpart to the male red pill movement. They really are, to use Pettitt's own slogan, an apron-clad army. Researcher Julia Ebner, who went undercover among red-pilled women in her book *Going Dark* (2019), estimated the number of red-pilled women to be around 30,000 at that time, and they congregated in a few forums. Today, it's impossible to know how many convinced tradwives there truly are and how many women are on the edge of the rabbit hole, looking on and wondering if a life of subservience to and dependence on men is truly a good idea. There are countless Instagram and TikTok influencers with hundreds of thousands and sometimes millions of followers. There are Facebook groups and Telegram channels dedicated to promoting conventional femininity, traditional gender roles and anti-feminist narratives.

If the manosphere is only one click away for most men, the tradwives are only one click away for many women. I first came across their representations of beautiful landscapes and familial bliss during the pandemic, yet just as with the wellness influencers, the algorithm took me to darker places.

I did not search for the tradwives; the tradwives found me, and if you are a woman of reproductive age, or a reasonably new mother, in all likelihood they will have made it into your social media feed by now. Once you click on these accounts, the onslaught is inescapable, and scrolling through endless images of women who seem to have enough time to make their own mozzarella from scratch feels soothingly addictive. A friend of mine confessed that looking at tradwife content is her guilty pleasure and expressed her own discomfort at finding them so appealing. Being a feminist and a lesbian, she is not exactly the target audience for influencers who sing the joy of heterosexual marriage and a life spent in the kitchen. Tradwives have also become something of a social joke. More than a few friends have facetiously suggested, when overworked, that maybe they should become tradwives and be forever relaxed.

While in her 1963 classic *The Feminine Mystique*, Betty Friedan spoke of the 'problem that has no name' – the feelings of dissatisfaction and unease that suburban American housewives experienced – influencers are telling us this lifestyle is the solution to our ills we didn't know we needed and managing to convince more and more that they are right. Media coverage of the tradwife movement has contributed in no small measure to its mainstreaming and to the collective fascination with the movement. Widely followed influencers have appeared in puff pieces run by conservative outlets and delighted tabloids, including the *Daily Mail* in the UK, which has gleefully run dozens of stories about self-described tradwives with titles like 'I live to please my husband': 'Tradwife, 37, reveals she lets her spouse have SEX with other women while she cooks, cleans and caters to his every whim – admitting "98% of her day" revolves around him.'[4]

When I started following the tradwife movement, I created an account to signal my interest, deliberately using a picture of a blonde woman dipping her feet in water and posting a couple of images of flowers and freshly baked cake to bait the hook. That was all it took to signal to social media platforms that I was fine with anything the tradwives sent my way, and the algorithm kept bringing me more. The entry point of the tradwife movement is that simple: a few visual cues signal you are open to receiving content. The tradwives follow me back. Many of them are discreet and have private accounts. Entering their groups online gives me deeper insight into their beliefs. While Estee Williams is doing TikTok videos dancing around her kitchen with an apron and instructing her followers on how to reproduce her look, and while we joke about being tradwives when the to-do list becomes a bit too long, there is an under-layer of tradwives dedicated to red-pilling women into male supremacist ideologies. This isn't surprising. The fringes are where they come from, and their aim is to radicalise.

Their uniting factor is their anti-feminism, but beyond that there are sub-types. Biblical womanhood tradwives are typically evangelical Christians who use selected Bible passages, particularly Titus 2:5 ('To be discreet, chaste, keepers at home, good, obedient to their own husbands, that the word of God be not blasphemed'), to advocate for traditional gender roles and cement the idea of the perfect Christian woman as a homemaker. These women advocate for homeschooling and sometimes cover their heads. Pagan tradwives overlap with wellness and New Age communities and combine wifely submission with talk of divine femininity, gut health and anti-vaccine talk.

Academics Sophia Sykes and Veronica Hopner, who have produced a tradwife Venn diagram, divide them into four categories: religious, political, militia and countercultural.[5] Religious tradwives primarily focus on promoting traditional marriage and femininity as a form of Biblical duty. For political (right-wing) tradwives, tradwifedom is essential to the restoration of national and conservative values. Militia tradwives, mostly based in North America, combine elegant femininity with gun culture and post pictures of themselves holding firearms. Countercultural tradwives, in their analysis, are the most extreme and see the tradwifedom and white motherhood as a key element in a 'race war'.

In the online attention economy, these distinctions sometimes blend into each other as each tradwife cultivates her own personal ideology and brand. Many tradwives, for instance, combine traditional Christianity and Biblical quotes with a bit of New Age paganism and its associated aesthetics, perhaps recognising the latter is more accessible for the educated millennial who is feeling burned out, was passed over again for promotion by a male colleague and is questioning her life choices.

In the midst of this, there is what can only be described as tradwife kink: stock pictures of 1950s housewives, the kind that adorn tacky birthday cards, with cheeky slogans. 'It's always wine o'clock!' is replaced with captions like 'Be proud of the patriarchy' and 'Patriarchy is the cure for disobedient women'. The existence of this kind of kink is entirely unsurprising. The tradwives offer male supremacists a fantasy image of the kind of women they want: modest to the outside world but sexually available to them and who do whatever they say. One of the core tenets of the Proud Boys, after all, is 'venerating the housewife' … as long as she knows her place, cooks and produces babies.

While AI apps that 'nudify' women are flourishing online, there is also DignifAI, an app created by 4chan users that digitally covers women up in modest clothing. In a world where women belong to men, they can be digitally stripped with AI as quickly as they can also be dressed as traditional housewives for male gratification.[6] One of those who epitomises these dynamics is Gwen The Milkmaid, a wellness-oriented tradwife whose TikTok and Instagram accounts are mostly about baking sourdough in willowy dresses and dancing in open fields. Gwen The Milkmaid owes her success to her narrative, which comes straight out of a male supremacist dream: she was an OnlyFans pornography performer who has now rejected 'sexual depravity', found God and gushes about the 'feminine urge to take care of your husband and make him delicious food all the time'.[7] Her past life also included producing bisexual ASMR videos, a fact she avoids advertising too much (as opposed to her OnlyFans history), recognising it is perhaps a bit *risqué* for her brand.

## Exploiting feminist fatigue

The appeal of the tradwives is not hard to see, not just for male supremacists who think life owes them one. The tradwives offer women an image of bliss, comfort and safety at a time when these feelings seem increasingly elusive, especially for young women who have grown up in the shadow of the 2008 economic crisis, a global pandemic and climate breakdown.

Many tradwives have a similar story to tell: the story of the career girl who is sick of the nine-to-five hamster wheel, feels cheated by the feminist promise of 'having it all' and finds fulfilment in the simplicity of home. Estee Williams told the *Daily Mail* she saw her mother 'run herself ragged trying to "do it all"'.[8] Pettitt said she 'pretended to be a feminist' to the outside world but was dissatisfied by 'working in London in the cut-throat and fast paced beauty industry'.[9]

The tradwives have found success online because they exploit women's fatigue, as well as feminist fatigue. Their message to women is clear: feminism has sold you a lie and left you dissatisfied, tired and working the third shift. They like to present a return to domesticity and traditional gender roles as a bold form of escape from late-stage capitalism, hustle culture and burnout, some of which the pandemic exposed by increasing the burden of care work placed on women.[10] While feminism was never about promising women they could 'have it all' – a marketing slogan put forward by former *Cosmopolitan* magazine editor-in-chief Helen Gurley Brown, which is also unfairly maligned[11] – many women have rightly identified that something about their lives is amiss, and tradwives are all too ready to blame this on feminism.

This explains why the tradwife movement is now also making forays outside of its initial target audience. While the movement is overwhelmingly white and has strong undertones of white nationalism and supremacy (though some tradwives will work hard to deny it), Black tradwife accounts have also sprung up.[12] They speak about the magnified pressures that fellow Black women experience but merely offer a life of subjugation as a response to societal failures. Indeed, burnout doesn't affect everyone equally. Studies have shown that women are more likely to experience burnout than men.[13] Data from the Study of Women's Health across the Nation in the US suggests that Black women are '7.5 years biologically "older" than white women' as a result of stress, hardships and the compounded effects of misogyny and racism they face.[14]

Given their careful branding and the expert management of their online personas, it will come as no surprise that a lot of tradwives are former urban millennial graduates and feminists who have renounced their ways but have specific skills (notably marketing and content writing) which they put at the service of promoting the tradwife lifestyle. Robyn Riley, who shares her experience of 'deprograming [*sic*] from the radical feminist mindset', has a degree in Film Studies and Mass Communication and writes for *Evie Magazine*, the '"Cosmo" for the far-right' as *Rolling Stone* describes it.[15] Presenting themselves as former insiders who have seen the bad and the ugly is central to presenting themselves as truth-tellers.

'I do know what feminism is; I've been in the belly of the beast. I was deep, deep, deep in the world of feminism and I chose to leave,' said Ayla Stewart (or 'Wife with a Purpose') in a 2015 YouTube video. Stewart was one of the early tradwives. She first gained notoriety with a YouTube video titled 'Welcome Refugees?? I blame feminism, this is why',[16] in the process attracting the attention of the neo-Nazi website Stormfront. She then infamously called on her followers to 'have as many white babies' as she herself had contributed, which was six at the time. These days, Stewart describes herself on her website as the victim of censorship and smear campaigns and is using discreet white nationalist cues which fly under the radar of social media platforms' content moderation.[17] One of the lesser-known aspects of her journey is that she pursued a degree in women's spirituality. In online videos, she recounts the experience of encountering derision during her master's degree for wanting to write about feminist perspectives on motherhood.[18]

Whether the story is true or not, she is styling herself as a woman who speaks to fellow sisters, particularly mothers, who have been scorned by feminists, and who has witnessed the problems with feminism first-hand: who has been in the belly of the beast, as she puts it. That metaphor has inspired the name of another anti-feminist far-right influencer: Rebecca Hargraves, aka 'Blonde in the Belly of the Beast'. Recounting how she learned to be proud of 'being descended from European civilization', Hargraves tells women about her career in finance in New York City: she says she worked with 'many feminists' and observes that 'if you're successful in a high-powered job, all that's waiting for you at the end is 80-hour work weeks and the inevitable decision to quit' when women realise they have left it too late for children.[19]

This isn't exactly creative rhetoric, but post-pandemic, these arguments have to do less work to convince than they used to. The fact that the tradwife message is finding a receptive audience testifies to widespread disenchantment with the feminism that is most often on display in the public sphere. This feminism has long sidelined women of colour and working class women, although these are not the audience Blonde in the Belly of the Beast is speaking to. The shallow message of empowerment that mainstream feminism has promoted for well over a decade feels increasingly alienating and vapid, even to the privileged and educated white women whom it primarily serves, as more women bear the brunt of technological alienation, inequalities and the climate crisis.

## The tradwife grift

While tradwives like to present themselves as canny individuals who have gamed the system, the immediate problem of their proposition is plain to see: for the vast majority of us, a single income is not enough to support a family and live in a cottage in the Cotswolds or on the American Plains. Far from being 'just' stay-at-home wives, tradwives are savvy content creators and businesswomen who use all the tools of the internet and social media to spread their ideas.

'They tap into pre-existing digital cultures, from selfies and travel writing to food and beauty blogging,' Eviane Leidig, author of *The Women of the Far-Right* (2023), tells me. They run multiple social media channels, which they use for different purposes.

Mrs Midwest runs a YouTube channel, a blog and a Pinterest account, selling her traditional and feminine way of life as an aspirational lifestyle. Followers can click on her 'Shop My Life' tab, which will direct them to a website listing everything from her skincare range to beauty tips.

By encouraging submission to men and staying at home, they put women in immediate positions of financial dependence, which can leave them at the mercy of abusive partners or trapped in unhappy partnerships. The only way to live the opulent tradwife lifestyle is to be independently wealthy, find a rich husband or monetise oneself well enough in the online economy, which is exactly what the popular tradwives are doing. While they promise an escape from end-stage capitalism, they are participants in the precarious online influence economy where relevance is determined by clicks and likes and where gender inequalities are entrenched:[20] most influencers today are women, but they earn 30 per cent less than their male counterparts.[21]

Huber's social media persona is carefully curated for maximum viewership. Her Instagram account includes discount codes for a range of products. Pettitt sells books and articles with advice. Some tradwives pay lip service to frugality, like Pettitt who told Holly Willoughby on ITV's *This Morning* programme that she uses the 'allowance' her husband gives her wisely. Viewers are, it seems, interested in knowing how they can make it work financially. On her FAQ, Mrs Midwest says she can afford their lifestyle by being frugal and that she likes to 'live an anti-consumerism lifestyle', all the while doing brand sponsorship and generating revenue through YouTube ads and affiliate Amazon links.

'I don't want to be a Girlboss,' these girlbosses assure us as they broadcast their lives to the world for clicks. As optimised content creators, they have a lot of things to sell and use the full gamut of influencer income generation: ad revenue, brand partnerships and merchandise. Many of them run online businesses where they sell clothing, sourdough baking kits, food supplements, skincare and more. What they also sell are courses and advice on how to become a tradwife: *not* a housewife, a tradwife who monetises her lifestyle. In this sense, the tradwife movement operates like one of the most exploitative economic practices of today's rapacious online economy: the Multi-Level Marketing Scheme

(MLM), where individuals earn money by selling products and by recruiting new members, turning them into sellers themselves. The most successful tradwives sit on top of the pyramid, living off other women's discontent.

Real MLMs mostly target women and have been on the rise since COVID-19, luring more and more in with promises of an income. They use emotional manipulation and cultic techniques to pressure their members to sell more and discourage them from leaving, as former members have testified. A report by the Federal Trade Commission found that only 1 per cent of people involved in MLM ever make a profit.[22] The Direct Sellers Association in the UK estimates that half a million people are involved in direct sales as of 2024.[23] MLMs include companies like doTerra, a Utah-based company which sells essential oils and has strong links to The Church of Jesus Christ of Latter-Day Saints (LDS Church or Mormonism),[24] which a number of prominent tradwives also belong to.

The growing popularity of MLMs is a reflection of decades of neoliberal politics and dismantlement of the welfare state, not just because these schemes become necessary in times of economic hardships but also because early MLMs were conceived partly as a response to the negative effects of neoliberal atomisation. Scholar Frankie Mastrangelo has noted that 'multi-level marketing schemes grew into an omnipresent force in the 1990s as neoliberalism ascended into a governing economic and cultural rationality.'[25] Early MLMs like Tupperware were a way for women to earn money from home at a time of economic deregulation, but they also provided opportunities for female sociability, the same kind of sociability that was under strain as a result of these economic policies. They also softened the blow of growing isolation at a time when feminist advances in the domestic sphere were slowly sidelined in favour of a strand of feminism concerned with personal advancement.

While early tradwife forums and groups provided a space for discussion and solidarity, influencer-era tradwifedom involves watching other women perform their lives online and competing with them for monetisation opportunities. Talk of sisterhood feels performative and the sense of belonging that comes with being part of an online community feels shallow as tradwives do not have much to say about community structures and real support for women.

## Finding your (white) knight in armour: from the mainstream to white supremacy

The emergence of tradwives as an increasingly mainstream movement promoted by influencers with carefully curated social media personas tends to obscure the darker politics these influencers promote. Dog whistles can be subtle in accounts curated for acceptability. Pettitt's content is mostly innocuous, putting aside its romanticisation of wifely submission and the fact that there are implicit undertones to her idealisation of a 1950s Britain and the time when 'you could leave your front door open and know that you were safe and you knew your neighbours in the street' as opposed to contemporary society where 'we don't even know the identity of our country right now.'[26] To be fair to her, Pettitt was one of the earliest tradwife influencers and has since expressed concern about what the movement has morphed into, quitting Instagram and telling the *New Yorker* 'It's become an aesthetic, and then it's become politicized. And then it's become its own monster.'[27]

Not all the tradwives are so innocent. Huber's 'YouTube content I've binged' on her website includes anything from videos of cream buns recipes to links to the channel of Brittany Sellner, an American-born white nationalist and wife to Austrian far-right Identitarian activist Martin Sellner. Her list of '20 things I recommend' includes a YouTube video of white supremacist Canadian YouTuber Stefan Molyneux slotted in between a peach pie recipe and her own compiled playlist,[28] showing how she straddles the line between commercially successful influencer and far-right red-pilled activist.

Other women are openly concerned with inculcating an anti-feminist and far-right view and recruiting women to their cause. Let's go back to the woman with the long brown hair and her dog. The fact that she keeps her face hidden in her photos is down to more than modesty or a desire for privacy. Amid pictures of idyllic campfires lurks a darker message, mostly conveyed through hashtags to maximise engagement and lure viewers in: popular hashtags like #cottage and #vintagestyle are used alongside #itsoktobewhite and #traditionaleuropean and #econationalism.[29] Other posts include more obscure references: #natsoc (National Socialism, or Nazism) and #tedkaczynski, a reference to the 'Unabomber' terrorist who carried out a series of terrorist attacks starting in the 1970s with the goal of bringing about the end of modern technological society. Kaczynski has become a key reference for eco-fascist movements, which combine white supremacy with back-to-the-land ecological discourse.[30]

The woman with her #itsoktobewhite hashtags is an unashamed white supremacist and eco-fascist who hides in plain sight on Instagram and sees the return to traditional gender roles as central to the new pure, white society she aspires to. 'If I can inspire at least one person to make some positive changes in their life, embrace modesty or live a more traditional lifestyle, I have achieved what started this page to do,'[31] she says in a post. Her account is an example of accelerationism, a form of far-right activism that welcomes the breakdown of modern society and political structures because it will lead to a return to nature and the rebuilding of society along racial and gendered lines: the rebirth of a white society.[32]

'People who are savvy and know how to use social media know how to signal through imagery. Words are not needed,' Noelle Cook-Bouton, a researcher based in California, tells me. Cook-Bouton spent 22 years as a stay-at-home mother raising three children and working as a community volunteer. 'I was married to an attorney, got a divorce and had a real decline in financial ability and social status. I experienced the difficulty of being an unmarried woman in the United States, especially if you're over 45, once your reproductive abilities are out of the equation,' she adds. Cook-Bouton travelled to Washington, DC, on 6 January 2021 to see the change of administration and ended up witnessing an insurrection. After that experience, she started following the trajectories of women in the far-right in the US.

'Tradwives are becoming bolder; the algorithm feeds you more and more – and you start to wonder if it is really as bad as they say,' she says. I can testify to that: scrolling through hundreds of tradwife videos served up by algorithms quickly desensitises you and the propaganda starts to sink in. The more extremist content starts to appear in hashtags and subtle visual cues, from the tradwife who bakes cookies in the shape of rune symbols used by Nazi Germany to the one slipping the hashtag #revoltagainstthemodernworld, after the book of far-right philosopher Julius Evola that bears the same name, on pictures of her spice cabinet.

While waiting for modern society to collapse, some of these tradwives are raising chickens and tending to their gardens on homesteads, in their Midwest farmsteads or in the European countryside, pursuing a dream of domestic submission and self-sufficiency. Amid anxiety about ecological collapse, they offer the twisted illusion that one can be shielded in the safety of one's cottage. 'Learning to grow your own food could be one of the most important life skills you will ever have, especially in times where the future is full of uncertainty,' says the hidden woman in the Instagram account ominously, conjuring the vision of elusive crises to come.

Some of this talk offers a sinister mirror image of the kind of rewilding, degrowth and self-sufficiency activism promoted by sections of the environmental movement. In 2015, French researchers Pablo Servigne and Raphaël Stevens coined the term 'collapsology' to refer to the study of the collapse of civilisation due to climate change. They also created a movement that advocates for the preparation of this event. Its approach is contested, but it has attracted former green politicians and left-wingers who have created their own self-sufficient farms. It is also increasingly appealing to far-right preppers.

The anxiety-inducing prospect of the end of civilisation lends itself to either of two main responses: a structural rethink of society itself along more equitable lines or a retreat into self-preservation. Both can be done at the same time, but the tension subsists and the focus on creating one's own safe haven inevitably takes something away from solidarity and structural change. It also inevitably lends itself into self-protective instinct that can veer into fascism and talk of returning to the land, which quickly comes with clear notions of where men and women fit.[33]

Pablo Servigne, who has an affinity with the mythopoetic men's movement and easily veers into New Age rhetoric, has stated that instead of a horror show where we all hold each other at gunpoint, we can get through the end of the world in a civilised fashion by creating structures of solidarity and mutual aid.[34] In this end-of-the-world scenario, we will find places to retreat and live in solidarity in small communities; men's circles will be involved. While I can appreciate the sentiment, I'm not sure I trust Servigne's brand of alternative preparation for the end of the world and probably won't be joining him in his ecological self-sufficient commune, not just because I don't have a place in the circle.

## Serving men's interests

The sinister turn the tradwives can take can be easily forgotten when mainstream tradwives assure us they have no links whatsoever to far-right movements, and most of them don't. As the tradwives went mainstream, their inbuilt hypocrisy hasn't gone unnoticed. Some anti-feminists and reactionaries have accused tradwives of debasing the movement and are concerned that the Estee Williamses will put other women off.

They want to steer the movement back to the core ideas: submission to one's husband, modesty and motherhood. American Christian commentator Allie Beth Stuckey called online tradwives 'narcissists' and stated that the movement is 'not Christian, and is not really conservative either',[35] or at least not enough for her taste. The right-wing paper *The Federalist* argued that there are 'no sourdough starters or prairie dresses required' in the anti-feminist cause and that traditional marriage and plenty of children are sufficient entry points.[36]

There have been anti-feminist women for as long as there have been feminists. In the late 19th and early 20th centuries, when the suffragette movement was in full swing, women-led anti-feminism took the form of organisations like the Women's National Anti-Suffrage League. In the 1970s, Phyllis Schlafly became a leading figure in the fight against the Equal Rights Amendment in the US. A key reference for tradwives is the Fascinating Womanhood movement (and the book of the same title) by the American Mormon and mother of eight Helen Andelin, in which she encouraged women to aspire to an ideal of traditional femininity, submit to their husbands and be the perfect 'angel in the house'. The book, released in 1963 like Betty Friedan's *Feminine Mystique*, presented itself as a deliberate counterpoint to the seminal feminist text. Andelin's daughter, Dixie, now runs Fascinating Womanhood, an online programme and support network for aspiring traditional women and housewives who are eschewing feminism.

The tradwives emerged entirely as a social media phenomenon, influenced heavily by internet culture and slang. While watching tradwife influencers offers little in the way of real sisterhood, early tradwife groups and their forerunners do offer spaces for discussion, especially for the management and negotiation of women's frustrations. A look at the r/RedPillWomen on Reddit shows that many women coming to these groups are navigating the complexities of contemporary relationships and the frustrations of married life. Here's an example of a conversation I find in the group:

> Here lately I don't know what is into me … I am usually always the type of woman who loves my husband, loves serving him, loves tending to our children and loves making a home.
>
> However recently I've been so bitter and angry. I feel inconvenienced by my children, I've been holding onto little irritations I have with my husband, and I've been looking at my wife and motherhood duties as like a maid servant and misery more than a joy.

Fellow women in the group offer words of comfort and encouragement and tips on managing wifely frustration, advising that the woman posting try journaling, self-care and taking up hobbies. Others deny the woman's feelings and tell her she wouldn't feel so bad if 'modern culture' valued stay-at-home mothers. When posters come to complain about their husbands' infidelity, the advice is to grin and bear it or put more effort into the relationship. Many women are also coming to these groups for advice on dating and finding a 'high value man' who will protect them and give them the opulent life they crave. One woman writes, for instance: 'I would really love to be a SAHW [stay-at-home woman] or SAHM [stay-at-home mother] to a man who is actually faithful and I don't mind being submissive so long as I am treated with basic respect.'

These sorts of exchanges make for a disturbing read because they show that the sort of self-erasure we thought belonged to the past is very much alive, and now promoted as a form of aspirational lifestyle, and perhaps explains why watching *Mad Men* today still feels so uncomfortable, as many TV critics noted.[37] They also suggest that for many women an illusory feeling of safety feels more appealing than an increasingly elusive vision of progress. Echoing Erica Jong's 1973 novel, Judith Warner wrote about women's 'fear of flying' in a *New York Times* piece published in 2011, a few years before the tradwife movement first emerged. She notes that many daughters of hippie mothers who sought to unshackle themselves from domesticity in the 1970s are themselves adopting different paths and retreating into domesticity, self-improvement and self-soothing practices (including yoga) to negotiate their frustrations. 'In the mid-1970s, women began to take flight,' she writes.

> Today the daughters of these runaway moms, having arrived at the shores of middle age, are taking flight, too. But they're not, by and large, dumping their husbands. They're not looking to the job market with expectations of liberation. Instead, they're fleeing to yoga, imitating flight in the downward-gazing contortion called the crow position.[38]

'Feminism exploits. Patriarchy protects', tradwives like to say.[39] The tradwife movement promises safety to women: the homebound flight is offered as an escape from objectification and sexual violence. One can understand where these fears come from. Discontent with online dating, hook-up culture and sexual objectification runs deep. One in four women in the UK has been sexually assaulted,[40] a third of women using dating apps have been abused and 20 per cent have received threats.[41] Choking during sex has become normalised to the point that many men now think it no longer requires consent (it is harmful regardless of whether it is consensual or not and can result in brain injuries), with studies in the US showing that 58 per cent of women in universities have experienced it.[42] Given this horror show, finding a traditionally minded protector-husband almost sounds like a good idea, if only these self-appointed protectors did not too often turn into abusers. In the UK, a woman is killed by a man every three days, most of them by a partner or ex-partner.[43]

Behind a veneer of promise that traditional marriage will protect women from sexual violence (which ignores the reality of marital rape) lies a darker message which implicitly condones or makes amends for sexual violence. Like their male counterparts, tradwives advocate for sexual availability to one's husband and for women to mould themselves to men's desires. Some tradwives have stern messages to women who want to 'deprive' their husbands of sex. One such Texas-based tradwife (a 'homesteadin' coffee lovin' mama'), who combines Christian tradwifedom with millennial-oriented wellness, writes: 'Just because you are "not in the mood" doesn't mean it's ok for you to deprive your husband of sex. Why do women resent this joyful calling?' She adds, 'Once you are married you do not have authority over your own body anymore. You also belong to your husband.'[44] Other tradwives have gone further and openly denied that marital rape exists.[45]

That tradwives work in tandem with their male counterparts is also clear from the fact that prominent anti-feminist influencers frequently credit men for their conversion to the cause. Riley credits Jordan Peterson's videos as a turning point in her ideological awakening and has promoted PUA Roosh V's book in her YouTube videos, describing him as someone who 'teaches men how to embrace their masculinity and not being afraid of approaching girls'.[46] Everything the tradwives and their fellow anti-feminist women say is music to the ears of the far-right and male supremacist men. Alt-right and MRA-associated blogger Matt Forney put it plainly by writing that 'no amount of phoney education or career "success" will scratch that deep itch in a girl's soul: the desire to serve a man' and that 'as men, it is our responsibility to bring girls back to their proper place. To lead them into their natural roles as wives and mothers.'[47]

For a long time, women had totemic roles in almost exclusively male-dominated far-right movements until the emergence around 2015-2016 of prominent alt-right women. One of these is Lauren Southern, who started out as an anti-feminist and went to SlutWalk demonstrations with signs saying 'There is no rape culture in the West', before becoming known for her anti-immigrant rhetoric and taking part in Identitarian campaigns to block search-and-rescue operations for refugees in the Mediterranean. Another alt-right YouTuber Brittany Sellner (née Pettibone) uses her Instagram as a façade for the representation of perfect millennial wifely devotion with coded references to white European identity peppered throughout. Pettibone shot to prominence before Trump's 2016 election and stated that immigration into Europe is a form of 'white genocide'.[48] She is married to Martin Sellner, who is the leader of the Austrian branch of the transnational ethnonationalist movement Generation Identity, who is permanently banned from entering the UK and who in late 2023 presented a plan at a secret meeting in Potsdam for the remigration (forced expulsion) of non-white immigrants from Austria and Germany to an audience of members of the far-right AfD party.[49]

The Sellners are an example of how far-right ideology, male supremacy and tradwifedom work together. They run a perfectly oiled PR machine and seek to imbue regressive and hateful ideology with a hip countercultural look, using their highly curated social media channels to project an image of a white nationalist 'power couple'. Brittany, though mostly cultivating a tradwife vibe, also leans into what Nancy S. Love calls 'fashy femme' aesthetics, with strong makeup and power poses.[50] Martin was the subject of multiple media pieces describing him as a far-right 'hipster' and Brittany has been described as a far-right 'Barbie',[51] images for which mainstream media has fallen.

Anti-immigrant plans hatched by Martin work hand in hand with Brittany's efforts to soften the image of the movement and promote motherhood as an integral part of a plan to revive white Christian culture. In recent years, her YouTube videos have been mostly dedicated to advancing anti-feminist views and the kind of arguments that male counterparts in the manosphere are articulating, with titles like 'WHY Is Masculinity Being Attacked?' and '7 Signs That Your Man's Masculinity Is NON-Toxic' and options to purchase her book *What Makes Us Girls* and to support her financially by donating, paying in cryptocurrencies or buying her items from her Amazon wish list.

## Loving men who hate you: the far-right's 'woman problem'

In her book on far-right women, Leidig writes that far-right women 'function as honeytraps for the male gaze'.[52] They show men the kind of life they would like to have – a beautiful woman and perfect family – as an entry point to other ideological beliefs. Another far-right woman who has cultivated a far-right Barbie image is the French Thaïs d'Escufon, the former spokeswoman for – until its ban – Generation Identity. D'Escufon first made a name for herself by carrying out anti-migrant campaigns. She has since reinvented herself as a red pill influencer distilling dating advice to men on TikTok and telling them what they would like to hear – for example, that 'marital rape' is an invention by women who would like to deny their husband sex and that the world abounds with promiscuous women with outsized 'body counts'.[53] She's a Gen Z blonde speaking to disenfranchised Gen Z men ripe for recruitment, to whom she offers workshops on 'how to hack the female brain'.

All these women epitomise the far-right's 'woman problem'. In 2016, Swedish white nationalist militant Marcus Follin reluctantly conceded in a YouTube video titled 'The Woman Question' that the movement needed to make overtures to them if it wanted to succeed.[54] By virtue of their gender, women are vital as sexual partners and mothers, and they do much of the invisible work of organising events, meetings and fundraisers. They have always been essential, although largely forgotten, in supporting the ideology of white supremacism: their role has been theorised as that of 'shieldmaidens' to soften and normalise.[55] The alt-right YouTubers who emerged as ideological figures in their own right changed that. Their purpose is still to normalise the extreme and give it a more gentle appearance, but these women, some of whom say they want nothing else but to serve their man, also seem to want a slice of the cake.

Andrea Dworkin wrote in *Right-Wing Women* (1983) that women who embrace anti-feminist views do so in the hope that they will achieve protection if they submit to patriarchy.

While that desire is clearly articulated by tradwives, there are more complex factors at play, including ethnicity and class considerations, as well as ideological motivations. Women might be doing more than seeking self-protection: they might also be strategising and making a conscious decision to prioritise other interests over that of their sex. In doing so, they submit to a set of rules that they need to negotiate. They might also hope that they will somehow be excused from the message of subservience they preach. Anti-feminist women are negotiating a role in movements that deny them one beyond doting subservience, only to find that they are not being repaid for their pro-man loyalty. Over time, Southern became increasingly sidelined and was herself subjected to misogyny and bullying.[56] After stating that she 'can't stand most of the manosphere' she received a violent slew of videos showing men beheading women.[57] In 2017, alt-right activist Tara McCarthy complained of widespread bullying and prejudice against women in the movement.[58]

Their content evolves as their lives change. Riley went from anti-feminist YouTuber and *Evie Magazine* columnist to tradwife and natural mama influencer after giving birth, having previously interviewed Sellner, Blonde in the Belly of the Beast and many other red-pilled women in a series of YouTube videos titled 'Girl Talk'. D'Escufon can play the red pill influencer because she is young and unmarried. Eventually, her expected role will become that of wife and mother, and anyone who fails to meet that model will have to fall on their own sword. Southern's trajectory exemplifies this: after being sidelined by fellow far-right men, she got married in 2019, moved to Australia with her husband and gave birth to a child. She lived a tradwife existence, before experiencing domestic violence, an experience she recounted to *UnHerd* in a May 2024 piece in which she never disavows the core of her ideas.[59]

The tradwife movement shows similar desires for influence. Despite being a dangerous grift dedicated to the promotion of male supremacy, it is a movement that is woman-led and where women are negotiating agency within their own self-imposed subservience. Culture writer and former LDS member Meg Conley, in an interview with journalist Anne Helen Petersen, spoke about women's lack of authority in the Mormon church and described social media influencing as a way for women to gain agency in ideologies or systems of beliefs where their subordination is encoded, as exerting influence (as opposed to making decisions) is considered an acceptable part to play for women.[60] She spoke about fellow Mormon Hannah Neeleman, the 34-year-old former Julliard ballerina, beauty queen and mother of eight who is the face of the online brand, ranch and ever-expanding business Ballerina Farm. It mostly sells meat from cattle raised on her and her husband's farm and a range of accessories for whoever wants to purchase a slice of the rustic dream projected by Neeleman, including a $71 sourdough kit or a $27 yellow apron. With over ten million followers, Neeleman's Instagram account features her cooking impossible meals from scratch, making raw milk turmeric lattes and doing plenty of ballet moves on the farm.

## Rooting for trad

Commentators have described Neeleman – who has been the subject of extensive cultural commentary and reporting on both sides of the Atlantic – as a tradwife, although she has not openly advocated submitting to her husband (the husband in question, Daniel Neeleman, is the son of the founder of JetBlue and four other airlines, which explains how she can make the lifestyle work) and her political views are more subtly coded. In a January 2024 *New York Times* profile where she is quoted, Neeleman denied she knew anything about tradwives and said she was 'unfamiliar' with the word, which by then already sounded implausible.[61] The problem lies less in what Neeleman herself does, says or thinks about gender norms – which is unclear – than in how her performance is weaponised: she has been described by the founder of the ultra-conservative Young Americans against Socialism, Morgan Zeders, as a 'DAILY inspiration on how to live out my values as a Conservative'.[62] *Evie Magazine* has devoted multiple pieces to Ballerina Farm (including 'How to Live Like Ballerina Farm on a Budget'),[63] which in themselves show how much she embodies the ideal that the magazine promotes. A profile in *The Times* offered an illustration of the cautious and seemingly apolitical brand that the Neelemans are cultivating, while suggesting a lot about the self-abnegation that the tradwife life entails (when her husband left the room to take a phone call during the interview, Hannah Neeleman whispered to the reporter that her one epidural had been 'kinda great').[64]

One could also argue that Neeleman embodies long-standing patriarchal norms – of beauty, modesty, fertility and wifely and motherly devotion – that feminists have spent decades trying to unshackle women from. Though this is slowly shifting, a close-to-tradwife existence is considered the pinnacle of success for women in large sections of society, as evidenced by vice-presidential Republican candidate J.D. Vance's misogynistic comment that the Democratic party is ruled by 'childless cat ladies'.[65] Not so long ago many women lived the life of dependency and service that the tradwives advocate for today. My paternal grandmother spent many years at home cooking two full meals a day. As a married woman, she needed my grandfather's written consent to open a bank account and to train as a nurse.[66] When I told her about the tradwife movement, she did not find it amusing or quirky, having lived through some of the realities that the tradwives romanticise when they tell us going to our husbands for our weekly allowance is a bold escape from the rat race.

These realities are easily skirted over by movements that romanticise the past and seek to make it desirable for disillusioned millennials and Gen Zers. Traditional conservatives and reactionaries have seized upon the tradwife movement to offer a seemingly more moderate and intellectualised case for traditional gender norms. Amid a backlash against girlboss feminism, 'trad' is making something of a comeback as commentators are working to convert young people to the idea of traditional marriage, presenting it as a transgressive choice, even as rates of marriage continue to decline in the Global North. William Bradford Wilcox's *Get Married* (2024), with its subtitle *Why Americans Must Defy the Elites, Forge Strong Families and Save Civilization*, is one among several titles playing on this desire for norm subversion.

These endeavours are aided by new 'anti-woke' movements, particularly Dimes Square, named after the trendy New York neighbourhood which became known for its rule flouting,[67] as well as its fascination for the tradwives and all things trad.[68] Promoting tradition as counterculture is also a useful distraction for illiberal projects. Writing in *The Cut*, Rebecca Traister has noted that the 'think-tank-economist-columnist class' increasingly promotes traditional marriage to curtail liberal marriage laws, including no-fault divorce, and to distract from housing and workplace reform.[69] There are other intellectual cases for trad, promoted by a growing strand of reactionary feminism, which puts forth critiques about the commodification of the body and the devaluation of the labour of motherhood. Tradwives may be baking pies on Instagram, but an intellectualised shift has emerged on both sides of the Atlantic that aims to capitalise on legitimate concerns about the shortcomings of liberal feminism to advocate for reactionary measures.

Louise Perry's *The Case against the Sexual Revolution* (2022) and Mary Harrington's *Feminism against Progress* (2023) – Perry calls herself a post-liberal feminist and Harrington is a self-described reactionary feminist – are representatives of this discourse. While Perry focuses on how the sexual revolution has sold women short, Harrington writes about the co-option of women's bodies by the market and the devaluation of motherhood and care work, critiques I broadly agree with. The answer, they say, is not to do feminism's unfinished work in the domestic sphere, have nuanced conversations about sexual politics or implement safety nets and economic measures to avoid making a life of submission and domestic chores the most appealing option available. Instead, both conclude that a return to traditional heterosexual marriage is the way. If it's easy for Perry and Harrington to make these arguments under the guise of attacking 'liberal feminism' – in which they lump together quite a lot and conveniently forget much of the work that feminist thinkers have done – it isn't because feminism has not articulated class or nuanced conversation about the body. It is because market-compatible feminism gets most of the headlines.

This is not limited to the Anglosphere. In France, a key proponent is philosopher Marianne Durano, who in her pamphlet *My Body Does Not Belong to You* (*Mon corps ne vous appartient pas*, untranslated, 2018) also describes her liberal and atheist upbringing and a period of sexual experimentation at university, before her conversion to Catholicism and her decision to give up birth control and to have several children in her 20s to honour her biology and ideal fertility window. Today, Durano, who has been profiled by major French newspapers, lives in a Christian eco-commune and has called on women to regain control over and 'love their bodies' – the kind of rhetoric that would not be out of place in a yoga class. Durano is part of a group of French reactionary Catholics who have protested gay marriage, oppose abortion and are promoting a reduction in women's rights, but are increasingly couching their views in anti-free-market discourse. It would probably be wrong to assume they are disingenuous in their critiques: concerns for sustainability are, I suspect, somewhat genuine, but these women are willing to sacrifice key advances in women's rights in the process. While Durano would ban abortion if she could, Perry is opposed to no-fault divorce and very reluctantly considers welfare for single mothers as a necessary evil.

Not all reactionary commentators are particularly enamoured with online tradwives like Gwen The Milkmaid and their gimmicks and are quick to point out they are not the real deal. Harrington has said that the 'tradwives are not trad enough' and that we should go back to pre-modern economic distribution of labour and gender roles to suit the modern day.[70] The conservative right might not like the tradwives much, but they do recognise they conveniently manage to spread their worldview to young women. This makes the male supremacist project a big tent, where very different people can get along, as long as no one forgets the end goal: ensuring that men stay in charge.

# 5

# The rigged game: men exploiting men

In this world, there is nothing that can't be monetised, and male supremacy is no exception. Anti-feminist influencers are turning resentment of women into a fully fledged business. The 'entrepreneur, risk taker, hustler and motivator' 'Coach Greg Adams', for example, runs a series of online programmes such as 'The Unapologetically Masculine Video Course', priced between $350 and $600 and promises 'a way for men to organise and prioritise their life in order to set himself apart from the men who lack masculine qualities.'[1] Streamer and Andrew Tate fan Adin Ross dispenses with courses. He has a clothing line – 'Brand Risk' – which features a selection of hideous black joggers, t-shirts or hoodies with the name splashed over in a lurid green font.

The anti-feminist 'influencers' of a decade ago were early adopters of crowdfunding platforms and understood quickly how to turn men's anger into profit. The male supremacist YouTuber Carl Benjamin, whose online pseudonym is Sargon of Akkad, kick-started his online career during Gamergate and infamously tweeted at Labour MP Jess Phillips that he 'wouldn't even rape [her]'. He had over 900,000 followers on YouTube at the height of his success and profited from his views via the crowdfunding platform Patreon. Following the rape comments, Patreon deplatformed him, and Jordan Peterson, expressing his support for Sargon, moved to the alternative monetisation platform SubscribeStar, before launching his own 'free speech' crowdfunding enterprise Thinkspot, which met with little success. It hardly matters. Today's manosphere influencers use mainstream social media platforms to redirect fans to a host of payment platforms and poorly moderated corners of social media which have become a haven for extremist communities. The website Rumble, for example, is the chief haunt of the male supremacist influencer Sneako, where he spreads misogynistic and homophobic messages to his audience of primarily young men.

## The art of the grift: the pursuit of money

Male supremacist influencers increasingly package their views as self-help. They sell books and guides, coaching sessions, financial advice, diet plans, exercise regimes, vitamins and supplements to name but a few – but like the tradwives, the main item for sale is the ideology. Kara Perez, a US-based financial educator who runs a company which provides advice for millennials on debt management, says that influencers 'rely on a sales funnel that is similar to traditional online marketing'. An incendiary post is created to maximise algorithmic amplification and will likely end up in the target audience's social media feed. It will include an 'aspirational pitch' wherein the influencer promises to teach men how to 'realise their potential', giving just enough information to hook them in. An 'exclusive workshop' will follow, a one-time offer that will require men to give their email address, which will allow the influencer to bombard the customers with marketing emails. 'The real aim is to rope you into a worldview that will turn you into a repeat customer and get you to buy more,' Perez says.

If men believe that their problems are caused by women and that the only way out is to become an alpha man, their insecurities can be used repeatedly to keep them hooked. The wealth of prominent anti-feminist influencers can only be speculated upon. In 2018, Jordan Peterson earned just shy of $1 million on the crowdfunding platform Patreon,[2] and he has an estimated net worth of $8 million (he also has a clinical practice and was until 2022 a tenured academic at the University of Toronto). In January 2024, Joe Rogan signed a $250 million deal with Spotify and reportedly earns over $100,000 per podcast episode.[3] The success of some big names also obscures the broader picture: thousands of influencers, particularly PUA and red pill influencers, are cashing in on misogyny. They use all the tools of the influencer economy to generate income: advertising revenue, crowdfunding, subscriptions, donations, affiliate marketing, brand sponsorship. What mostly sells is discourse about a manufactured problem: men's disadvantage in society. The success relies on recruiting ever more men into the worldview, turning the male supremacist operation into an MLM or pyramid scheme.

The US Securities and Exchange Commission describes pyramid schemes as sharing these characteristics: the promise of a high return in a short period of time, the fact that no genuine product or service is actually sold and that the primary emphasis is on recruiting new participants. By this definition, some male supremacists' operations are true pyramid schemes. Andrew Tate's online academy where members earn commission by recruiting new members is one, but the male supremacist influencer model itself is an MLM, necessitating the recruitment of ever more men into the worldview to feed the misogynistic money-making machine. In this respect, male supremacy has parallels with the weight loss industry. It too sells solutions that largely fail, is based on a narrow definition of health that places responsibility on the individual and distracts from broader socio-economic forces that determine weight and health. It also keeps customers coming back for more when the magic pill fails to work.

Decades of evidence from the weight loss industry have proved one thing: diets fail, yet the weight loss industry still thrives by plugging the belief that if one just makes enough personal effort, one will succeed. The minority of individuals for whom diets are successful are just enough to perpetuate the myth. The weight loss industry is itself a by-product of a broken food system that generates profits by selling customers ultra-processed foods and has a financial interest in making sure they fail in their goals. It's a useful analogy, because despite all its hatred of women, the manosphere relies on men failing too.

Just like the weight loss industry, male supremacists need to hook men with promises of salvation that disregard the underlying causes of their ills and keep them coming back. They need to inject a constant sense of insecurity, which can then be turned into revenue, which can be reinjected into manufacturing yet more insecurity, creating a loop that researchers have likened to a 'protection racket'.[4] There are plenty of insecurities to exploit. Influencers draw direct links between financial insecurity and sexual discontent, amplifying them with pseudoscientific stories about female hypergamy and a sense of grievance and entitlement. In a society that wants to rob men of the livelihoods and sex they think they deserve, influencers have plenty of advice on how to acquire women and resources.

Take the case of Canadian alpha coach Richard Cooper and his website, podcast and multiple social media channels. Cooper started out by promoting debt management and entrepreneurship before branching out into dating, having discovered the 'cold hard truth' about heterosexual relationships. He tells men they have been sold a lie:

> Western culture is a scam for men. You get up early to pay for a house you hardly live in, you don't own the land it sits on, to pay a mortgage to a bank that lent you pretend money made out of thin air you pay interest on they didn't even have on deposit in a vault …

'All this', he continues, to 'usually to impress a woman enough to commit to you, that has already shared her body with dozens of other men, that brings baggage to the table, that if you live with or marry, can take half your shit, and your kids, if she changes her mind about you.'[5] Luckily, Cooper has the solution to this nightmare in his book *The Unplugged Alpha: The No Bullsh★t Guide to Winning with Women & Life* (2020) and on his online store with its 14 supplements.

The feelings of insecurity and loss of control are real. In many Western countries, it takes the form of stagnant wages, rising debt, insecure housing and broken social safety nets. In the US, rates of male unemployment have increased as the decline of traditional industries has left an employment vacuum. Meanwhile, women now comprise the majority of university graduates and have more choices in their personal lives than at any time in the past. While the patriarchy continues to work extremely well for most men, some – correctly – sense that it does not quite deliver as well as it used to. Influencers like Cooper explicitly link men's financial insecurities to thwarted patriarchal claims to women's bodies.

The obsession with the sexual marketplace and one's hierarchy in it mirrors a loss of economic status. Successful influencers promote a crude neoliberal message: men can achieve individual salvation with enough resolve and enough willingness to exploit others – and enough cash to buy their coaching programmes. They have an interest in ensuring men don't examine the real societal causes of their suffering, because they themselves are prime representatives of an economic system that harms men and that relies on the exploitation of the many for the success of the few. Men's failure is baked into the manosphere's evolutionary worldview as much as it is in the commercial model. If 80 per cent of women go for 20 per cent of men, as the pseudoscientific theory goes, only a small proportion of men will be alphas. Targeting men in an insecure economy and an alienating dating culture, male supremacists promise them a meritocratic go at gaming the sexual and financial market while also implicitly admitting that most of them won't succeed.

Like every get-rich-quick scam, nothing male supremacist influencers offer in the way of financial advice is sound or sustainable. Tate's course is a mix of cryptocurrency, Amazon drop-shipping and 'freelancing' or recruiting new members into the pyramid scheme. Influencers also encourage men to invest in forms of ownership where they can exert control over others and pursue dreams of unaccountability. Myron Gaines from *Fresh&Fit* is a proponent of buying 'real estate' – private property gives one control over tenants[6] – and has encouraged men to ignore any mainstream news warnings about the dangers of certain investments.[7] Male supremacists also like cryptocurrencies.

A report by independent investigator Tara Annison found that male supremacist influencers generated over $40 million in this way. Adin Ross, a Twitch streamer who visited Tate in Romania after his arrest, promotes crypto-gambling websites and cryptocurrency scams.[8] The red pill influencer Donovan Sharpe has a crypto-focused website, which he uses to attempt to 'orange pill' men or get them to invest in cryptocurrency. Cryptocurrencies, once the preferred currency of right-wing libertarians, have become a go-to of far-right and white supremacist groups, who have embraced them because they offer privacy, anonymity and independence from mainstream institutions, allow them to monetise their activities without scrutiny and accountability,[9] and fit in with their conspiratorial worldview: mainstream institutions are considered corrupt, infiltrated by various enemies. Decentralised modes of ownership with no accountability reflect the male supremacist ideology writ large: a vision divorced from any idea of collective good but one in which a minority of men can preserve their power and pursue a dream of unaccountability and dominance while exploiting others.

To become financial alphas, men are encouraged to coerce and exploit women. Tate allegedly forced women into webcam scamming work and has been accused of running an online pimping operation, which he boasted allowed him to earn $600,000 a month. His online 'War Room' (priced at $8,000) advertises itself as a 'global network in which exemplars [*sic*] of individualism work to free the modern man from socially induced incarceration' and teaches men how to groom women online. A BBC investigation found that at least 45 women were groomed into prostitution by members.[10] To think Tate is an outlier would be a mistake. A report by Prism found that male supremacist influencers have encouraged men to set up scam agencies to lure sex workers on OnlyFans with promises of revenue. These men targeted women who might be less aware of their rights and more vulnerable to scamming, including those in the Global South who did not speak English.[11] The Spanish-speaking TikToker Sergi Berenguer, for instance, ran a Discord server called Pimp School, which instructed men on how best to recruit women to these scamming agencies, echoing Tate's Pimpin' Hoes Degree.[12]

## Incels are not sex socialists: the pursuit of women's subjugation

It's unclear whether Robin Hanson thought he was in need of an attention boost, but after a self-described incel drove a rented van through a business district of Toronto on 23 April 2018, killing 11 people and injuring 15, he got one. A few days after the attack Hanson, a libertarian economist from Virginia's George Mason University with a history of ill-advised forays into sexual economics, questioned why progressives who are so fond of wealth redistribution had not considered that the problem of incel violence could be resolved by giving sexually aggrieved men access to what they want: sex. 'One might plausibly argue that those with much less access to sex suffer to a similar degree as those with low income, and might similarly hope to gain from organizing around this identity, to lobby for redistribution along this axis and to at least implicitly threaten violence if their demands are not met,' he wrote, reassuring readers (lest they might be worried) that 'rape and slavery are far from the only possible levers.' Possible solutions, he suggested, could include giving men cash handouts to become more attractive to women, paying sex workers or giving incels access to sex robots.

The comments earned Hanson the title of 'America's creepiest economist',[13] but he was not alone in his views. Other conservative commentators became compassionate voices for poor sexless young men who, they suggested, would not act out if only women met their needs. While Hanson provided the techno-pragmatic side of the argument, more traditional conservatives touted marriage and sexual restraint. Christian columnist Ross Douthat nostalgically pondered if our societies might be willing to embrace 'older ideas about the virtues of monogamy and chastity and permanence and the special respect owed to the celibate'.[14] Jordan Peterson weighed in and suggested that 'enforced monogamy' – the modalities of which remained vague – would remedy the problem. Paraphrasing arguments from the incel community, Peterson said 'a small percentage of the guys have hyper-access to women,' adding that 'no one cares about the men who fail' to marry and have relationships and that this is a crisis that merits a serious response.[15]

To see these mainstream debates about distributing women to a movement of angry men who had just been linked to a terror attack was bizarre. That giving in to the wishes of violent men could even be discussed is because – contrary to other forms of terrorism – incels' extremist ideology sits on a continuum of entitlement to women's bodies that patriarchal norms promote. These discussions moved the issue squarely onto the terrain of male supremacists, where sex and women are a resource and incels can be depicted as unjustly deprived and a marginalised community in a cruel sexual market. Incels have tried to portray themselves as something of a socialist movement, their desires a battle for social justice. A post shared on Reddit, for instance, attempts to equate incels' demand for sex to an equity movement, offering a series of proposals akin to 'socialist' state policies. They include: preventing women from wearing makeup and dating 'above their league', state-mandated 'sexual market value cards' (complete with points systems) and forcing single mothers and women with a history of more than nine sexual partners to have sex with incels.[16]

Mainstream institutions have become complicit in the normalisation of incel beliefs. A 2019 essay written by an incel with the pseudonym Alexander Ash attempted to distance the majority from a violent few and decried the 'often sensationalist overtones' of media coverage – even though some members of the incel forum that he founded and runs expressed extreme misogyny and were charged for plotting to shoot women.[17] Ash argues that incels are not a movement at all but simply people trapped in a life situation and frames much of the language on his forum as 'venting' and 'locker room talk'. He has since been invited to sit on panels alongside academics from the International Center for Study of Violent Extremism and is listed as a co-author on some of the Center's research papers on incels. It is unusual, to say the least, to have a prominent member of a community linked to extremism so closely involved with the writing of an academic report on that very same movement.

Feminist scholar Amia Srinivasan in *The Right to Sex* argued that incels' claim that they are victims of life's injustice is abhorrent, but like any conspiracy theory, it points in twisted ways to real injustices. Many people do not have the sexual relationships they would like to have, due to racial, ableist and other biases. Srinivasan writes:

> Some men are excluded from the sexual sphere for politically suspect reasons – including, perhaps, some of the men driven to vent their despair on anonymous forums – but the moment their unhappiness is transmuted into a rage at the women 'denying' them sex, they have crossed a line into something morally ugly and confused.[18]

Meanwhile, speaking about her series of interviews in *The Hairpin* with people who are single not by choice but because of trauma, disabilities and other factors, writer Jia Tolentino noted that, contrary to incels, none of them 'believed that they were owed the sex that they wished to have'. The interrogation of prevailing norms and a reconditioning of their desires are not on the table for incels and their supporters, who prefer state-mandated tradwives.

Ironically, the commentators who argued for sex redistribution are otherwise libertarians or free-market liberals who claim to believe in 'meritocracy'. In other words, they believe in the sort of economic policies that put men in vulnerable positions in the first place. Peterson and his ilk, who are in favour of minimal state intervention, are willing to make an exception when it comes to furnishing angry men with sex. Of course, sex, as Srinivasan and others have noted, is not a resource to be distributed like a subsidy. But false equivalences suit entitled men who can argue that not having sex with attractive women is a case of inequity. Srinivasan wrote about Elliot Rodger's fixation with 'hot blonde sluts' and the racism and class superiority complex he exhibited. Behind the veneer of discussions about equity lies entitlement. Political scientist Alan Finlayson argued that though the language of male supremacists superficially sounds like a critique of neoliberalism, it actually 'celebrates heroic individualism, expressed as manly and victorious conduct in marketplaces of all kinds'. The PUAs want to game the market and the incels want it to look different,[19] but no one is escaping.

## Men who refuse to apologise: the pursuit of power

'We love dogs because they express so honestly and without dissimulation what we also are and want … Women are, in their natural state, close to this condition as well, or closer on the whole, which is where they get much of their charm and power from.'[20] This insight comes from a 2018 pamphlet by Bronze Age Pervert (or BAP as he is known to his devotees), a fascist and self-described 'aspiring nudist bodybuilder'. His social media feed is a collection of homoerotic pictures of ultra-tanned muscular men, musings about the grandeur of classical civilisation and lament about the depravity of contemporary society. Mixing esoteric language and bits of Nietzschean philosophy with internet jargon and anti-feminist and racist diatribes, BAP exhorts men to lead a life of 'sun and steel' and return to a new form of masculine political vitality and aestheticism inspired by classical antiquity. Another of his pearls of wisdom is: 'The "liberation" of women makes democracy into a terminal disease … one that doesn't just end a particular government, but the civilization.'

Contemporary Western societies are, in BAP's considered opinion, an ugly feminised 'longhouse', a matriarchy populated by 'obese high-fructose-corn-syrup-guzzling beasts'. The only way out of them is by regaining control and returning to a world of masculine strength and beauty. If nothing else, BAP is blessed with a fertile imagination, which he allows to wander freely. He wonders what would happen if Mitt Romney was 'capable of acting like he looks', started a war with India and slept with Vladimir Putin's wife. He dreams of nations governed by pirates. BAP is also firmly against 'xenoestrogens' – substances mimicking the female hormone oestrogen that saturate our water and food supplies and, he says, are silently emasculating men.

Bronze Age Pervert is as absurd as his name. This did not prevent his book from quickly achieving a cult following in US far-right circles, apparently becoming a favourite read among Trump's junior staffers and being reviewed by Michael Anton, a former spokesman for Trump's National Security Council.[21] While incels rage at women and PUAs optimise themselves, in the constellation of online male supremacists BAP is an ideologue who is trying to shape a new political movement. While his work contains antisemitic and racist content, one of the key features is that it is deeply anti-feminist and articulates a reactionary form of politics centred on masculinity. He is the perfect fascist influencer for the age: he combines overt misogyny and bigotry with tongue-in-cheek internet slang. His attempts at intellectual substance are compatible with the imperatives of Instagram marketing – pictures of bodybuilders reading the book contributed to its success – and an anxious health discourse. After media outlets outed a Romanian American with a PhD from Yale, Costin Alamariu, as the person behind the account, he used the notoriety to publicise another book, in which he argues that prehistoric societies were matriarchies (like today's, apparently). The book briefly became an Amazon bestseller.

Like other male supremacists, Alamariu channels the energy of the man who takes without asking and does not apologise for it. While today's men are feminised and docile, he dreams of conquering continents. He is a pagan who dispenses with religious pieties and gives men permission to coerce and hate women without having to give their feelings a veneer of acceptability. The dream of male supremacist 'pirate' leaders is not so far out of reach as BAP might think – ever more far-right leaders are embracing unapologetic male supremacist language and the policies that go with it. Donald Trump's 2016 election was one of the first examples. Trump, who said he could 'do anything' to women because he's a star and who was accused by multiple women of sexual abuse, is the man who takes without asking: the perfect candidate for male supremacist communities. Alex DiBranco of the Institute for Research on Male Supremacism says Trump's election was a victory for a 'secular version of hostile misogyny', in contrast with the evangelical Christianity embodied by George W. Bush or Mike Pence.

Male supremacy and hostile misogyny did not disappear with Trump's 2020 election defeat. They have become central to far-right organising in the US and have taken hold in the right wing of the Republican party. 'Anti-feminist conspiracies have become a motivating force for the right,' DiBranco says. The right of the Republican party now has no qualms about using male supremacist language as a deliberate strategy to win votes and achieve their political aims. A 2020 recording of North Carolina's 2024 Republican gubernatorial nominee Mark Robinson shows him saying he 'absolutely want[s] to go back to the America where women couldn't vote',[22] which has the merit of stating plainly what the project is about. Fellow Republican Matt Gaetz, when asked in a TV interview about the risk of losing women's votes because of the unbridled misogyny, said the party was in the middle of a 'realignment'. 'For every Karen we lose, there's a Julio and a Jamal ready to sign up for the MAGA movement' was his defiant response,[23] a prediction that proved partially true as Trump increased his share of Latino men's vote while still winning white women's vote. The same Gaetz hired a male staffer who described sexual consent as a 'pernicious fetish'.[24]

Male supremacy is what far-right groups are using to seek mainstream influence and to build coalitions. The Proud Boys, the 'pro-Western fraternity' turned street gang that took part in the Capitol insurrection, is the far-right group for those who 'refuse to apologise for creating the modern world' and who see the restoration of traditional masculinity as necessary to the survival of Western culture. Despite being anti-immigration and white nationalist, the Proud Boys understand the need for priorities. The group's chairman Enrique Tarrio, who is of Afro-Cuban origin, has downplayed its links to white supremacy and neo-Nazi groups and has described it as 'rough around the edges' but welcoming to men of colour. DiBranco says it is a strategic move. 'If they were successful in their current goals, white nationalism would be the next intention.' The key messages focus on traditional family, 'free speech' and guns. Gavin McInnes, however, has used classic male supremacist arguments, stating that 'by every metric, men have it worse than women, including rape, when you include prison.'[25]

Far-right and authoritarian leaders are trading in men's rage and winning elections by promising to take rights away from women while adopting the kind of economic policies that are likely to reinforce men's economic struggles. In Poland, where manosphere influencers are flourishing, nearly half of young men aged between 18 and 25 back the far-right Konfederacja party, more extreme than the right-wing nationalist Law and Justice Party.[26] The leading figure of the movement, Janusz Korwin-Mikke, has promoted Holocaust denial and said he opposes women's right to vote. In the space of a few years Konfederacja, once a fringe party, has become a key political force in the country.[27]

In December 2023, the ultra-libertarian, chainsaw-wielding Javier Milei, who described abortion as a 'tragedy' and said he would 'not apologise for having a penis', won the Argentinian election in no small part thanks to young unemployed men who voted for him, lured by his promises of rolling back of women's rights, widespread economic deregulation and new rules on gun ownership. Since his election, women's rights organisations have reported waves of harassment and threats, and prominent feminist activists have gone into exile, fearing for their lives and safety. Ahead of Spain's general election in April 2019, the Spanish manosphere group ForoCoches, which started out in 2003 as an online forum to discuss cars and became a key place for men to discuss the scourge of false rape accusations, established an alliance with the far-right Vox Party, which ran on an explicitly anti-feminist platform, railing against 'supremacist feminism' and 'feminazis'.[28]

In March 2022, Yoon Suk Yeol won the Korean presidential election by speaking to the *idaenam*, disillusioned 20-something male voters with shrinking economic prospects and resentful of greater gender equality. Yoon promised to abolish the Ministry of Gender Equality and Family, accused feminism of being responsible for the country's low birth rates and promised to crack down on false rape accusations. These were all themes dear to the country's male supremacists, who congregated on the Ilbe Storage forum, the Korean equivalent to the English-speaking Red Pill Reddit page. One of the most-visited websites in Korea,[29] Ilbe Storage has, over several years, contributed to popularise the idea of a feminist conspiracy against men. In a 2021 poll, a staggering 84 per cent of Korean men in their 20s and 30s said they had been discriminated against because of their gender.[30] The election results showed a stark divide between Korean men and women: nearly 60 per cent of men in their 20s voted for Yoon, while a nearly equal proportion of women in the same age bracket voted for his Democratic opponent, Lee Jae-myung.

That election followed a clear backlash pattern. In recent years, South Korea's #MeToo movement has gained visibility, leading to the 2020 resignation of Bun's former mayor Oh Keo-don over allegations of sexual assault.[31] The bestselling novel *Kim Ji-young, Born 1982*, published in 2016, became a cultural touchstone of the country's feminist movement. The same year, a woman was murdered in the toilet of a karaoke bar in a busy district of Seoul by a 34-year-old man who said he had been 'ignored and belittled' by women.[32] Korean-born scholar Min Joo Lee, who focuses on feminism and gender relations in Korea, believes the last elections took on the form of a 'gender war' where feminism became a rhetorical tool to win the votes of aggrieved men who resented greater opportunities for women. She tells me, 'anti-feminism was growing before the elections, and celebrities who expressed support for a feminist cause experienced backlash.' When Yoon promised to dismantle the ministry in charge of gender equality, his opponent also started pandering to anti-feminist arguments. 'Each side decided to flex their power, and feminism ended up being caught in the middle,' she adds.

Male supremacist talk may be a rhetorical tool to grab the votes of red-pilled men but it has an impact on policies and on normalising supremacist behaviours. Korea has seen a rise in online sexual violence and exploitation of women. The use of *molka*, small spy cameras hidden in public toilets, changing rooms and other public spaces to film people without their consent, has increased and become a growing tool of sexual violation used by men to reassert power over women. In her book *Flowers of Fire*, Korean journalist Hawon Jung quotes a viral post from an online forum about spy cameras, showing it is as much about the joy of putting women down and reasserting one's masculinity than it is about sexual gratification:

> Did you feel hurt when the above-average-looking bitch who just walked into the subway looked down at you as if you were a cockroach and turned her head in 0.1 second?
>
> … Then watch the toilet *molka*.[33]

Between 2018 and 2020, a group of men ran Nth Room, a sexual trafficking operation on Telegram which coerced women into sex work and then blackmailed them. Like other similar sexual trafficking schemes elsewhere, it primarily targeted economically deprived women.[34] Even in countries where overt male supremacists have failed to win elections – Éric Zemmour in France proved too alienating to female voters but still managed to get 7 per cent of the votes with a previously fringe conspiracy theory – the Overton window of acceptable conversation has shifted. Meanwhile, election gains by far-right parties across Europe have been stark and this has allowed their ideas to enter mainstream conversation and influence policies on gender norms, climate commitments and migrants' rights. In September 2024, Germany's far-right AfD party won its first parliamentary seat election since WWII.[35] The same month, Austria's Freedom Party came first in the country's election.[36]

## Male fantasies, climate anxieties and fossil fuels: the pursuit of resources

In August 2022, as summer-time barbecues were coming to an end after an extreme heatwave hit Europe, French Green MP Sandrine Rousseau told the crowd at an event that 'we have to change our mentality so that eating a barbecued entrecôte is no longer a symbol of virility,' citing data which shows that men in France eat twice as much red meat as women. The controversy was ready-made. Rousseau, not just a green political figure but also a leading figure of the French #MeToo movement, received a torrent of abusive messages from men who poured out their hate alongside pictures of meat, barbecues and sausages, which left little to the psychoanalytical imagination. News outlets and political figures across the political spectrum jumped on the spat, condemning Rousseau's 'deconstruction of men'.

Heterosexual men's totemic relationship with the barbecue elicits 'last bastion of masculinity' jokes. As journalist Meghan Casserly noted in a widely commented piece in *Forbes* a few years ago, the image of men cooking meat is one that is closely linked to a post-war American suburban ideal but one that has little anthropological reality:[37] in many human societies throughout history, women have been in charge of cooking meat on the fire. Thanks to the new brand of alternative health and wellness influencers, though, meat has become a new way to signal identity in a perceived battle for men's survival.

From the far-right's predilection for the insult 'soyboy', which was popularised by Mike Cernovich and is based on the pseudoscientific idea that soy decreases men's testosterone levels,[38] to the love of the carnivorous diet advocated by the likes of Rogan, Peterson and Tate, eating meat is what alpha men do, as opposed to 'woke' tofu-eaters who love gender equality. This would be comical if attempts to reduce meat consumption and other measures to slow carbon emissions and mitigate climate disaster were not increasingly presented by their detractors as an assault on Western masculine identity. Indeed, a shift has taken place in anti-climate discourse recently. Climate denial is no longer convincing to the majority of voters, who can see the reality for themselves as they experience ever more suffocating heatwaves. Studies of anti-climate rhetoric around the COP summit have found that those who want to undermine climate action have a new strategy: deceive the public and delay climate action by turning environmental policies into another battle in the culture wars.[39]

This gives us another manifestation of outrage activation and 'mirror world' politics. Climate sceptics use a range of tricks, from 'woke-washed' criticism of elites flying in their private jets to climate conferences (which sees them opportunistically using the same language as Greta Thunberg) to misinformation about electric cars, which have a heavy environmental cost in their own way and which climate experts agree are not a panacea. Blaming countries like India and China for their lack of climate action is another useful distraction. The use of legitimate criticism is of course merely rhetorical and aimed at justifying inaction rather than holding anyone to account on their climate goals. It also mirrors the male supremacist project: using a kernel of truth to keep us hooked on ways of life that destroy us and undermine any political efforts to solve the real crisis.

The conversation about climate change is increasingly linked to conspiracy theories about tyranny and elite control, as well as culture wars discourse about attacks on 'our way of life'. This is good fuel for right-wing media outrage and reactionary backlash, and gives us, for example, moral panics over vegan barbecues. Amid debates about the Green New Deal, US right-wing media stoked fears of liberals coming to steal honest Americans' beloved steak. Fox News journalist Larry Kudlow claimed that the deal would put an end to Independence Day barbecues,[40] while QAnon-supporting Republican Lauren Boebert urged President Biden to 'stay out of her kitchen'. Culture warriors are not the only people attached to beef. A study in Australia found that three quarters of men would rather give up a decade of life than give up meat and that this was significantly linked to wanting to appear manly.[41]

No wonder the love of meat is pervasive in male supremacist and conspiracist communities. Plant-based diets, they argue, are a plot hatched by 'Big Pharma', the World Economic Forum (WEF) and other malevolent institutions, to control and poison populations and emasculate men. Fears of contamination and elite overreach have spawned a range of food-related conspiratorial beliefs. The 'Great Reset' conspiracy theory, the idea that elites led by the WEF will enslave the world's population and force people to 'eat bugs' while they continue enjoying their steaks, has spread widely in conspiratorial wellness groups and international far-right circles.[42] Discussions about edible insects and lab-grown meat, touted as possible responses to the climate emergency, have become imbued with dark purposes. Pro-Trump Republican Marjorie Taylor Greene, for instance, claimed that the US government would force people to eat meat grown by Bill Gates in a 'peach tree dish'.[43]

Faced with the prospect of living in a feminist 'soyciety', where men's testosterone levels are falling fast, far-right conspiracy theorists are glugging raw eggs, drinking raw milk and eating pounds of meat as an act of masculine resistance, rejecting progressive 'cucked' climate policies. French influencer Baptiste Marchais (aka Bench & Cigars), who relocated to Texas and now courts the US far-right, previously made meaty far-right discourse something of a speciality and produced many videos where he eats a 'lord's dinner' and tucks into obscenely large steaks while chatting to various far-right guests. A range of far-right influencers and conspiracy theorists with unfortunate names see diet as a way to restore Western civilisation and masculinity, allegedly under attack. They include Raw Egg Nationalist, an anonymous writer, social media personality and Great Reset believer who has advocated eating 36 raw eggs a day (and other 'pure' animal-based products like raw milk and honey), to escape attempts by elites to implement social control. He has his own magazine, *Man's World*, a cookbook and a pamphlet, *The Eggs Benedict Option*, which is half agricultural treatise in favour of regenerative farming and half feverish musings about plots hatched by the WEF to enslave the world's population.

While far-right activists and self-optimising primal men are gnawing on liver in YouTube videos for clicks and views, others are making more political arguments. Climate change has become a favourite topic for Peterson, who has interviewed climate deniers on his YouTube channel, shared claims made by fringe climate-denying outlets on social media[44] and spoken at anti-climate conferences sponsored by fossil fuel companies.[45] During an appearance on Rogan's podcast, he claimed that scientific climate change prediction models are 'useless'.[46] He has devoted multiple videos to attacking climate science, with titles like 'The World Is Not Ending'. Peterson's recent predilection for climate denial is not surprising. A study of the language of climate deniers by Swedish researchers Jonas Anshelm and Martin Hultman found that they 'described themselves as marginalised, banned and oppressed dissidents' and saw climate action as an attack on the 'masculinity of industrial modernity'.[47]

Political scientist Cara Daggett coined the term 'petro-masculinity'.[48] The extraction of fossil fuels, she argues, is inseparable from the model of post-war white Western consumption it helped build. The economic prosperity of the 1950s powered by cheap fossil fuels made a certain ideal possible for white Western men: supporting their family on one income and enjoying new levels of consumption, at a time when men ruled their households. The prosperity of this era, along with its gender and racial norms, is what many male supremacists and their tradwife counterparts hark back to (when not singing the praises of Ancient Greece). After several decades of merrily burning fossil fuels to support Western consumption, we are now reckoning with impending climate catastrophe and the need for drastic policies. It's a time of reckoning for harmful practices – but that's not something that the men who 'refuse to apologise for making the modern world' are interested in doing.

Climate action is of course broadly associated with progressive politics, but it is also perceived, more or less explicitly, as a thwarted male privilege. The eco-feminist movement which emerged in the 1970s has described the domination of nature and the coercion of women as two interlinked aspects of the patriarchy. Men dominated nature and extracted resources the way they dominated women, with no limits or accountability. It can now be seen in the almost exclusively male practice of 'rolling coal' – retrofitting diesel engines to emit large clouds of black polluting smoke. 'Coal rollers' have used trucks and heavy engines to threaten Black Lives Matter protests and have featured prominently in the Canadian 'Freedom Convoy' in early 2022, a protest movement against COVID-19 vaccine mandates led by an alliance of right-wing truckers, extremist groups and conspiracy theorists. While falsely presenting itself as a movement of ordinary truckers (90 per cent of truckers got vaccinated), the Freedom Convoy had close links to the previous far-right movement United We Roll, which combined opposition to the Canadian government's carbon tax with demands to build more fossil fuel pipelines and opposition to immigration.[49]

The kind of destructiveness exhibited in rolling coal is not a failure to understand the reality of climate change: it is about asserting one's right to continue unimpeded. It will perhaps come as no surprise then that backlash against climate activism increasingly takes the form of heinous abuse and threats to those at the forefront of the climate movement. A 2023 poll of 468 climate scientists by Global Witness found that 40 per cent were harassed because of their work and over 30 per cent of female scientists received a significant amount of gender-based threats (compared to 3 per cent for men).[50] Prominent figures in the climate justice movement including Greta Thunberg and Alexandria Ocasio-Cortez have been targets of violent misogynistic abuse; Ocasio-Cortez has been deepfaked in porn.[51] On 4chan and other fringe platforms, calls for the rape and assault of climate activists are rife.[52]

While male supremacists love fossil fuels, some also love nature and long for a pristine land, free from pollution. There are extremist and Instagram-friendly versions of this kind of fantasy. At the extreme end, you have Mike Ma, the founder of the eco-fascist Pine Tree Party. A Breitbart writer and former collaborator of Milo Yiannopoulos, Ma is a leading voice of 'accelerationism'.[53] He and his devotees feel that the world we live in, with its widespread environmental degradation, is unsustainable. They hope for an acceleration of climate collapse to rebuild a clean and unpolluted society, free from immigration, industrial degradation and technological encroachment, where men are strong and women are fertile. Racial hate combined with seemingly environmental discourse underpinned several deadly terror attacks in recent years, including the 2019 Christchurch attack (the terrorist's document before the attack included calls to 'kill the invaders, kill the overpopulation and by doing so save the environment') and a 2022 shooting in Buffalo. Terrorism experts say this trend is likely to increase as the climate crisis intensifies.

In addition to cultivating an audience on social media, Ma sells a self-published novel called *Harassment Architecture*, which features fantasies of violence against women and shooting gay people at nightclubs. In social media posts, he has urged his followers to buy weapons to 'oust illegal immigrants with zero mercy',[54] as well as expressed his desire to have friends with whom he can be his authentic misogynistic and racist self. He has also given aesthetic consideration to his ideology, stating that whether terrorists will be remembered and praised after their death 'depends on how well they were dressed' (he also sells pine-tree-emblazoned clothes).

This is an extremist movement celebrating violence, but softer versions of similar purity fantasies underpin male supremacist wellness discourse and the tradwife movement, in which dreams of masculine men and feminine women go hand in hand with the obsessive avoidance of toxins of all kinds. Carnivore Aurelius and others are urging their audience to 'live off-grid', grow their own vegetables, avoid hormonal birth control and have large, strong, healthy white families. All share what feminist scholar Françoise Vergès calls the 'dream of docile, domesticated, and privatised lives', with clearly delineated national, ethnic and gender lines. In addition to the obvious male and racial supremacy at the heart of this project, the thing that's absent is any sense of collective responsibility or care for others.

The escape from polluted modern society and the reckless burning of fossil fuel may look like opposites but they are not as far apart as one might think. Both are attempts to escape solidarity and accountability. What underpins this kind of behaviour is the fantasy that a minority who answers to no one can thrive while the planet burns. There is, however, some grim reality to that: climate change and environmental disaster might be coming for us all, but it is not coming for us in the same way and at the same speed. The countries that are most vulnerable to climate change are the ones that emit the least carbon dioxide.[55] The climate crisis has already had a disproportionate impact on women, minorities and the poor. In early 2024, women and girls made up 80 per cent of the people displaced by climate change and were 14 times more likely to die as a result of climate disasters.[56] Both in the UK and the US, poorer communities bear the brunt of air pollution.[57]

If fossil fuels are partly about identity, appealing to a male identity under threat can secure votes. Trump's 2016 slogan 'coal is back' was one such example. The mining industry declined during Trump's first term so the promise of bringing back coal was merely rhetorical. However, for individual men, the promise was emotional because real livelihoods, which also mean identities, were at stake. For many men, the decline of the fossil fuel industry is a story of lost jobs, hollowed-out communities and a loss of a sense of purpose. The closure of oil rigs and associated layoffs have been linked to increased suicide rates among men.[58] Michael F. Smith, who wrote about his experience of working on an oil rig, has detailed the seismic change that quitting oil represents for men who worked all their lives in oil extraction. Between 2008 and 2017, 1,566 workers (nearly all men) died in the US while extracting oil, pretty much the same number of US soldiers who died in Afghanistan in the same period,[59] a statistic which I find deeply saddening because it symbolically encapsulates the parallel between the male supremacist project and fossil fuel extraction: in both cases, men exhibit attachment to that which harms them, but individual men suffer from the 'oil soaked' – to use Daggett's adjective – dreams of the men sitting on top of the pyramid.

## So what can we do?

Today's male supremacists and their allies rehash old tropes and promote reactionary agendas but use modern tools to make them look innovative and countercultural. Their project is rooted in and benefits from ordinary misogyny, and nothing less than a deep shift in societal norms and structural socio-economic changes will fully address the problem, which is arguably daunting. Male supremacy is also a multi-pronged political project. It has online and offline campaigns, its zealots, its funders, its opportunists, its amplifiers, its complicit allies and its victims, and as a political project it can be fought. We all intuitively know that for all its benefits, the internet can be bad for us. To a greater or lesser extent we also understand that social media platforms need to keep us browsing and, in doing so, funnel us into more extreme and polarising content, while harvesting our data for profit.

As a policy researcher, I am invariably asked in my job: what can we do? I have spent a lot of time arguing for tech platforms to be accountable and for governments to regulate them. In everyday life, having seen my friends fall down their rabbit holes, having heard men around me parrot the arguments of previously fringe groups and having myself realised how easy it is in moments of isolation and vulnerability to be sucked into an online vortex, I have reassessed the solutions to the problem. I would like to believe we can treat it as a challenge that can be met. The challenge is big, because it touches on the very nature of our social norms and structures and is underpinned by powerful corporate and political interests. It is linked to the state of our polarised political discourse and fraught information space.

I have met many people in my professional life who are trying to address the crisis of radicalisation and polarisation we are experiencing, and their passion and commitment to the work, despite waves of abuse many of them have experienced, has convinced me this is work worth pursuing. Part II of this book considers responses. I am by no means claiming to offer all the solutions but attempting to shine a light on different ways of addressing the problem, with pragmatism and nuance. There are immediate risks associated with the male supremacist project, like the normalisation of coercive and violent behaviours towards women. The male supremacist project aims to change social norms, erode women's rights and achieve legislative wins.

In a tired and cynical age, there is a risk of political disengagement and individualistic self-protection at the expense of a collective vision of progress. While I have seen these trends in the rise of New Age and far-right conspiracies, and many women's disengagement from feminism, I'm seeing a movement of public educators who try to tackle these issues with compassion. I'm also seeing vibrant feminist activists and intellectuals grapple with the complexity of contemporary gender politics to give us new ways to think about the way we live now. Beyond the Twitter pile-ons, there is a movement.

# PART II

# Fighting back

# 6

# Can there ever be girls on the internet?

Mia Landsem had recently turned 18 and, like many young people, was enjoying her first legal beer with a group of friends at her local bar in the central city of Trondheim when she saw a group of men in a corner glancing at her and laughing. She ignored them but the laughter continued. Exasperated, she got up and confronted them. 'Aren't you that porn star?' they said and showed her a picture of herself having sex with an ex-boyfriend. Mia had come out of a bad relationship with the ex a few months before. Weeks before she turned 18, he had posted intimate pictures of her online. By the time of the bar incident, the pictures had been posted on porn sites and were circulating in online groups and on social media, spreading throughout her home city, unbeknownst to Mia. In the weeks that followed, dozens of people started messaging her. She reported the case to the police. They said there was little they could do.

Mia started conducting some online research to track how far her pictures had travelled. What she found marked her for life: intimate pictures of hundreds of other girls and women. 'They were categorising us: by age, height, hair colour. I contacted these girls and started telling them because the way I found out about the pictures was horrifying.'

Image-based sexual abuse – commonly referred to as 'revenge porn', a term heavily contested by organisations and experts studying the phenomenon for its implication that victims are somehow to blame – is a very gendered phenomenon, overwhelmingly affecting women and girls. In the UK, studies estimate that 60–90 per cent of victims of image-based abuse are women. The Revenge Porn Helpline has reported that 75 per cent of calls are from women.[1]

When we speak on a winter afternoon, it is dark outside Mia's Oslo flat. She is direct and says exactly what's on her mind when she tells me her story. After the sex pictures, Mia tried to move on. She always had an interest in online gaming but she also loved sports and martial arts. She made it onto the Norwegian Taekwondo national junior team, eventually becoming one of a handful of young athletes to enter the Norwegian School of Sports Sciences to study for a bachelor's degree in sports science and coaching.

During her second year in school, she sustained a knee injury and was in crutches for six months. The dream of going to the Olympics was over.

The two ordeals she endured led her down an unexpected career path at a time when she felt she had nothing to lose. 'I suddenly thought "fuck it, I'll study IT". Who knew girls could do that?' She quit her bachelor's degree, Googled 'IT studies', found a two-year online course, and the week after she applied she was told she could start. After studying computer science, she landed a job as an 'ethical hacker' at the IT multinational Orange. Over the last few years, she has worked in IT security systems, while also doing pro bono work from home to help female victims of image-based abuse. More and more women came to her for help, including a Norwegian handball star to whom she helped give media exposure.

For a long time, Mia did not tell her story to the media outlets who asked her about her path, first opening up to *The Guardian* in 2022. That attracted media attention, both in Norway and internationally. Now, she has given over 500 talks around the world and written a children's book about online safety. 'I didn't want to be the victim who became a hero, I wanted to focus on the problem itself. I don't care about my picture anymore. It is everywhere,' she says. Whether she is helping a teenage girl or a professional athlete, Mia never charges people.

Non-consensual images on revenge porn websites are almost always pictures of women. Despite that, Mia is keen to stress that she does not help just women and girls. In fact, she has deliberately adapted her discourse in her media appearances and says that many young men are now approaching her with cases of online abuse, doxxing and identity theft. She says we need greater involvement of women in cybersecurity, not just as a career path but as a safety consideration that is built into systems. 'We need female developers, and female everything in cyber. When I do security testing, I always keep in mind: how can this be used not just to find someone's personal information but also to stalk and harass them?' she adds.

As she became more prominent and in the public eye, she has attracted waves of abuse and backlash from men who resent her very involvement in cybersecurity. 'Suddenly, men felt I was taking away their toys,' she says. When we speak, she has just come home from work, cooked dinner and taken the dog for a walk, and she is about to embark on the night shift of answering emails asking for help. During our interview, her mother calls her to ask her for some credit card advice for her grandmother. A lot of people depend on her, something which has evidently taken its toll as Mia confesses she is 'working too much'.

Mia's path is not the result of a choice but of incredible resilience, strength and talent in the face of trauma. She is one person helping countless women every day, doing the job that the police should be doing and addressing a problem that laws and regulations should be addressing. These days, she refuses most interviews and says she has learned to prioritise her wellbeing and focus on her family, relationships and hobbies. 'I have stopped being this "yes person".' She continues: 'The impact of seeing child abuse is horrifying, but being able to help one child makes it all worth it. You're looking for clues to identify the perpetrator, you learn to disconnect.'

When it comes to online violence and sexual abuse targeting women, social media platforms have been slow to react and legislation has been inadequate. Individuals and activist organisations are stepping in where the law and tech platforms have failed. Mia says we need to apply greater pressure on social media platforms and demand laws to force them to follow abuse compliance. Many avenues that she could take to help people are not open to her for privacy reasons: 'I can't do a lot of the stuff the police could do; I have to stay on the right side of the law.' Over the years, she has built a library of resources on her website on online safety, providing guidance on anything from how to create a good password to how to react to digital sexual blackmail. She continues to investigate more complex harassment cases, doing passive reconnaissance. This involves open-source research tools to gather metadata on accounts perpetrating abuse and works on discrete projects investigating more coordinated or deeper networks of abuse.

## Dealing with trolls

Among the feminist activists who focus on online abuse, there is some resistance to considering individual cybersecurity and safety advice as a form of response at all, for fear of encouraging victim blaming. Yet there is a growing recognition that enhanced cybersecurity skills are a necessary tool for individuals and an indispensable component of education for youths and adults alike. Mathilde Saliou is a technology expert based in Paris who focuses on the impact of technology and AI on gender equality. She writes a regular newsletter for women, sharing cybersecurity advice and tips, and advocates for cybersecurity knowledge to be made more accessible to women. In the UK, research conducted by King's College London found that men were more likely to be well-versed in anti-tracking technologies such as virtual private networks and anti-malware, noting that online safety advice needs to be more tailored to women's needs.[2] This is something that Saliou agrees with: 'We need to break the myth that knowing these kinds of skills is a man's thing.'

Books such as *How to Be a Woman Online* (2022) by disinformation expert Nina Jankowicz offer practical and immediately applicable advice to women on how to navigate the risks of online abuse, protect themselves online and deal with the male trolls who demand women's attention. Nina Jankowicz, using an expression coined by Australian activist Van Badham in a particular stroke of genius, calls this men's 'engagement boner': the gratification they obtain from receiving the attention they feel entitled to. To deal with the engagement boner, her advice includes using the mute and block buttons liberally, ignoring men's pleas for attention and navigating platform settings. She also encourages women to find online and offline communities of support they can rely on. In her book *How to Stay Safe Online* (2022), activist and CEO of Glitch, the first UK charity focused on ending gender-based online abuse, Seyi Akiwowo advocates for 'digital self-care', which she defines as 'non-negotiable self-love in the face of so much negativity and harm', giving women, particularly women with intersecting identities who face particular forms of online abuse, encouragement to do what they need to do to cope both online and offline. 'Digital self-care is about acknowledging when you need to take a break from the online world. When we talk about online abuse, recognising how it causes trauma can help you create boundaries to minimise how it can harm you,' she tells me. But none of these writers, who have worked tirelessly for tech regulation, have suggested that personal safety tips are an alternative to tech accountability or a long-term response to male supremacist attacks.

A strong password or double authentication will not prevent anyone from being targeted with abuse, smear campaigns and deepfake pornography. 'Manosphere networks know exactly what they are doing. They can doxx someone in two seconds,' Saliou tells me. Human rights academic Agnes Venema, an expert on deepfakes, agrees and tells me that getting justice for individuals is impossible:

> Finding the exact perpetrators is difficult. You also run into jurisdiction problems, where the perpetrator is in one country, the server is in another and the platform on which it was posted in yet another. To get them to work all together is very difficult; people are unlikely to get the justice they deserve.

What personal safety does is give agency. While online safety tips can only ever go so far to protect individuals, experts have also documented how feminist ideas can help us reshape a safer internet. They say that until we fix the gender bias in AI, we will not solve the problem. While the technology itself is neutral, its design is informed by societal biases. 'Until we have a diverse group of people developing AI, we're not going to get rid of this,' Venema says. 'The problem isn't AI; the problem is the dataset. Women are not welcome in the field, although some people, including men, are really pushing hard for inclusion.' Diverse representation in designer teams would go some way to the problem, while the involvement of women in cybersecurity would also lead to a major shift. When Landsem says that in her cybersecurity work she thinks about how a certain technology can be used to harass women, she is touching on the key question: who is cybersecurity designed to protect?

The answer is that cybersecurity is primarily geared towards helping states and businesses, and not much of it is developed to help individuals, particularly women. Julia Slupska, an expert on feminist cybersecurity, says that tech companies could apply some of the principles of corporate cybersecurity to individual online safety. The cybersecurity field that focuses on insider threat can inform responses to intimate partner online violence. 'If you're fired from a large company, your access to company files is revoked via cybersecurity tools; if we think of intimate relationships, we could design processes that could allow you to revoke access to a file after you break up.' This is a step which would go some way in increasing people's agency instead of attributing responsibility to victims, as is often the case with image-based sexual abuse. Too often, the default response to women victims of image-based abuse is to ask them why they shared the pictures in the first place, the equivalent of telling women not to wear short skirts if they don't want to be raped.

This kind of thinking could also be applied to social media platforms. In recent years, the notion of 'safety by design' has become more prominent in discussing how to hold tech giants accountable for the harms perpetrated on their platforms. The idea of safety by design, when applied to social media platforms, rests on the notions of accountability, user empowerment and transparency.[3] Safety by design encourages social media platforms to address any emerging harm and give users greater control over what they see online. This requires a radical shift of assumptions. Slupska says that tech companies could build in mechanisms that do not assume that users want to see their picture widely shared online: 'We need to develop privacy tools that shift the underlying assumption of who has control over what we put online.'

The tools and technologies which could make a difference exist. Getting large tech companies – profit driven, male-led, with male-designed products and increasingly politicised CEOs – to adopt them is another story. Tracy Chou knows all this too well. A software engineer in Silicon Valley, she was one of the first employees at Quora and Pinterest when these platforms started. Chou was key in building these companies' content moderation tools. She also became what she calls an 'accidental activist for diversity and inclusion in tech'. After attending a work conference on diversity in computing, she became curious about representation in tech companies and the lack of reliable data about the number of women employed in technical roles. She wrote a blog post, which went viral, urging companies to disclose data on the topic. This led to her creating an open-source repository. Within a week she had collected responses from 50 companies.

As a result, Chou became the target of racist and misogynistic abuse campaigns, coming from the cesspool that is 4chan. She says:

> For a long time, I brushed it off, I listened to people who said 'don't read the comments, don't feed the trolls', but I realised how bad it made me feel to see this all day long. Even though I get a lot of benefit from being online, there is a severe mental health impact.

She also became the victim of severe stalking and spoke to a private investigator. 'One of the pieces of advice they gave me was that it can feel debilitating to feel like there is nothing you can do and what can help is to reassert agency and think about the ways you can be more proactive.' These experiences led her, in 2021, to design and launch Block Party. Block Party is an anti-harassment online tool which allows users to block any messages from accounts that are likely to harass them and mute any posts that include abusive language, preventing that content from reaching users and effectively creating a protective shield. When it launched, it had free and paid-for options. Having gone to university with many people who went on to have senior leadership positions in large tech companies, every time Chou posted on her social media feed about the abuse she received, her contacts at large companies swiftly dealt with the problem. 'This was also something that frustrated me about my own privilege: I wanted these protections for everyone.'

Block Party is what's known as 'middleware', a type of instrument that stands between the platforms and the users. For advocates of tech regulation, this can feel like a distraction and a Band-Aid. Chou argues for realism and says this type of tool needs to exist because of the difficulties of regulating tech platforms and getting them to embrace safety by design. 'It's not that social media platforms don't care about user safety, it's that they care about other things more,' she says. 'Instead of banging on Facebook's door and telling them that they need to fix their algorithm – which assumes there is one algorithm that Facebook has control of – it allows people to have choice about what they see online.'

Chou has tested the limits of this thinking. After Elon Musk bought Twitter, Block Party lost its application programming interface (API) access and had to shut down the tool. This shows that without regulations mandating access to the API, such initiatives are at the mercy of the limited goodwill of the sort of tech CEOs who are welcoming Andrew Tate back on to their platforms with open arms. Unless tech companies are forced to grant access to their API, they will be able to rescind it at any time. After losing access to the renamed X, Chou and her company have created a new tool, a free browser extension which identifies online vulnerabilities in one's social media accounts and automates privacy settings.

Browser extensions aren't sexy, but they can have a significant impact on online safety, pointing to the disconnect between the incentive to create safety tools and the impact they may have. What makes the most difference to people is not what is shiniest or most rewarded. As Chou tells me, 'No one gets promoted for working on a settings page; you get promoted for working on a fancy new feature.' Anyone who has tried to navigate the privacy settings on LinkedIn and Instagram can testify that they don't make things easy. No one wants to spend time fiddling with privacy settings, but they can be the key to preserving one's safety and sanity.

## Design and outrage

Social media algorithms lead users towards more extreme content, and anti-feminism is often the entry point into darker male supremacist and extremist depths. Outside of rabbit hole dynamics, however, researchers are now paying more attention to how platform design shapes our online actions, encouraging certain types of networked behaviour. Anger, polarisation, outrage and mob mentality: these dynamics may be rooted in real emotions and structures, but they are encouraged by the design of platforms themselves. Whitney Phillips' *This Is Why We Can't Have Nice Things* (2015) showed that the design of 4chan – with its anonymity, focus on offensive humour and format of posts and replies – encouraged the most offensive memes to go viral and fuelled the misogynistic culture of online trolling that came to characterise the alt-right and made a lasting imprint on the state of online political discussion. The pornographic deepfake images of Taylor Swift which emerged in early 2024, a report by Graphika found, originated from a weeks-long challenge on 4chan where users competed to find ways to beat safety features on generative AI technology which were meant to prevent users from creating deepfake porn. Users took on daily challenges to find words that could allow them to bypass filters, rejoicing at being able to game the system.[4]

The structure of mainstream platforms promotes similar behaviours. Technology designer Tobias Rose-Stockwell has shown in *Outrage Machine* (2023) that the functionalities and features of these platforms encourage polarisation, dehumanisation and outrage. We log into our social media feed and immediately read a tweet that uses shocking language. We feel angry, and without pausing to think we retweet it or insult someone because they are only a theoretical person behind a screen. In doing so we simply feed the outrage loop further. This leads to what Rose-Stockwell calls 'outrage cascades'. Of course there are many injustices in this world about which we should feel outrage, but in this form it is toxic, not justified or not well thought through but an immediate response to a fleeting stimulus. Social media platforms want to keep us engaged and clicking; they demand our reactions, facilitate knee-jerk responses and reward moral outrage.

This leads to the polarised state of online discussions where it is increasingly difficult to engage with people in good faith but it is easy to attract widespread abuse and vilification for the flimsiest reasons and become the internet's 'main character of the day', as the expression goes.[5] As an article in *Vice* detailed, those who have become the main character and the centre of the daily pile-on include a woman who tweeted: 'My husband and I wake up every morning and bring our coffee out to our garden and sit and talk for hours'; the tweet triggered widespread rage for her alleged lack of consideration for the less fortunate who don't have a garden and the leisure to sit in it for hours.[6] This outrage has ruined social media for many of us who are wary of participating in any online discussions and don't believe we can have good-faith debates. Shouting at people who think differently from us is unlikely to make them pause and reconsider and can entrench people further in their views. While incivility and outrage are not the unique preserve of a particular group, outrage has fuelled organised male supremacist campaigns, which trade in and thrive on these feelings. Moral outrage has sparked powerful movements like #MeToo, but it also can also lead us to being swept into waves of abuse and take part in harassment when we think we are morally in the right, even though we might be egged on by a few bots.

The outrage machine that amplifies disinformation and violent speech while simultaneously stifling reasonable debate thrives because we are poorly equipped to deal with an online environment that wants us to be angry. Technology researchers including Tristan Harris have argued that our brains cannot cope with what technology encourages us to do. Researchers are now advocating for tech platforms and third-party organisations to implement various forms of compensatory mechanisms and brakes to help us regulate our emotions when we are online. Rose-Stockwell advocates for the introduction of features that slow down the process of sharing articles and mechanisms that allow content that is going viral to be temporarily suspended and reviewed by moderators before it spreads further. Harris says that we should embrace services that encourage us to get offline, take breaks from technology and wean us off the dopamine hits of likes. This is analogous to ultra-processed food: asking us to resist being sucked into an algorithmic vortex is like asking us to resist ultra-processed snacks, when they are designed to be cheap, addictive, widely available and pushed onto the consumer.

Caroline Sinders is a designer, visual artist and technology researcher who studies coordinated harassment campaigns and advises victims of online abuse. She says a key problem is that 'we do not live in a harassment literate society.' Even millennials and Gen Zs who have grown up with the internet are surprisingly ill-equipped to deal with harassment and have gaps in their understanding of online safety. 'The clients I work with think online dating, for instance, is incredibly safe; it's just a way to meet people. They give away their phone numbers and after a few dates end up being stalked. Many people underestimate the risks involved.' She also believes that, 'Harassment cases require a lot of context and understanding of power dynamics.'

This is something most of us, not being experts in domestic abuse or harassment and living in societies where misogynistic biases prevail, are lacking. This societal gap is also what allowed millions to tune into the *Depp v. Heard* trial and decide that they could analyse Heard's performance of victimhood and look for evidence of guilt without a proper understanding of what counts as evidence in an abuse case. Male supremacists can easily weaponise that knowledge gap. Backed up by conservative media, they work hard to promote the broad narrative that we live in a 'woke' society where women who come forward with accusations of abuse have overwhelming amounts of power. 'It's easy to engage in misogynistic lines of thinking, even if it's not your intention,' Sinders says. While many people spent time rationalising Depp's behaviour, the same consideration was not afforded to Heard.

All social media platforms started with only a few users; they never fully adapted to having millions or billions. There are design steps platforms could take to address this, reducing the risk of backlash-driven harassment and assisting victims more quickly. If tech companies tried to design platforms with greater user safety in mind the way an urban planner designed a city to make it safer, they could, Sinders suggests, create tools that allow a victim of coordinated harassment to gather evidence in a few clicks. On a platform like X, simple tools could be made accessible to users to collect several hundred tweets, report batches of data to platforms and clean up mentions (tweets where one's social media handle is used) in one go. Tools could also give greater privacy options. While these measures would not make platforms a utopia of civility, they would counterbalance their most toxic aspects and would help abuse victims feel immediately safer, as opposed to waiting three days for a content moderator's decision.

On Facebook, individuals can set up a legacy contact to take care of their account after their death; they should also be able to nominate a contact to help them gather evidence in case they become a victim of harassment. Platforms could also create a new user visibility setting that sits somewhere between public and private, with greater control over privacy settings: women leaving social media entirely sends the signal to harassers that they have won.

At a broader level, social media platforms need to have teams that are trained in specific contexts and recognise specific forms of harassment and disinformation. For example, someone who focuses on political disinformation is unlikely to understand what can affect a person with eating disorders: unless one is an expert it can be easy to miss words and terminology that could drive someone towards restrictive or harmful patterns of eating. 'Gamergate was misunderstood due to lack of widespread knowledge of gaming,' Sinders says. For the first few months, mainstream media covered the event as a form of infighting in the video game community rather than what it truly was: coordinated harassment driven by misogyny. Over-reliance on tropes about gaming meant that the long-term impact of Gamergate was underestimated. Similarly, lack of nuanced understanding of harassment and power hinders the understanding of a trial like *Depp v. Heard* and what will come after it.

While rationalisations abounded in the *Depp v. Heard* trial, the broad reality of misogynistic harassment, backlash campaigns and sexualised retribution is that there is no rational explanation for it. Men who abuse and harass women do it because they feel entitled to it; it gives them a sense of power and control and, against a backdrop of perceived victimhood of gender equality, becomes a tool for retribution and coercion. Abuse and the silencing women are rooted in men's desire to punish women for existing or expressing 'sentiments that differentiate them from a doormat', to use Rebecca West's famous words. They are embedded in cultural standards which normalise men's control over women's bodies and the viewing non-consensual images as a form of entertainment. Putting brakes on platforms and regulations can only go hand in hand with a shift in these norms. Public discussion and education are important in areas where regulation is non-existent or slow moving.

## The online porn wild west and the misogynistic abuse frontier

One online sector has managed to evolve outside of almost any regulation: the online porn industry, which has for a long time avoided scrutiny by presenting itself as a space of free sexual expression in which the state should have no say. Porn is often presented as a domain of sexual agency and individual consumption, as if porn sites too were not driven by algorithms which curate content and shape users' preferences and behaviours. The scale of the online pornography industry is truly immense. Pornhub is among the top ten most-visited websites in the world.[7] In a single month in 2023, it received more visits than Instagram, Netflix, Pinterest and TikTok combined. It is also the one that tends to be discussed in mainstream media (though Xvideos is the largest porn website in the world). A 2020 exposé in *The New York Times* titled 'The Children of Pornhub' highlighted the prevalence of non-consensual videos and child rape on the site, also reporting on how the company made money out of videos of rape on unconscious women and various forms of torture.[8]

I speak to Fiona Vera-Gray, who has worked on the issue for many years and interviewed women on their usage of pornography. 'My concern as a researcher, citizen and parent are the ways in which these platforms are narrowing our sexual freedoms because they are streamlining us towards harmful content that maximises their profit,' she says. In 2018, with a team of researchers at Durham University, Vera-Gray investigated what the three largest porn sites, Pornhub, XHamster and Xvideos, recommended to people visiting them for the very first time. Researchers found that one in eight videos on the front pages of these websites included sexual violence.[9] Once you click on something you will be recommended more of the same type of content, and more extreme versions of it, to keep you engaged. In the UK, the British Board of Film Classification classifies all pornographic films that are sold in sex shops and that can be watched in cinemas, but its remit does not extend to online content.

The UK's Online Safety Act became law in the UK in October 2023 after many years of crafting and debate. With the stated ambition of making the UK 'the safest place in the world to be online', it imposed rules on social media platforms to mitigate a range of harms. Under this legislation, platforms which host pornography need to ensure that children do not encounter their content, including by introducing age verification measures. Notably, it also bans the creation and distribution of deepfake pornography, effectively making the usage of widely advertised nudifying apps illegal. Legal scholar Clare McGlynn, a leading authority on online harms, isn't hopeful that the legislation will change much in practice in the UK where the regulator – Ofcom – is tasked with setting obligations for platforms. 'The guidance coming out of Ofcom is quite weak. It's an important legal change, but the extent to which it will have a significant impact on individuals or at a systemic level is open to question,' says McGlynn. By making deepfake pornography a criminal offence, the law sends a powerful message to those who might be tempted. The same applies to other cyber offences. In March 2024, the Online Safety Act led to the first ever conviction for 'cyberflashing'; the perpetrator received a 66-week jail sentence, but he was already on the sex offender register. McGlynn doubts law enforcement will have the same incentive to pursue other perpetrators.

Child sexual exploitation was illegal before the Online Safety Act, but that did not prevent porn sites from hosting this type of content. 'It is almost impossible to hold pornographic sites to account,' Vera-Gray says. Illegal content, horrifying enough as it is, is only part of the story. For Vera-Gray there needs to be a broader conversation about what these websites encourage and normalise and why things which are not allowed elsewhere are allowed on porn sites. This is a social conversation that has been delayed by stigma. In the UK, the broadcasting code and advertising standards don't allow women to be represented as animals or being spat on, but both of these are common in online porn. 'Many men have known for a long time what is on these sites, and what it says about women, and they've navigated it in whatever way they've navigated it but they haven't tried to do anything about it,' she adds. Women's understanding is also growing as more of them consume online pornography.

Linguist Alessia Tranchese of Portsmouth University has found that the language of incels mirrors the language of mainstream pornography very closely.[10] Extreme misogynistic communities and mainstream porn promote the same dehumanisation of women and their education on body parts, which shapes men's understanding of what women are for and what is acceptable to do to them. Choking or strangulation during sex is harmful even when it is consensual, as it can lead to brain damage,[11] but it has increased among members of Gen Z, a rise that has been attributed to its normalisation in porn. It helps to think less about the consumers of porn themselves (around 50 per cent of men, though the percentages are much higher for younger men, and 15 per cent of women in the UK),[12] as opposed to the corporations who profit from it.

Meanwhile, the harassment frontier keeps shifting. Where new technologies develop, abuse follows. In early 2024, UK police launched the first ever investigation into the rape of a teenage girl in the metaverse. The girl, aged under 16 at the time, said her avatar was assaulted in a virtual reality (VR) game.[13] Researchers who investigated metaverse harassment and created a female avatar found that VR reflected real-life harassment patterns. VR harassment and abuse has become a new frontier, one which is very difficult to prosecute barring a reconsideration of existing laws. The term 'virtual reality' itself can lend itself to misconceptions and convey the false idea that since abuse is virtual, it doesn't impact victims, when in fact VR technology is designed to be as immersive as possible and to elicit physical sensations, and VR headsets are capable of producing ever more realistic images.[14] Meta's CEO Mark Zuckerberg has said he wants the metaverse to supplant mobile phones in the next decade: whether this aim is realistic or not, the fact that the metaverse is being designed without safety considerations and is already showing the same patterns of violence as other forms of technology – and with fraught legal implications for regulation – does not bode well.

## Disrupting the male supremacist machine

Along with ideology, financial rewards are what drive the internet's 'chaos entrepreneurs' while social media platforms profit from their extremist views and keep us hooked with more of the same. Tech platforms do not have the financial incentive to address polarising views and harassment. It might be in their interests to look better than their competitors, although Elon Musk has given a bullish response to advertisers expressing concerns about the direction X has taken. Campaigners including Seyi Akiwowo have lobbied for part of the UK government's digital services tax to fund anti-online abuse work. These recommendations recognise the fact that not only is fighting abuse and harassment costly but the only way to incentivise social media platforms to take these problems seriously is to make inaction costlier for them too.

Demonetisation and no-platforming have also proved effective. Take the case of Milo Yiannopoulos, who a decade ago used his various media platforms to spew antisemitic, misogynistic and racist commentary under the guise of anti-political correctness and was not only indulged by conservatives in the US but was also depicted by mainstream media as a tantalising, if naughty, provocateur. The more the media cheered, the more he played his role. Feminist author Laurie Penny once called him a 'charming devil and one of the worst people I know'.[15] This went on until 2017 when footage emerged showing Yiannopoulos endorsing child sexual abuse, leading Simon & Schuster to cancel his lucrative book deal, universities to call off his speaking engagements and media outlets to shun him. What is notable is the many opportunities he was given by these institutions in the first place. Yiannopoulos has since faded into complete irrelevance. Likewise, between 2015 and 2018 conspiracy theorist Alex Jones reportedly made $165 million in sales of supplements and survival gear while peddling conspiracy theories about the

2012 Sandy Hook massacre, the moon landing and 9/11. His deplatforming immediately hit his viewing figures and online sales of supplements.

Other attempts to cut off extremists' funding have emerged in recent years. The activist group Sleeping Giants, an activist organisation specialising in demonetising hate, led a campaign to encourage brands to stop advertising on Breitbart, which was central in shaping anti-immigrant rhetoric during the 2016 US elections. This kind of work inevitably leads to accusations of censorship. If this argument resonates, it is because the notion of what is acceptable has evolved, and hate speech is increasingly couched as reasonable. Cutting off funding from media outlets that spew misogynistic, homophobic and anti-immigrant hateful rhetoric, or indeed dangerous health misinformation, is not curtailing freedom of speech; it is recognising any responsible company should not allow harmful discourse to shape public conversation. A handful of people like Milo Yiannopoulos a few years ago and Andrew Tate have a disproportionate impact in spreading hate. At the height of the pandemic, a study by the Center for Countering Digital Hate found that a dozen anti-vaccine influencers accounted for nearly 70 per cent of anti-vaccine content online,[16] with their disproportionate reach having significant public health consequences.

The demonetisation and no-platforming of key figures can be swift and effective, but a similar approach aimed at disrupting the activities of male supremacist entrepreneurs could be applied across the board. Carl Miller says, 'we need to disrupt misogynists' online influence campaigns, make them costlier and more difficult and inject chaos into them.' He sees it as a war and borrows from the military concept of a 'kill chain', the series of steps required for a military operation, to illustrate how we can undermine male supremacist influence. 'We need to cut different segments of the chain. If they have assets, we need to cut access to assets; if they capture attention, we need to divert attention; they should be deranked on search engines and denied access to unfair influence techniques.' Agnes Venema agrees and says that simple steps such as banning social media apps that host deepfakes or image-based abuse from app stores would go a long way to incentivise platforms, which would suddenly be cut off from their consumer base. 'The app stores have immense power as to what you can and can't download. If we told these platforms that they're not allowed to be in the store until they fix things, it would go a certain way in addressing the problem.' While tech giants have long allowed hate and extremist to fester on their platforms, there are a few signs that the tide might be turning, and that governments are willing to take strong steps to show tech companies they are not above the law. In August 2024, French authorities arrested Russian-born billionaire and Telegram founder Pavel Durov, ostensibly over the platform's failure to stem illegal child sexual abuse images. Days later, a Pennsylvania court ruled that a mother whose son died after imitating a self-asphyxiation video on TikTok, could sue the company. In Brazil, a Supreme Court judge ordered the country's telecommunications agency to suspend access to X across the whole country after Musk failed to ban several accounts from the platform.[17]

Making the life of the manosphere's loudest voices more difficult works to a certain extent. We should focus on the individual influencers with outsized audiences while bearing in mind the more important fact, which is that they give a voice to feelings that will not go away by deplatforming them. The collective fixation on someone like Tate, who sealed his own fate, can make us forget that in the era of fleeting fame and clout chasing, hundreds, if not thousands, of PUAs and red pill influencers are reaching young men on social media. The resentment, misogyny and lack of vision that drove young men to one influencer will not disappear without a societal reckoning with the ideological and socio-economic factors that underpin these feelings. This is why in recent years, education, counter narratives and digital literacy have become the second default solution advocated to tackling online harms.

# 7

# How do you argue with a male supremacist?

The divorce had been difficult. Now, though, the difficult process of separation was over, and for Aileen Barratt, it felt like the start of a new life chapter. It was time to take advantage of her new-found freedom and get back on the dating scene. A lot had changed in the time she had been married: internet dating had become commonplace and even entered a new phase of evolution. The era of swiping had arrived. The apps that invented this functionality had launched in 2012; it was still just four years old and felt fresh and new. So Barratt joined Tinder in the hope of putting the spark back in her romantic life. She created a profile, logged in and got her thumb to work. Left, left. Left, right, left. The matches started to come in, but soon she was struck by the amount of misogyny she experienced and the overtly crude accounts she encountered on the platform.

Others were less directly offensive but wrapped in double-speak and misogynistic entitlement: 'I want a woman who is comfortable in her femininity, takes care of her body and can challenge my perspective on things to help me grow.' Barratt started an Instagram page called TinderTranslators, in which she translated men's Tinder profiles for other women. 'I'm looking for someone who takes care of herself' she translated as 'I want someone slim, not someone who goes to therapy.' Or, 'Married but looking, please don't judge, I have my reasons' equals 'Married but attempting to cheat. My reasons are that I want to cheat, but I'll pretend there's some complicated situation that makes it okay.' The translation for that original profile, in case you wondered, is: 'I want a woman who's comfortable with gender stereotypes, is thin and can challenge my perspective but, like, not too much, because I'm the man.'

If her Instagram struck a chord, it is probably because most women who have used dating apps have encountered similar Tinder profiles. My own fleeting experience with dating apps was disappointing and mercifully short-lived: I encountered all the types that Barratt excoriates in her online profile. Barratt started interacting with thousands of women who spoke about their experiences with dating apps. These stories were transformative for her. She broadened TinderTranslators out into wider coverage of dating and relationships and started covering misogyny and the manosphere. Today, she is the host of *Manosphere Debunked*, a podcast she co-hosts with a male psychologist known only as 'Dan' who protects his anonymity online. Her account features explainers on concepts such as misogyny and the patriarchy and debunks common male supremacist refrains from 'women only date up; it's called hypergamy' to 'marriage doesn't benefit men'.

Quite by accident, Barratt has become one of an eclectic cohort of people who have built an online following by engaging with male supremacist arguments, bringing facts to counter myths. Many are women; some are men; there are data nerds and silver-tongued debaters; psychologists and misinformation experts. Most fell into their role by chance rather than by a burning desire to pick battles with male supremacists; indeed, some of them have a degree of reservation about what they do. This chapter profiles a few and explores their motivations and tactics. It asks the question: does any of it make a difference and to whom?

Having spent the last few years tracking misinformation about the pandemic, climate change, global conflicts and elections, I have been asked by journalists more times than I can count: 'What can we do about it?' Working in this field can feel like a frustrating game of whack-a-mole and a race to track the latest conspiracy, which dwarfs any sensible attempt at engaging with the crises that we face. During COVID-19, research showed that the reach of conspiratorial websites significantly outweighed the reach of World Health Organization (WHO) and the US Center for Disease Control (CDC).[1] Awareness that online misinformation is a democratic and public health threat has grown, but societies are struggling with the pace, shape-shifting and technological advancement of misinformation. After COVID-19, conspiracy theories spread to Ukraine and the Israel–Hamas war and are increasingly polluting discussions about climate change. For many years, researchers have advocated for truth-based solutions as a remedy to the ill. While political fact-checking has a long history,[2] the first dedicated fact-checking websites appeared in the early 2000s when disinformation looked quite different from the 'conspiracy smoothies' we are now drinking.[3]

Truth-based solutions are complicated. This is because while today's influence campaigns do still use blatant lies, their main weapon is outrage activation and distortion: making some truths more visible than others, cherry-picking data and manipulating in other ways. Facts can be viewed subjectively, even in areas where accusations of ideological bias are more difficult to make, like health and science, and influencers can play on widespread distrust of politicians, journalists or any type of expert. They also play on emotions. Movements like QAnon have explicitly used the language of critical thinking with slogans like 'do your own research' and recognised our desire to understand and have a grasp of the world around us. Alternative health practitioners selling snake oil use the language of patient empowerment and liberation movements. Anti-abortion movements produce activist guides on how to undermine the work of reproductive rights organisations. Male supremacist entrepreneurs invite men to think critically about gender relations. All have built the mirror world which Naomi Klein talks about in which words are increasingly losing meaning and where incels' entitlement to sex can be framed as a reasonable political demand worthy of a #MeToo movement.

Conspiracy theories are by definition a bastardisation of critical thinking, when healthy scepticism goes off the rails. Recent years have seen renewed interest in what underpins conspiratorial thinking: some research has found that people who rely on intuition and gut feeling as opposed to analytical thinking were more likely to believe in conspiracy theories.[4] It is a strange paradox of conspiratorial thinking that the people who intuitively believe in wild conspiracy theories also spend a lot of time doing research and backing up their beliefs. Thanks to the internet they are now blessed with unlimited content to pore over and find new 'evidence'. If today's politicised conspiracy theories are the distorted mirror image of insufficiently addressed scandals and injustices, as Klein argued, one could say, if one wanted to be especially generous to them, that conspiracy theorists are people with a misguided sense of justice. To view them purely as irrational would be a mistake.

The pandemic, which took our lives online and led to the widespread circulation of conspiracy theories, has resulted in a confused world where we do not know who to trust anymore. The erosion of expertise has been long in the making. The 2016 Brexit referendum and US election campaign saw political figures on both sides of the Atlantic proclaim that people have 'had enough of experts'.[5] On the one hand, the reaction to the pandemic and the fact that most people adhered to the lockdowns that were imposed showed that the world at large does still have some base level of trust in experts; on the other, it revealed how conspiracy theories have gained a mainstream foothold in public discourse and led to the abuse of medical professionals.[6] At the height of the pandemic, US chief medical advisor Dr Anthony Fauci reassured millions of Americans (a *New York Times* poll[7] in September 2020 found that 84 per cent of American trusted medical experts' advice about the management of the pandemic, regardless of partisan divide) but was also the subject of conspiracy theories and received death threats after being undermined by Trump. Speaking after Joe Biden's election, Fauci expressed relief at being able, again, to 'let the science speak'. The relief has been short-lived. Scientists have come under growing attack post-pandemic and are facing various forms of abuse and threats. The playbook of personalised, often misogynistic, attacks that targeted politicians and celebrities is now being deployed against medical professionals and climate scientists.

This is the landscape in which the counter-speakers – those seeking to debunk male supremacist arguments – are working. It is a daunting task, not least because their opponents have inserted themselves into so many different corners of online life. Perhaps the one that touches the lives of the largest number of women, however, is dating.

## Spotting 'red flags': the Tinder translator

In early 2023, close to a quarter of American adults and just under a fifth of the British used dating apps.[8] There are thousands of these apps, from mainstream ones such as Tinder, Bumble and Hinge to more niche offerings such as NUiT ('let astrology empower you to make more meaningful connections!'), Veggly ('If you're looking for herbivorous love, we're here to help you find the right plant-based match!') and Christian Mingle, which inspired a 2014 film of the same title.

Lamenting the state of online dating is not the preserve of male supremacists, although they certainly like to do so given the opportunity. The subreddit r/WhereAreAllTheGoodMen (96,000 followers) – a parody of women's complaints about online dating – is a place of choice for men to vent about hypergamous women and spread various incel and red pill talking points. It is 'dedicated to exposing all the women who complain about wanting a "good man", to show what happens when women reject decent men for jerks and promiscuity, along with showing the unreasonable standards many women have while offering little to no value themselves'.[9] Given the existence of large subreddits like these, it is no wonder that online dating has turned into such a minefield. A 2022 study by the Australian Institute for Criminology based on a survey of 9,987 app users found that three quarters had experienced some form of online sexual violence on dating apps, with 79 per cent of women reporting online violence[10] – presenting an unflattering picture ten years after the launch of Tinder. In the UK, dating apps have been linked to increased cases of offline violence and rape.[11]

These are the most extreme forms of violence taking place on or via dating apps, but other complaints have emerged too: disenchantment with online dating, casual misogyny and a commodification of relationships which plays directly into the transactional view of romantic relationships that male supremacists promote. It's a problem the apps are all too aware of: part of Bumble's brand proposition has always been to be the safest dating app for women, while dating app Plenty of Fish ran the ad campaign 'The Gallery of Dick Pics' featuring attractive pictures of different users called Richard (Dick) on billboards in New York's subway. It was an attempt, in the words of its global director of brand marketing, Mitra Shad, at 'making online dating more welcoming – using humour to take the worst dating behaviours that exist and flip them on their heads'.[12]

Aileen Barratt had always worked as a writer, and so TinderTranslators came naturally to her as she became interested in seemingly innocent words in Tinder profiles and their hidden meaning. She became aware of the manosphere a few years ago and says its language has seeped into men's dating profiles, becoming increasingly pervasive. Words, for Barratt, are not innocuous: 'I started using these little phrases you find online as a way to interrogate dangerous ideas and behaviours.' Among the linguistic quirks she noticed were generalisations ('women are like this'), references to male supremacist influencers and talk of hierarchies of men and women and of the body count.

Barratt says,

> Something quite revolutionary has happened with women who date men in the last five or ten years, in that there are more women just choosing to be single, rather than feeling like they need the validation of a relationship: I'd rather be alone than be with somebody who doesn't respect me or make me feel good about myself.

She adds, 'Men have come up against that, and manosphere influencers have given them someone to blame.' Barratt helps women unmask potential bad dates and recognise the language of male supremacists: 'There's almost a script that you can see repeated verbatim in dating app bios. Things like: "80 to 90% of women only go for the top 10 to 20% of men".'

Barratt knows incels will not be tuning into her podcasts to hear what she has to say about the patriarchy. She wants to speak to women on Tinder of course, but also to a broader audience of women and men who might not realise they are hearing male supremacist arguments distilled on popular lifestyle podcasts, two clicks away from their YouTube search for high-protein pancake recipes. 'I want people to know that when they hear someone talking about sexless young men or hypergamy on a popular podcast, they know where these ideas are coming from.' She is not talking to the manosphere or men who hold these beliefs but is reaching out to the people in their lives who might be concerned about it. 'I don't have empathy for Andrew Tate, but I have sympathy for the 21-year-old who has not been lucky in love, who feels crap about himself and who becomes a disciple of Tate and spends all his money trying to be part of his club.'

Barratt also has a ten-year-old son, older than the youngest demographics exposed to male supremacist influencers (according to polling by Women's Aid/ORB International, 21 per cent of 7–11-year-olds had seen posts or videos featuring Tate[13]), and hopes to reach parents of young boys and teenagers who are becoming radicalised online and teach them how to spot warning signs. Parents need to understand what their children are talking about when they get home and start speaking in unfamiliar language.

> I think it's really important that we are aware of this language if it comes into our homes, that we're able to recognise it and engage with it, and say, 'Oh, where did you hear that?' It's really important that boys know what sexism is, before they know who a misogynistic influencer is.

She has produced digital literacy tools which allow her listeners to quickly access resources to fact check common male supremacist claims. For example, the idea that family courts favour women has long been a talking point of MRA, but debunking it requires time-consuming research.

'I focus on educating people who don't disagree with me already,' Barratt says, 'so that they have the tools to talk to people in their lives.' Despite the fact that she doesn't seek to engage with male supremacists directly, as a woman talking about feminist issues with enough followers to be officially an influencer, Barratt is no stranger to online abuse. She has to balance her desire to build an audience with managing her feelings of personal safety. Like many women with a social media following and with something to say, Barratt has to negotiate the trade-off between exposure and the potential negative blowback that comes with it: as could be expected, organised male supremacist trolls and networks have targeted her with the lazy tactics they favour. 'If one of my clips goes viral, I am suddenly inundated with identical messages copy-pasted by multiple accounts' she explains. The aim of these tactics, she says, is to grind her down, and she switches between different privacy settings, limiting who can see, comment and send her private messages.

This adjustment in behaviour is the online manifestation of what Vera-Gray and her colleague Liz Kelly call 'safety work', the strategies that women and girls adopt to keep themselves safe from violence, particularly sexual violence (for example, changing their route when walking home at night), and the associated thinking and planning that goes into it.[14] Intimidation tactics are part of the reason why she doesn't try to accrue more followers – she feels she has the right audience size that doesn't pressure her to compromise her speech. Barratt stresses the importance of finding the right tone that is educational but keeps people engaged through humour. 'If you're just kind of going "oh, this is all awful" then you disengage viewers.' A challenge she encounters is discussing complex ideas on platforms that do not allow for fine distinctions and complexity. 'A lot of these things are nuanced, terms like the patriarchy, but that's hard to get across on social media. People like simple slogans and messages about what to do.' She emphasises the need for integrity over reach or success. 'The thing with content creation is not to be bent to the shape of who we're trying to counter. We have to be better than them.'

## Appealing to the youth: the extremely online left

**Erudite CALLS OUT Sugar Baby for BANKRUPTING Men!**

**Erudite Finally LOSES IT in Debate with a Rad Feminist!**

**Alpha Male RAGEQUITS Panel on Relationships!**

Kyla is the queen of clickbait. She's a raven-haired, 20-something former psychology student who is known online as @notsoErudite. Erudite or not, she is certainly eloquent. When in full flow in one of her YouTube debates, she barely pauses for breath, rattling off cold facts and hot takes with the assurance of a fire-and-brimstone preacher. At other times, she leans back and stretches in her chair, waiting for another speaker to finish before coming in with a view of her own. The debate may be serious, but her near-50,000 YouTube subscribers surely come for the drama. Kyla is a YouTuber and Twitch streamer who engages with male supremacists and isn't afraid to face them directly, producing videos on deliberately provocative topics (Do virgins make great wives? Are 'weaponised white woman tears' a real thing?). In a world where angry men make a lot of online noise, @notsoErudite is playing them at their own game, speaking to a generation raised on memes and internet slang. Rather than letting male supremacists' videos go viral on YouTube, she has plunged into the cesspool. She produces videos commenting on clips of influencers, addressing their arguments for a youth audience and offering her own left-wing counterpoint.

She says that social media provides a distorted picture of the conversation on masculinity and its discontent, and the 'most deranged minority is the loudest'. The @notsoErudite debates are typically robust but actually not so very ill-tempered. If Barratt bemoans the lack of ability to express nuance on social media, Kyla's trick is to give nuance a deranged headline. When we speak, Kyla is as articulate, confident and outspoken as you would expect a YouTuber to be. She describes herself as left-wing, which in internet terms is 'basically communist', she tells me. Though a feminist who disagrees with everything the manosphere stands for, she still describes herself as being 'sympathetic' to manosphere arguments. Kyla sums up her beliefs as the fact that there are 'gender-specific issues young men are dealing with that the manosphere is good at putting its finger on, but not at identifying the causes of'. Although she is extremely online, she tells me her real interest lies in community work. 'My goal is to open a centre for young men leaving the judicial system to help them transition back to regular life. I'm interested in gender dynamics and the way societies interact with femininity and masculinity and what healthier gender expectations would look like,' she says. Despite that, she has managed to build an audience with progressive live-streaming and the appeal of the clicks looks strong: she has appeared as a guest on the *Fresh&Fit*

podcast, trying to resist giving the podcasts' host bait but feeding their podcast machine all the same.

It is quite clear that Kyla tries to appeal to men who are going down misogynistic rabbit holes by offering a progressive internet youth discourse. In doing so, she is adopting what she calls 'reasonably pro-men' positions and uses the kind of terminology that the manosphere has made pervasive online. Speaking on *Fresh&Fit*, she has answered in good faith questions put forward to her by male supremacist podcasters on women's 'body count'. She believes that while 'toxic masculinity' has received a lot of discussion in mainstream conversation, it has not been replaced by a form of masculinity that appeals to young men in popular culture and offers them aspirational images of who they could be. 'I see the manosphere as a reaction to an emptying that occurred and that wasn't replaced with anything else,' she says. Kyla's unapologetic style and choices of debate topic have won her a dedicated following, but she has received abuse from both misogynistic accounts and feminist accounts, who accuse her of betraying the cause – a reflection of the current state of online discussions as well as the fact that progressive communities can also be unforgiving. But even here, she is able to take advantage. 'Intellectual DESTROYS NotsoErudite in HEATED Debate about Peer Review' is the title of one YouTube video. You might think it was a brutal attack from some alpha male podcaster, except it's on @notsoerudite's channel and it's Kyla's headline. The clicks keep on rolling in.

There are surprisingly few left-wing YouTubers who try to debate male supremacists or engage with their arguments with nuance, while producing appealing content at the same time. If Natalie Wynn, or ContraPoints as she is known online, stands out, it's because she is one of the few progressive voices providing political commentary who has achieved substantial reach on YouTube, the platform which has done a lot for the rise of the alt-right and is a playground for right-wing and conservative influencers.[15] Wynn is perhaps the most visible figure in a small constellation of successful left-wing YouTubers who originally emerged as a counterpoint to the alt-right and are now frequently found on Twitch. Labelled 'BreadTube' (after the 1892 anarchist text *The Conquest of Bread* by Russian author Peter Kropotkin) when they first emerged (though many refuse the word), they include a number of content creators with a predilection for one-word abstract avatars such as Vaush and Destiny. @notsoErudite is part of this constellation of progressive voices who don't shy away from provocation. Another is the self-described socialist Hasan Piker who became Twitch's top streamer during the 2020 presidential elections in the US and is no stranger to controversy.[16]

In interviews, Wynn has said the spark for making YouTube videos was Gamergate. After the 2018 Toronto van attack, she gained wider public attention with an influential video about incels, which was viewed over four million times. Speaking to the *New Yorker*, she said: 'I sometimes imagine a hypothetical 19-year-old boy looking for answers.'[17] While having no sympathy for them, her video attempts to understand how incels come to embrace their ideology, while exposing the deep flaws of their thinking.

A trans woman who has had to face society's gaze and expectations of womanhood, Wynn speaks to the self-hating, looksmaxxing incels obsessed with fevered theories about the size of their jaws:

> I mean I'm just as obsessed with bone structure as the goddamn incels. Because I think certain parts of my face make me look like a man, and I worry about it every day. We're all obsessed with the bones, honey. We all have bones inside us, we all love touching bones.

Wynn is so appealing because her videos provide nuanced and thoughtful commentary with humour and strong aesthetics. Videos come with props, lavish costumes and carefully designed sets. Wynn's taste for the gothic and baroque is clear, with plenty of costumes that are best described as 1990s vampire chic, but other settings include 'fantasy garden party' (flowers and paper lanterns), nightmare circus (clown makeup and a whip) and Garden of Eden (she clutches an apple and two daisies cover her nipples).

In her videos, Wynn adopts a range of personas. In her personal life, she has agreed to debate with conservative YouTubers and commentators speaking to similar audiences as her: the 'extremely online' youth who might be tempted by far-right discourse, manosphere influencers or indeed a particular brand of left-wing online engagement. She has also run into controversies after featuring Buck Angel, a transgender educator and former porn producer who has proved divisive in the trans community, in one of her videos as a voice-over, resulting in a call-out campaign to which she responded with a video titled 'Cancelling'. In another video, from April 2023, Wynn said that 'there's still a part of me that wants to see the best in people and to believe that people can change if you just talk to them and make a good enough argument … maybe.'[18]

De-radicalisation is slow and requires a lot of time and investment, and its impact is largely measured by a negative: how much worse would it be were it not for the likes of Kyla? According to Maeve Park from Groundswell, who works on de-radicalisation, 'several incels [she encountered in her work] credited Wynn with shifting their views'. Likewise, a study at Australia's Monash University on subreddits dedicated to helping men get out of the manosphere found that two such groups – r/IncelExit and r/ExRedPill – helped a few boys and men to change their minds.[19] In one cited example, a college student asked the forum how to move past his feelings of hurt after being rejected by a woman. While red pill forums promote manipulative dating strategies and incel forums offer nihilist solutions, r/IncelExit's commenters offered empathy and nuanced advice. The authors of the study also found posts from teens who had actively joined these forums to hear something else, suggesting that the pain that drove them to male supremacist influencers can also take them elsewhere, and that their cries for help should be heeded.

## Setting the record straight: the (evolutionary) psychologists

Male supremacists are using bad science to support their talking points. They have capitalised on men's resentment and disillusionment at a time when science and facts are under assault. For many years, the answer to political disinformation of any kind was: debunk, debunk, debunk. In an age of ubiquitous conspiracy theories which feed on emotions, the issue is now not so much whether 'facts care about your feelings', as right-wing pundit Ben Shapiro put it a few years ago, but whether feelings care about your facts. While male supremacists rely on pseudoscience to support their made-up hierarchies and theories about the conspiracy against men, it is impossible to ignore the fact that they, like other conspiracy theorists, have capitalised on grievances which feel real and on men's desire for knowledge. While pseudoscience gives their power fantasy an air of scientific plausibility, there are people who engage with them on their own bad science turf.

Alexander is one such person. He calls himself a 'reluctant debunker', but when you are a man whose interest is research around dating and romantic relationships, you will inexorably find yourself bumping up against male supremacist arguments online. On social media and in real life, Alexander keeps his private life very private, hardly surprising given the controversial topics he talks about and the people he brushes shoulders with. But he agreed to talk to me. A muscular 30-something, Alexander speaks fluent English with a hard-to-place European twang. He says he has a degree in psychology and cognitive neuroscience and runs the website DatePsych, where he shares dating data, sexuality statistics and research on romantic relationships. DatePsych answers, in graphs and charts, the questions that male supremacists are losing sleep over. Questions such as: are women having more sexual partners than men? Do women prefer 'alphas'? What is a high body count, and do men have double standards when it comes to the issue? He uses personality-based surveys to do his work, which are not peer-reviewed, but the conclusions he shares frequently address and contradict key manosphere talking points. His conclusions are not surprising to anyone with a bit of life experience and who is not buried deep in misogynistic rabbit holes: that average-looking men ('normies') really do get girls,[20] women don't find alpha men that attractive,[21] and men have double standards when it comes to the so-called 'body count'.[22]

Like Kyla, Alexander has attracted the wrath of some of the most vocal male supremacist influencers after conducting surveys of women rating the attractiveness of the top red pill influencers and wounding some egos.[23] If his charts are disproving male supremacist misinformation, it is by coincidence and not design. 'I never wanted to focus too much on being the manosphere debunker, but it's hard to talk about dating and relationships without crossing over to that,' he says. One of the reasons Alexander pushes the manosphere's buttons is that figures from that world obsessively look for data to support their preconceived theories about women. In particular, 'the manosphere focuses on women who are high in socio-sexuality [the term that some psychologists use to refer to willingness to engage in uncommitted sex] and infer patterns from anecdotes,' says Alex. His own research simply hammers home the obvious truth that anecdotes do not amount to evidence.

I can see why Alexander might be a credible voice among those who might be drawn to male supremacist arguments. He is not affiliated with a 'mainstream' institution, and though he monetises his work through Patreon, he appears not to be driven by corporate interests.

Alexander's motivations remain somewhat unclear, however. Despite no background in evolutionary psychology, he frequently appeals to evolution and biology to explain behaviours. His surveys on the 'body count', whatever they may reveal, reinforce the idea that this is an important sociological data point, rather than plain misogyny. His X biography also signals an affiliation with an AI-driven matchmaking service called Keeper.ai, which promises to revolutionise matchmaking by using evolutionary psychology principles. He has also appeared on manosphere podcasts, recognising that they are good publicity for his work. When I ask him who he thinks he is speaking to and whether statistics convince anyone, he recognises it depends on how ideologically convinced people are. 'I get a lot of emails and feedback from people who said they were getting more immersed in manosphere communities, and that gave me a more nuanced perspective. Equally, though, some people will say: "Your surveys are fake, it's not even women answering them."' Data can have a de-radicalising effect but only if people are open to listening in the first place.

Evolutionary psychology is a controversial and much-debated field, not least because it has been seized upon by male supremacists. While many evolutionary psychologists are producing robust research and do not seek to support reactionary agendas, research has found that male supremacists use and misuse evolutionary psychology for their agendas,[24] particularly evolutionary psychology that focuses on dating. William Costello is an evolutionary psychology PhD candidate at the University of Austin, Texas, who focuses on incels and says they are 'giving evolutionary psychology a bad name'. His research lab focuses on sexual conflict and competition, and 'mating psychology', and thanks to male supremacists' strong investment in the topic, he is in high demand: 'From my perspective this is the only game in town: it concerns everyone, we're a sexually reproducing species, we build billion-dollar industries based on dating apps.' Disgruntlement around dating means there is plenty to cash in on.

According to Costello, 'incels overemphasise the importance of looks, status and money, where plenty of evolutionary psychology talks about women's preference for kindness, humour, and resources.' He believes evolutionary psychology can help shine a light on incels' dating struggles and inform responses. Based on his own research and a sample of incels he studied, Costello believes that around '30% of incels are autistic' and therefore lack traditional flirting skills.[25] He also believes there is a stark mismatch between the current and past structures for meeting partners. Indeed, for centuries, many marriages were arranged (a fact which incels use to justify their entitlement and demand wives), and even when they weren't, most people encountered only a couple of dozen potential partners.

Costello points to widely acknowledged problems with dating apps. 'They expose you to an unlimited quantity of potential mates, which is problematic for wanting to settle for one. Incels can rack up more painful rejections in one day than would have ancestrally been possible in a lifetime so that creates a social pain.' He says before we even think about sex education in schools, we need to teach young people basic social skills, which includes courting: 'If you don't help men improve, more nefarious people than evolutionary psychologists will step in,' which is perhaps what you would expect an evolutionary psychologist to say. The current popularity of evolutionary psychology means that plenty of experts in the field are having a moment in the public eye. They have achieved media coverage in mainstream outlets while their findings are also widely celebrated in far-right publications.

Evolutionary psychology, by its focus on explaining behaviour through the lens of natural selection and evolution, lends itself to dangerous musings about 'natural' racial and gender norms. Academic evolutionary psychologists will say they promote nothing of the sort. 'To overcome those evolutionary instincts or darker aspects of our nature, you need first to understand them,' Costello says, adding that 'shying away from the darker findings from the discipline only gives power to male supremacists.' While many researchers will argue that their findings are neutral, select findings (which merit deeper interrogation) can serve as fodder for reactionary agendas, even when they claim to provide evidence that serves women. Texas Christian University psychologist Sarah Hill's book *This Is Your Brain on Birth Control* (2019), a mix of neuroscience and evolutionary psychology, is mostly a warning about hormonal birth control, which plays into anti-feminist arguments.

Hill has framed her findings cautiously in progressive publications like *The Guardian* and presented her book as a tool to equip women with facts and give them full knowledge of the good, the bad and the ugly of hormonal birth control. Meanwhile, she has been interviewed by Jordan Peterson, and on social media has suggested that women who use hormonal contraception are detached from their natural femininity. 'Women on HBC [hormonal birth control] tend to prefer less masculine faces. They aren't as dialled into stereotypical "male" features, like strong jaws, deep set eyes and the like, as naturally cycling women are,'[26] she says – a finding that incels who think they don't match conventional male beauty standards might be thrilled to learn – but also cautions that 'women look, walk, sound, and smell sexier to men' when they are not taking birth control because they are sending 'fertility cues', conjuring up the image of women who are not in tune with their 'natural' fertile bodies. 'You might be choosing the wrong husband,' *Evie* wrote, citing Hill's research.[27]

Evolutionary psychology does make for compelling headlines. Recent years have shown that there is public interest in evolution and space for more nuanced considerations of human evolution. Authors like Cat Bohannon have written about women's contribution to human evolution, which is under-explored.

Bohannon, recognising the threat of evolution being used for reactionary agendas, has spoken about her ambivalence when writing her book *Eve* (2023). 'I want women and girls of all types to live better lives. And I don't want to be part of the problem. And there are lots of people who are going to weaponize science against the bodies of marginalised folk.'[28] The nuanced science might be out there, but it largely disappears when red pill influencers turn selective studies into a one-minute Instagram clip geared towards virality.

This context can lead to a rethink about how we approach digital literacy. While the focus of digital literacy has long been on developing critical thinking and engaging in depth with data, some experts believe we should rethink this approach in an era of pervasive bad science and assaults on our attention. This is the belief of Mike Caulfield, who says being drawn into spurious arguments online leaves an imprint and doesn't help non-experts make sense of them. Rather than burying ourselves in evolutionary psychology or complex medical studies about side effects that we don't understand, Caulfield urges us to use the SIFT method when we encounter online claims: **S**top; **I**nvestigate the source; **F**ind better coverage; **T**race the claims. Caulfield also writes,

> It would be comforting to think that when you engage deeply and earnestly with neo-Nazi literature or tobacco-company research that you come out more informed, provided you note all the logical traps and rhetorical fallacies. In reality, whenever you give your attention to a bad actor, you allow them to steal your attention.[29]

And male supremacists are experts at capturing attention.[30] From my own experience of struggling with health disinformation, I can understand why Caulfield's method is compelling. Practising 'lateral reading' as Caulfield calls it – identifying the source of a claim and swiftly moving on instead of deeply engaging with it – is one of the best things I have done.

## Making robust science available: health communicators

While I have found disengaging from bad science helpful, I have also found credible sources who address my health concerns with a level of seriousness. These are important: where there are injustices, murky science and grifters will step in. The neglect of women's health – and some of the health challenges that men are also experiencing – is a prime target for manipulation. Krishana Sankar and Magda Byma of ScienceUpFirst are all too familiar with this. Launched in January 2021 by Canadian senator Stan Kutcher and legal health scholar Timothy Caulfield (no relation to Mike), ScienceUpFirst, in collaboration with the Canadian Association of Science Centres, aimed to counteract vaccine myths and boost vaccination rates during the pandemic. Now a cornerstone in Canada's fight against health misinformation, ScienceUpFirst unites skilled communicators to craft engaging, clear content for healthcare leaders to share with their communities, including in person. Byma, the initiative's director, highlights their strategy of harnessing social media to connect experts with the public to address concerns without alienating the vaccine-hesitant, understanding that dismissing people's fears would only push them away.

ScienceUpFirst stands for disseminating trustworthy information tailored to community needs. It's not just about 'finding better coverage' as per the SIFT method; it's about providing essential coverage for underserved groups. 'Canada is so huge and diverse and we leverage our members' understanding of communities, including different religious and ethnic communities,' Byma tells me. 'We started in anticipation of the disinformation that would come about vaccines, but quickly we were inundated with so many pieces of misinformation, we ended up focusing on misinformers' tactics and how understanding their tactics could help us address other forms of public health misinformation.'

Their secret to combating health misinformation: addressing real needs. Post-COVID-19, ScienceUpFirst sought to understand the concerns of Canadian communities. The area that quickly stood out, unsurprisingly, was women's and queer health. Byma explains:

> in an age of clickbait and scary headlines there are a lot of emotions around information: some information you understand and feel great about but it doesn't address the need that you have. Then there's information you don't understand and makes you feel incompetent and angry, and results in you turning away and not doing anything. Where you find the information that is accessible, understandable and addresses a need you have is where the magic combination happens.

Timothy Caulfield and his team have led studies on the effectiveness of 'debunking' and found that counter-messaging can work, when done right. His findings: provide facts, avoid jargon, use trustworthy voices to spread the message, use stories and expose misinformers' flawed strategies.[31] Byma and Sankar acknowledge the challenge they face against those sowing medical mistrust. Sankar says: 'We want to give people the tools to understand misinformers' tactics,' adding that 'a key learning from our conversations with the communities we work with is the importance of being able to have difficult and polarising conversations but still being able to maintain relationships.'

Another area with a pressing need for nuanced communication and education is sex and romantic relationships. Sophia Smith Galer, who has mastered the millennial art of building a portfolio career, is a former newsroom (now freelance) journalist, active TikToker and a certified sex educator who speaks in schools across the UK on the subject. She participated in a pilot initiative with Brown University's Information Futures Lab, leading digital literacy workshops for British youth. Mirroring Caroline Sinders' findings that young people are badly equipped to understand harassment risks and digital safety, Smith Galer observed a significant gap in young people's digital literacy and their grasp of the risks associated with their dream of becoming influencers. More than half of Gen Zers in the US have said they wanted to become influencers.[32] In 2024, being an online influencer featured in the sixth position among young British youngsters' dream jobs.[33]

'When I asked young people to cite an example of positive social impact from the world of content creation and online influence, an overwhelming majority could not cite one example, and when they did, Tate's name came up,' Smith Galer tells me. Similarly, students are ill-equipped to name a single harm that results from online harms. Smith Galer knows that many teenagers dream of lives as influencers. 'For me, these were media literacy conversations masked as career talk,' she says. 'Young people want to become content creators but it is not a structured career path.' Young people overestimated how many posts on social media platforms were removed, and they did not know how many videos are uploaded to TikTok per day. Smith Galer's takeaway is that the existing curriculum fails to meet the needs of school-aged children, who, despite spending every waking moment on social media and being exposed to its myriad risks, underestimate its potential perils.

Similar gaps are visible in sex education, which she believes is both inadequate and subject to conservative backlash. After all, a British Conservative MP claimed (with little evidence) that current sex education in schools promotes 'graphic lessons on oral sex, how to choke your partner safely and 72 genders'.[34] While Relationships and Sex Education was made statutory in England in September 2020, experts argue that the current provision inadequately addresses the complex issues that young people face, from changing digital sexual abuse threats to widely available pornographic scripts and the normalisation of harmful practices such as choking.[35] Sex education, Smith Galer argues, should tell students about sex, relationships and consent, but also about medical conditions and their bodies. 'Teachers are under-resourced and cannot deliver good quality sex education, particularly when it comes to digital harms,' she tells me. 'Violent sexual acts for which consent has not been asked beforehand suggests to me that that behaviour has been normalised and no one has stepped in.' Discussing sexual behaviours and addressing young people's concerns is not the responsibility of schools alone. In an ideal world, Smith Galer says,

> every young person in the country [England] should have a teacher, a school nurse or medical figure to whom they can ask a question; outside of schools there are local sexual health services, and in the online

> world you would hope they get access to high quality information that they may not feel comfortable asking someone in real life. All in all, they should have access to a rich information diet.

In Britain, a decade of austerity has taken its toll on sex education. The funding given to local councils for sexual health services was reduced by over £1 billion (24 per cent) between 2015–16 and 2020–21.[36] As of 2022 the UK government had only spent half of the original £6 million it originally promised in 2019 for teacher training in Relationship and Sex Education.[37] Reports have also shown that over a quarter of local authorities in England did not offer up-to-date training for teachers.[38] It is quite clear that British youths are receiving anything but the rich information diet required to counterbalance the male supremacist onslaught.

Engaging in an information war with male supremacists is a difficult and time-consuming mission. Reducing the impact of their arguments can happen only if men are less receptive to their seductive appeal. There is a growing cohort of people who are trying to counter the power of male supremacist lies by trying to make its targets happier, more secure, more resilient. They are anti-supremacist alphas. Is it possible that men can save each other?

# 8

# The anti-supremacists: can men save each other?

'Dead inside. Emotionally retarded. Those were the words that were thrown at me in my 20s. And I was just like, "Yeah, just that's me, you know?" And it wasn't even an insult. It was just who I was.'

The man speaking looks like he ought to be hurling a discus across the sun-bleached amphitheatre of some ancient Olympiad. The body of an athlete, a jawline as defined as his muscles and a handsome, sensitive face. The eyes that gaze out steadily from beneath a haircut that's ever-so-slightly Brad Pitt in *Troy* look soulful – not those of someone dead inside at all. But then, Ben Bidwell has managed to break free from his past shackles, and now he helps other men do the same.

'I had no intention of disconnecting from emotion or closing myself off – I just lived in a society that grabbed me and did its thing and took me down that road,' Bidwell tells me. 'And then it is hard to come to the realisation that actually "this is just the way I am" might not be true. That in fact I learned to be this way and that maybe I can be different.'

In her 1949 work *The Second Sex*, Simone de Beauvoir wrote that 'a man would never get the notion of writing a book on the peculiar situation of the human male.' Just walk down the aisle of your local bookstore and you will find things have changed. The rapid advances of feminism in the past few decades have been accompanied by a new reckoning with what it means to be a man as well as renewed panic about men's alleged loss of purpose in more gender-equal societies. Indeed, the manosphere as it exists today has its roots in men's activism, which came as a response to the rise of second-wave feminism in the 1970s.

The original men's activism movements started in the 1980s and were intended as a force for genuine good. They critiqued traditional gender roles as a form of solidarity with feminism: movements like Men against Sexism in the UK and the National Organization for Men against Sexism in the US, which still exist today, initially had a strong focus on gender equality and social justice. By the 1990s, some of these groups turned their focus to men's rights, as opposed to gender equality and solidarity with women, which they perceived as increasingly antagonistic with the advancement of women's rights.

As more women entered the workforce and key advances in women's rights were secured, men's activists became concerned with conceptualising men's role in a world where they felt their dominance was being questioned. The 'mythopoetic' movement of the 1980s and 1990s in the US, spearheaded by Robert Bly and his book *Iron John* (1990), which wanted to be a third way between men's feminist movements and the burgeoning MRA movement, argued that men had lost their purpose in the modern world.

Through male-only workshops and retreats in nature, which involved various rituals, including singing and ceremonies in sweat lodges (ceremonial huts appropriated from Indigenous American communities), the mythopoetic movement encouraged men to regain a form of authentic manhood connected with nature and focused on brotherhood. In doing so, it presented itself as a remedy to aggressive masculinity and stated that men needed an outlet for their impulses to avoid acting on them. Though *Iron John* attracted mockery when it first came out, it remained on the *New York Times* bestseller list for weeks. While Bly's 'wild' man was to be an antidote to violent and savage – one could say toxic – masculinity the movement had (and still has) an implicitly anti-feminist flavour because of its belief that men have lost their way in more gender equal societies.

The mythopoetic movement is also one concerned with myths and psychoanalytical archetypes, particularly those developed by Carl Jung. A key text of the movement is Robert L. Moore and Douglas Gillette's *King, Lover, Magician, Warrior* (1990), which was inspired by Jungian psychology. Jordan Peterson is also fascinated with myths and their alleged representation of fundamental truths. Seen as true rather than culturally constructed, myths can lead us to view groups of people in reductive terms, an argument that religion scholar Robert Ellwood made in his 1999 book *The Politics of Myth*. Writing about the mythologists who became key references of men's movements, including Joseph Campbell, Pankaj Mishra noted that they had distinctly reactionary ideas, or as he puts it, 'the modern fascination with myth has never been free from an illiberal and anti-democratic agenda.'[1]

Though the manosphere has twisted much of what the original male activists stood for to suit its own nefarious ends, there are still those who remain true to the feminist spirit of the movements of the 1970s and 1980s or who are trying to shape more modern iterations of men's mythopoetic groups. There are many other groups and movements of men who sit somewhere on a spectrum between the manosphere and feminist men's groups, many of them borrowing from the mythopoetic movement. There are also counter-influencers and coaches who seek to offer an alternative discourse on masculinity for men undergoing crises.

Bidwell's road to enlightenment came through therapy. On his website it sounds a tantalisingly erotic journey: 'When a hypnotherapist accidentally entered my life over 10 years ago, I wasn't looking to change. I was just intrigued to see if I could enhance my sexual experiences,' he writes. The full reality, as he has shared freely on TV and social media, is somewhat more clinical: Bidwell suffers from anorgasmia, a difficulty in achieving orgasm, and was seeking help for this condition. But the hypnotherapist he went to see quickly made him realise the goals he had been pursuing – 'financial success and female adoration' – were bringing him no fulfilment. Perhaps the revelation that money and sex isn't everything sounds trite, something that could have been gleaned by watching a made-for-TV film about a dog that saves Christmas, but for Bidwell it was a hugely important turning point.

'I was being the man I had learned to be rather than the truth of who I really was. Society presented me with this narrative of who I should be and I learned to numb myself from my emotions, and I take full responsibility for that,' he says. Bidwell has reinvented himself. Gone is the previous career in finance; now he is a self-described 'human potential coach' who focuses on masculinity and men's mental health, promising men a life of wellbeing and emotional fulfilment.

## The men who help men

'I came out of the military after ten years. I was 26, and I was dead. I was a zombie. I couldn't feel anything.'

It's probably no coincidence that another coach who focuses on healthy masculinity uses the same form of words as Ben Bidwell when describing his past. This one is Bryan Reeves, and he describes himself as a 'life and relationship insight ninja' – implausible-but cool-sounding job titles being very much in vogue in the world of self-help gurus. Reeves is as handsome as Bidwell, with smiling eyes and an open face. He too charts his journey from an emotionally stunted high achiever – US Air Force Captain turned successful businessman in this instance – to a contented 'spiritual warrior' helping men become their best selves.

Reeves and Bidwell are part of a growing industry of life coaching for men, helping them deal with the emotional pain and dissatisfaction that the manosphere has successfully identified and exploited to monetise an anti-feminist message. Market research company IBISWorld estimated that coaching is a $2.1 billion industry in the US, and more and more men are customers.[2] Life coaching is an unregulated industry and has no governing body or set of ethical standards. Anyone can in theory call themselves a life coach and no specific requirements are needed, although many institutions now offer a range of courses. It is a sprawling industry, where the offering ranges in quality.

Contrary to therapists, coaches do not offer advice on clinical conditions like anxiety or depression but help clients lead more satisfactory lives. Reeves and Bidwell are not short of customers. The demand for their services shows that men are in search of guidance on everything from relationships to careers. Both feel that men are struggling to find their place in the world.

There is evidence to suggest that. A 2021 Australian study found that over 50 per cent of millennials and Gen Z reported regularly feeling lonely.[3] A 2019 YouGov poll in the UK found that 30 per cent of millennials felt lonely 'always' or 'often', while a 2022 study by the Cigna Group found that rates of loneliness were almost three times higher among 18–34-year-olds as opposed to the over 55s.[4] While loneliness among young people does not appear to be uniquely gendered, certain groups of men – such as Black and Latino men, younger men and men on low income – were more likely to report such feelings. The 2023 'State of American men' report by Equimundo found that nearly 50 per cent of the men polled found their online lives more rewarding, only 22 per cent had three or more close connections in their local area that they could depend on and 40 per cent of all men say they trust one or more figures from the manosphere (a proportion that reached nearly half for young men).[5]

Male malaise and moral panics about the disappearance of men are not new. The post-world wars period was marked by discussion about the 'crisis of masculinity' both in Europe and in North America. Thanks to the anti-feminist backlash and efforts by sections of the manosphere to draw attention to men's plights, plenty of airtime has been given to what ails men. Here are examples of recent columns: 'A crisis of masculinity imperils the foundations of the West' (*The Daily Telegraph*), 'Is masculinity in crisis?' (*The New York Times*), 'The new crisis of masculinity' (*Vox*) and 'What's the matter with men?' (*New Yorker*). In his book *Of Boys and Men* (2022), the self-described 'conscientious objector in the culture wars' Richard Reeves (no relation to Bryan), a research fellow at the US-based Brookings Institute, has documented the ways in which young men, particularly in the US, are struggling, in education, in the workplace and in relationships, offering policy-based solutions to address the unease. Growing societal concerns about the 'crisis of masculinity' has given greater visibility to Reeves' work. He has since set up the American Institute for Boys and Men, a think tank which conducts research on and runs programmes to improve men's wellbeing and has received $20 million in financial backing from the Melinda Gates Foundation, showing that the message he has conveyed in the public sphere has been heard.[6]

Men, according to Reeves, are threatened with 'cultural redundancy' and falling behind in education, dropping out of the workforce and failing as fathers. Socio-economic shifts are feeding the feelings of irrelevance, and there is no consensus about what a healthy model of masculinity looks like. The conversation about the crisis of masculinity is trapped in a strange dichotomy. As Reeves noted, boys might be struggling at school and women may be fast outpacing men in education, but men still out-earn women significantly and dominate political leadership, essentially holding the money and the power. By most metrics, men as a class, particularly straight white men, are doing okay.

Women also take a hard hit in the workplace when they have children, and that's before the overwhelming risk of sexual and physical violence women continue to experience. Yet in an era when societal norms have changed rapidly, many men do feel adrift, a change partly driven by socio-economic factors and the decline of manufacturing jobs in favour of services-based roles, which men are reluctant to take. While men at the top continue to thrive, these societal shifts have been enough to leave many others struggling with a feeling of 'aggrieved entitlement' – the term coined by sociologist Michael Kimmel to describe the wounded feelings of a person who feels entitled to something and fails to receive it and their attempt to rationalise their perceived failure. Reeves and others have rightly cautioned against confusing the success of a handful of powerful men and the broad trend with the lived experience and feelings of the many young men whose status is less rarefied. A minority may be thriving, but countless men are suffering and need attention, so the argument goes.

This sits uneasily with some progressives and feminists. By focusing on men's feelings, some argue, we may be diverting attention away from addressing gender inequalities, which overwhelmingly still fall on women, and indulging the wounded pride of men who cannot bear the thought of women overtaking them. Feminism has long cautioned against seeing gender equality as a zero-sum game, but in the face of persistent inequalities and continued violence against women, there is an understandable reticence about paying attention to men's problems. Many feminists rightly argue that it is not women's job to 'fix men', and figures like Bryan Reeves and Ben Bidwell fill a need: they are the men that other men who want to sort out their lives turn to.

By addressing male distress and insecurity, however, they position themselves in a space occupied by red pill influencers. In some ways, they share similarities with the manosphere's darkest figures. Like their male supremacist opposites, Bidwell and Reeves run courses aimed at fulfilling men's desires but without the coercion and manipulation, a form of non-toxic self-improvement that emphasises taking responsibility. The language they use sometimes betrays a similar sense of entitlement. 'I help you create the life and love you deserve,' promises Reeves on his website: 'Turn your biggest dreams into everyday reality … Attract (& keep) an amazing romantic partner … Create an exquisite intimate relationship.' They are the anti-Tates, addressing the same fears that male supremacists exploit but offering an alternative to anger and grievance with self-improvement and personal responsibility. For good or ill, the fact that the duo are handsome and successful is important in gaining the respect of those men who might otherwise be attracted to male supremacists.

Their charisma is essential to their appeal. If there is someone who understands the dynamics of charismatic influencers, it is Derek Beres, a writer and fitness instructor based in Portland, Oregon, and the co-host of a podcast on conspirituality (and co-author of *Conspirituality*, 2023, with Matthew Remski and Julian Walker). Beres has been documenting the phenomenon for the last few years and has seen the spread of manosphere ideas in the wellness world. He has also witnessed an anti-feminist backlash in fitness as more women have turned to the gym and are exploring exercises traditionally performed by men, such as weightlifting.[7] 'We're in a place where men feel abused in ridiculous ways and they have to leave a mark everywhere and this started pervading the world of wellness when more women became involved in it,' he says.

Beres says he has a good relationship with his father and a supportive group of male friends who provide him with a system of checks and balances, but he understands the appeal of charismatic gurus. He was overweight for several years and developed orthorexia, a form of disordered eating focused on an obsession with 'clean food', and has taught various forms of fitness and exercise in California, including yoga, kettlebells and weight training. Male supremacist influencers who project an image of strength can be appealing to men in search of control. Beres says,

> I think Andrew Tate is a train wreck, but some people really like him because he is strong and he's big, but he also just says whatever is on his mind. If I was a teenager growing up right now, I can understand being drawn to that, because he exudes confidence.

## Back to the future: the new men's circles

Bidwell and Reeves may have felt 'dead inside', dissatisfied, confused at what their role in society ought to be, but like Beres, they never felt the appeal of male supremacist influencers. That may be partly because they simply weren't exposed to it at the time of their crises, but they were probably largely immune to its temptations in any case. Both had enjoyed genuine success – Reeves in the air force and then business, Bidwell in his sales and marketing career. In male supremacist parlance, they are alpha males.

These coaches and public communicators are aware that they are competing with red-pilled men whose content is more favoured by social media algorithms. While Bidwell avoids the topic of where male supremacy fits in his work, Reeves positions himself more openly as an alternative to male supremacist depictions of masculinity. By promising men romantic success, Reeves is treading the same territory as PUAs, but he sees his work as a counterpoint to them. 'I've always been suspicious of that community,' he says, adding,

> I never studied pickup artistry. These guys – they know how to get the girl, but they have no idea how to have a healthy relationship. You know, they might intrigue a woman, know the tricks about how to get attention and how to play the polarity dynamic, but they have no idea how to be in an actual relationship with a woman.

Reeves understands conspiracy theories. He became estranged from his father during the pandemic, as the latter became drawn to QAnon. He says:

> The thing about discussion around masculinity is that it kind of quickly veers into conspiratorial thinking, and I have sympathy for that in a sense. Not for those beliefs, but I understand what it is to go down the rabbit hole. At the heart of it, it's appealing because it tells you that 'Oh, well, it's not your fault. It's feminists and progressives and other people out there that are out to get you.'

Bidwell, too, knows he is speaking to the men who might be tempted by the manosphere. He says that some of his – apparently right on the money – marketing advisors have encouraged him to parrot the language (but not the content) of the manosphere and tell men what they want to hear to accrue clients. 'A lot of it is marketing and telling them what they think they need and then giving them what they really need.' He adds, 'If we tell people they're wrong and they can't see it, there's going to be resistance.' Bidwell frames the offering as giving men more things, a better relationship with others, more happiness. He says you have to 'speak the language of the dominant culture'. One has to grant it to him: he knows how to attract attention and gained social media traction with something of a PR stunt – he posted naked pictures of himself under the pseudonym 'the Naked Professor' while encouraging men to reconnect with healthier masculinity. Bidwell also stands out in his frank discussion about sexual vulnerability amid plethora of male gurus who leave little space for it.

How do these coaches promise to turn men's lives around? Bidwell's is an amalgamation of breathwork and logotherapy – a type of existential analysis popularised by psychiatrist and Holocaust survivor Viktor Frankl. Reeves runs relationship coaching for couples and a programme for men called Elevate Your Relationship, which involves embodiment work, learning relationship skills and working on relationship challenges. The for-men programme involves openly talking about relationship struggles – an intimate and difficult subject – in the presence of other men. 'I get groups of men, you know, these are fighter pilots, lawyers, business owners, first responders, construction workers, who just met other dudes and they are coming together to discuss their relationships, and not in a way that is cynical, mean spirited or dismissive.' Men's retreats of all kinds are a boom industry: searches for 'male-only detoxes' increased by 200 per cent between 2022 and 2023, according to bookretreat.com.[8] Men's circles and male-only retreats are increasingly populating lifestyle columns of mainstream newspapers.[9]

This includes the retreats of former Irish professional rugby player Anthony Mullally, who now runs wellness workshops for men. Marketing material for the retreats on Instagram shows men jumping into icy water, meditating in the middle of the forest and doing yoga in circles. Pictures of men's retreats look invariably similar, showing middle-aged white men walking in the woods and doing breathing exercises. These retreats are firmly part of the privatised wellness industry and come with the latest health trends, from ice baths to sound gongs. They are also direct descendants of the mythopoetic movement and like to rely on similar archetypes and New Age language. If the mythopoetic movement sometimes attracted mockery in the 1980s, its contemporary iteration in the shape of 'inner warrior' retreats shows the idea of cultivating one's 'deep masculine' energy sells.

Today there are legacy organisations directly descended from the 1980s movement, like The ManKind project, which has local chapters in several countries and organises weekends of initiation called The New Warrior Training Adventure. Another mythopoetic-adjacent coaching organisation, the Embodied Men's Leadership Programme, runs a six-month programme or 'six-month container of impeccability to sharpen your consciousness and clarify your mission in the world' ($9,900), where participants will learn, among others things, to become 'an artist of dark sexual energy'. The programme involves a few hours of coaching, access to an online group and a 'private desert immersion'. The same organisation runs intimacy weekends for couples (priced at roughly $2,500 per person), many of which appear to consistently sell out. A seven-month programme for women promises to teach women how to 'create a devotional and unshakeable relationship with the divine masculine'. Talk of the perfect polarity between divine masculinity and divine femininity is something of a warning sign, but the price tag alone makes the Embodied Men's Leadership Programme a response to the mid-life crisis of Silicon Valley executives, which does little to help the majority of struggling men.

Some retreats aim to appear accessible. Mythopoetic groups have made efforts to be inclusive to men of colour and gay men and look progressive. The ManKind Project, for instance, is going to great lengths to erase its anti-feminist roots, presenting itself as a 'direct outgrowth of the feminist movement'.[10] Yet, despite its moderate website statements, a dozen cases of male supremacist radicalisation linked to ManKind project retreats were reported to Miviludes, the French government agency in charge of monitoring cults,[11] showing that seemingly well-intentioned programmes focusing on healthy masculinity can sometimes go wrong.

Many existing programmes rarely address men's issues from the perspective of greater gender equality and reducing men's violence against women. Bryan Reeves, who does not cultivate the image of a wellness guru, stands out in that respect. In his programme he incorporates reflections about women's experiences, and on the for-men-only course, he brings this issue into the conversation. One of the most rewarding aspects of the coaching, he says, is helping men gain awareness of women's experiences. 'One of the things that often comes up is when I'm able to help men understand what women experience daily – the lack of safety, for example – that men don't feel, certainly not in the same way,' he says.

> When men start [the programme] we have that conversation. I don't frame it as 'It's your fault, guys, you're fucking this up.' I'm simply shedding light. I'm helping men understand, but I'm not going to pretend to know what it's like to be a woman. But I have gotten the message, from my partner, from other women in my life. I'm trying to bridge the experience.

Reeves talks about the resistance he receives when calling out men's responsibility. 'It is confronting to men that they are not absolved of the responsibility that we have for our impact on others. And I think a lot of men, at first, are not ready to accept that,' he says.

> Most who come to work with me have already been brought down to their knees by life, and often it is relationship with a woman that has brought them to me because they have finally come to the realisation 'I don't know what I'm doing, I am clueless, and I want things to be different. And I don't want to lose this woman, or I have already lost her, and I'm starting to see my part in why it happened.' These are the men I love to work with the most, because they are ready to change.

Bidwell is uneasy at the suggestion that men work alongside women to challenge anti-feminist discourse and manosphere ideas, saying:

> The way I would look at it is that if we tell people they're wrong, and they can't see it themselves, there's going to be resistance. They're not going to go, 'Oh, that's really interesting, thank you, please share more.' Some might be open to it but the majority will push back, whereas if we offer men the opportunity to be better, it will reach more of them.

It seems clear that some coaches are willing to take more risks to confront men, while others make sure that men are not faced with any uncomfortable feelings about their place in the world or asked to do anything more than focus on themselves. They may be healthier alternatives to male supremacist influencers but do little to challenge men's underlying assumptions or invite men to think about male violence against women. This lack of accountability can sometimes result in complicity with abusers.

Both Bidwell and Mullally took part in Russell Brand's annual wellness festival, before a Channel 4/*The Times* investigation exposed allegations of rape and sexual harassment against the comedian but at a time when Brand had already used the pandemic to spread conspiracy theories and around whom allegations of abuse were already starting to swirl.

When I speak to male coaches and influencers, the influence of male supremacist arguments looms large. During our conversation one mentions Warren Farrell's *The Boy Crisis* (2018), a key text for the MRA movement, describing the data as 'compelling'.

Bidwell's website reads: 'Masculinity is under fire; men are increasingly becoming unsure of who they are meant to be in today's world,' which could be interpreted as carrying an anti-feminist subtext. Any conversation about masculinity inevitably involves some intellectual engagement with books that are part of the canon, including some texts that later became associated with the Men's Rights Movement, which in itself isn't a problem, as long as we can move past that canon. Similarly, the similarities between today's wellness retreats and their 1980s ancestors does point to a lack of renewal in the offering for men.

## Leaving the man cave

I meet Neal Allistone outside a pub on the English south coast on a late summer afternoon. A former business analyst and police intelligence officer, Allistone has a similar background of stereotypically 'manly' life experience and career success to Reeves and Bidwell. He works for A Band of Brothers, a charity which offers mentoring by older men (defined as 30+, the oldest volunteer is 82) to young men at risk of falling into the criminal justice system. For the past few years, he has also been working with men in prison, in child custody proceedings or going through adoption. Where Reeves and Bidwell have thriving businesses, Allistone is doing community work and leads a free community-based project, catering to the working-class and marginalised men that expensive programmes rarely reach. With his curly, mid-shoulder length hair and an esoteric symbol hanging from a thread round his neck, his interest in spirituality is apparent. 'I was baptised Methodist as a child, and then I hit my 20s and I joined a Buddhist monastery,' he says, sipping on a lime soda. 'And then I lived over in Ukraine for a while and got baptised as Russian Orthodox and now I'm like … actually, you know what, I still do believe in sort of that kind of Scripture, but I disagree with organised religion so I'm finding my own roots.'

While he may have moved away from organised religion, Allistone laments the decline of the kind of community ties that church, mosque, synagogue or temple used to bring. Describing the work of A Band of Brothers, he says: 'We come from the point of view that community is dying, men don't hang out with men anymore, men don't grow up with older consistent male role models in their lives, men tend to see other men as competition or threat.' The young men he works with are at higher risk of loneliness, and since the pandemic Allistone says he has seen their feelings of isolation increase. Simultaneously, the prisoner rehabilitation system has buckled with an ill-fated experiment by the UK government in which the probation system was temporarily privatised. 'Since COVID, a lot of guys released from prison or care get phone calls as opposed to face-to-face meetings,' Allistone says.

He also recognises the men he works with have trouble forming romantic relationships: 'Guys don't know how to behave towards women and the growing use of social media has made that worse. They are warriors behind the keyboard, but in person they don't know how to talk to women.' Some of the men he works with have been the subject of allegations of sexual abuse, although none of them are on the offenders' list. A Band of Brothers offers a ten-month-long free mentoring programme supporting men with the following: mental health, money, addiction and relationships, which, Allistone is keen to stress, are relationships in the broadest sense and involve anything but romantic relationships.

The starting point of the programme, however, is a 'rite of passage' weekend. This resembles the kind of retreats offered by other private events for men – though stripped of the wellness and New Age elements, it seems, and without the price tag. Allistone remains vague about what the weekend entails and the men taking part are kept equally in the dark – 'We never tell them what we're going to do, because if they knew what would happen, they wouldn't join' – but it involves a weekend of camping in the wilderness without technology and contact with the outside world or distractions. The cohort of mentees go to a countryside spot. Their phones are confiscated and they build a camp from scratch on a Friday, before being asked to share their darkest fears and confront their vulnerabilities on Saturday. Then, 'on the Sunday, we come out into joy and we look at joy.' Allistone says the weekend is cathartic but not a long-term solution, stressing that long-term change happens when men take part in the programme in full:

> The guys ride out of that weekend on a high and feel fixed. We tell them that they will come down from that high, but by then their relationship with the mentor has been cemented and they have started experiencing community. And it's a long, long journey – it takes years, you know, doing the work and revisiting and looking back at it to make changes.

The weekend is ritualistic and dramatic but has a long-term purpose, to start men on a journey.

The men who Allistone mentors love male supremacist influencers and podcasts. The day before I met him, one of his mentees sent him a video titled 'The CONSEQUENCES Of FEMINISM In Modern DATING' [*sic*], a YouTube video from *Whatever* (over 200,000 views), another dating podcast which regularly recycles key male supremacist talking points. *Fresh&Fit* is also popular, and most of the men have read Jordan Peterson's *12 Rules for Life*. Individual influencers are where real life collides with the online world. Allistone says that the men often share video clips of male supremacist influencers in WhatsApp groups but rarely do so in person. 'Deep down they know it would get called out and they would get challenged, because it's an influencer doing your shouting for you.' The way Allistone and his colleagues deal with the issue of charismatic influencers is by 'putting the question back to the men, saying "So what is it you're trying to say here? What does it do to you?"' The fact that charismatic influencers' content is mostly shared online is closely linked to the dynamics that these influencers are creating. The video and podcast format allows them to speak loud and fast and create a hypnotic effect on listeners. Male supremacists who appear as guests on each other's podcasts ensure that their ideas are never challenged.

There is a real difference between the online outrage peddled by male supremacist influencers and men's real life. Many men struggle to escape the feelings of isolation that makes the online man-cave so attractive. This is the work A Band of Brothers is trying to accomplish. A recurring theme from everyone I speak to is an emphasis on accountability and personal responsibility. Reeves says:

> A lot of men when they first discover my work, they get angry. They're confronted by it. I think a lot of men are still caught up in that victim mentality: I'm the victim here, it's women's fault. I'm the one that means well, I'm the one that has good intentions. If you would just listen to me and see it my way, everything would be okay.

Another topic that everyone returns to is the importance of offline support networks and role models. 'I mean, I had a dad, but not one who necessarily showed me the healthy aspects of masculinity that we look for in today's world,' Bidwell says.

> I'm not criticising him: he came out of the Second World War, and at that time, there wasn't space to be open to being vulnerable. It was important at that point for him to grin and bear it. There are a huge number of men who grew up with fathers like that: dads who are there, but who aren't actually offering any guidance. Society is so quick to judge the behaviour without understanding where the behaviour might have come from.

I would argue that feminists have plenty to say on where that behaviour comes from.

How much these influencers can compete with their counterparts in the manosphere is open to question. 'If you have 100,000 followers on Instagram, and you're able to make a living by coaching a small number of people, that's still nothing compared to 11 million people per download for an episode of *The Rogan Podcast*,' says Beres. Bidwell and Reeves have built online communities but are individuals with a specific clientele. Allistone works with a more disadvantaged community but initiatives like A Band of Brothers remain too few. 'Toxic masculinity' has become devalued as a phrase,[12] despite the fact that the new guidance released in 2019 by the American Association of Psychologists describes 'traditional masculinity ideology' as harmful to men and associated with negative health outcomes. Many men resist engaging with these ideas at all. 'Using terms like toxic masculinity is not helpful,' says Reeves. 'I understand it, but many men hear an attack on masculinity itself, and so I think messaging is very important. I do believe it has to be approached delicately, if we're going to make any movement forward.' Getting men to embrace change, even among well-intentioned influencers, seems to involve a lot of coddling and very little discomfort.

Nevertheless, men's coaches do understand the significance of human contact and community in addressing men's feelings of insecurity, and they know how to communicate with men who might otherwise be attracted to violent and coercive belief systems. And they do make a difference. Allistone ends our drink with a story of a man he worked with who had just come out of prison.

> He'd done 14 years inside. He wasn't allowed to be anywhere near children or anything at all because of the level of violence that had been in his life. I worked with him for a year, and he's now got a wife, and her child that was taken and put into care has come back, so he's raising a stepson. And they're doing amazingly. They've got a little business that they're working on together and every now and then he sends me texts and pictures of his kid and tells me how they're doing. And it's lovely to hear stories like that. Our successes have gone away and been able to live fulfilling, independent lives.

# 9

# The backlash to the backlash

'Men who don't like women call feminists "man-haters" to make sure that their arguments can't be heard. Instead of reassuring these men, I thought: you know what, why not hate them?'

The woman speaking is bestselling author and self-described misandrist Pauline Harmange. After graduating with a degree in communication in 2018, Harmange, then in her mid-20s, was seeking her career path. She loved writing and had been involved in feminist activism since high school. She freelanced as a copywriter and volunteered at L'Échappée, an NGO fighting sexual violence against women in the French city of Lille, where she lived. She wrote an unpublished novel. She blogged. Life ticked along, until Monstrograph, a micropublisher of 'weird little books' noticed one of her blog posts and offered her the opportunity to write a book. It printed 400 copies of the 80-page polemic *I Hate Men* (*Moi les hommes, je les déteste*). It might only have been read by devotees of Harmange's blog, had it not been for an overzealous government official.

Just before its release in the middle of the pandemic, a male advisor to the French government's department for gender equality took umbrage to the book, accusing its author of promoting 'incitement to hatred' against men, and threatened to sue the publisher if it was not retracted. The case attracted widespread media coverage, turning *I Hate Men* into an instant bestseller in France, and soon internationally. Suddenly, Harmange was notorious. If *I Hate Men* has been so successful, it is because it unapologetically says what many women feel but dare not express aloud for fear of conforming to clichés of 'man-hating feminists'. 'We're always told we're not allowed to hate men; this is not about hating individual men, but understanding patriarchal systems and how men use them to behave badly,' Harmange tells me. When we speak, she strikes me as confident, direct and assured in her beliefs. Considering the many interviews she has given to media around the world, she has had a chance to stand her ground and own her misandry.

Harmange gives women permission to be angry – at societies that fail them, at men who don't do the mental workload of informing themselves about gender inequalities, and at their own complicated feelings about societal norms and how they continue to mould themselves to them. She also gives women permission to stop feeling obliged to stroke men's egos, making themselves smaller in the process. 'Before being a feminist, I was a girl, and that's it, and I didn't sweat it. Then I became a feminist and I had to call everything into question,'[1] she wrote, embarking on years of feminist activism which, she says, left her hollowed out. Harmange is not alone: feminist writers have spoken about what comedian Lindy West called 'sexism fatigue', the exhaustion that comes from feeling that progress towards gender equality takes one step forward and two steps back. In this particular moment, fatigue for many is reaching breaking point.

When her book was published, Harmange was inundated with abuse, rape and death threats. Since then, male supremacists have only become emboldened, a fact she finds validating. 'I received waves of abuse from the manosphere and hardened misogynists, but also from ordinary men who felt personally attacked,' she says. 'Globally, we hear women express anger at not being heard and respected. When I wrote my book, I hoped that men would change but I see that a vast majority of men don't want to seize that opportunity.'

Male supremacists preach to anyone who will listen; they try to influence public opinion, shape policies and public discourse and capture a growing number of men's attention with a simple narrative that does not ask them to engage in uncomfortable introspection, be better human beings and take part in a collective vision for good. Instead they encourage them to focus on the individual pursuit of what they feel entitled to. They also ask for society's attention and women's compassion for men's plight. Harmange is reluctant to give it. 'Feminists have always focused on men's problems and how the patriarchal system is selling men short; it is a bad faith argument to say that we don't care about men's incarceration and suicide,' she says. 'If women are tired of listening to men's problems, it is because we do that all day long, and when male supremacists tell us to listen to their problems, it's a just way of not listening to ours.' She has a point: while equality is not a pie, public attention and policy resources are not infinite, and growing mainstream discussion on how men are falling behind can feel like a distraction and a desire to reassert dominance and maintain the status quo, because it is indeed an objective pursued by male supremacists who are doing a lot of work to hold the microphone.

## Women's payback

Harmange says, 'society underestimates women's anger.' Other feminists have embraced the idea of misandry as a legitimate right to hate patriarchal behaviours and to prioritise women. French novelist Chloé Delaume is a proponent of misandry as a legitimate form of self-defence. Her first novel, published in 2000, follows a heroine who dreams of different forms of male castration and wonders if she should implement the radical feminist Valerie Solanas' 1967 *SCUM Manifesto*, which called for the elimination of men. According to her fellow countrywoman, feminist comedian Typhaine D., 'misandry saves lives',[2] and other feminists in France have adopted the slogan. Women's separatism has a long tradition. Second-wave all-female communes, notably lesbian communities or Womyn's lands, emerged as a radical demand for women to live on their own terms, unshackled from patriarchal structures. Many of these radical feminist experiments declined and are now historical relics, although there has been renewed interest in women-only spaces of late. In 2023, the doors opened at New Ground, the UK's first co-housing community for women only (men are not allowed to live in the community, though women living in the community can have male partners).

Radical women's separatism has also emerged as a form of retaliation for male supremacist violence. The radical feminist Korean online group Womad became known for using male supremacists' tactics against them in retaliation, including hateful speech, abusive memes and trolling – acting as fodder for male supremacists' talk of widespread misandry. Members of Womad also took nude pictures of men via spy cameras as retaliation for the epidemic of molka abuse. The group, an extreme case and outlier rather than a reflection of the kind of widespread hate of men that male supremacists like to agitate against, also used homophobic and transphobic language, having splintered from the less radical Megalia, which does not allow this form of hateful speech.[3]

As male supremacist groups have developed, women's communities which act as counterparts to the different sections of the manosphere have also emerged, creating something of a fast-growing 'femosphere'. This includes online communities of 'women going their own way', who reclaim the right to just focus on themselves and eschew contact with men as a means of self-protection. Splintering from men is at the heart of 4B, a movement of South Korean women who vow to renounce sex with men, dating men, marrying them and having children. On Reddit, the group /r/WGTOW: Women Going Their Own Way counts over 13,000 members at the time of writing; it encourages women to live a life without men and provides an online discussion space for 'asexual, aromantic, or just generally happy single women' where members exchange life tips and reading recommendations and come for support with various life challenges. In practice, there also appear to be a lot of not-so-happily single women in the group who acknowledge they made the choice to give up on men out of frustration. Discussions about loneliness and sexual deprivation are, naturally, prevalent. 'I miss being held and touched. I feel so touch-starved. I'd really like to self-soothe this but the suggestions I have read haven't really helped,' says one poster who has considered – and rejected – 'hookups' as a solution. The group allows 'venting about sexism' and encourages posts which tell women why it is better to be single; posts focusing on men need to be kept to a minimum.[4]

Among straight people at least, whether it's men or women who are Going Their Own Way, the urge seems to stem in part from distrust of the other sex and a lack of belief in the possibility of harmonious relationships between them. Femcels are the female counterparts to incels, though incels and other male supremacists deny their existence and claim that 'they are just women who don't like their options,'[5] immersed as they are in beliefs that they are uniquely deprived and hard done by. All of this is of course ironic given the original founder of the incel movement was a queer woman. Like incels, femcels lament not being able to have sexual relationships, because of misogyny and the impossible beauty standards imposed by men. Alongside incels, Reddit has banned femcel groups. Emerging media coverage of these groups has sought to create equivalence with male supremacist communities. A Channel 4 documentary called 'Radicalised: Are Femcels the New Incels?', released in March 2024, sought with its sensationalist title to ask whether femcels might be an equivalent threat, broadly reaching the conclusion that they aren't. Jilly Kay, a feminist media academic who studies the femosphere, says that 'while you can't discount the possibility of a violent attack, femcel communities don't exhibit the hate and objectification that characterise the manosphere,' though it would no doubt suit incels to suggest they do. Limited studies of femcel forums have found that violent speech and antagonism towards men were significantly lower than violence towards women on male forums, and rather than blaming men for their situation, femcels tended to blame themselves.[6]

The idea that women's payback is growing in popularity is unsurprising to Harmange. 'It's proportional to the inefficiency of the system that surrounds them,' she tells me. In India, where over 30,000 rapes are regularly reported per year (and this is likely a fraction of the actual number), the Gulabi Gang, a women's vigilante group, tracks down rapists and beats them with sticks.[7] Women PUAs and dating coaches and podcasts have also emerged to tell women that they need to protect themselves against manipulative men and give them a taste of their own medicine. Female Dating Strategy (FDS), a Reddit group turned website, calls out misogyny and male entitlement and in the process describes poorly behaved and violent men as 'scrotes'. The anonymous women behind FDS use a mix of feminist empowerment rhetoric (urging 'queens' and 'babes' to 'level up') while mirroring male PUA communities in their views of dating as a ruthless market with winners and losers, where low-value members of the opposite sex need to be weeded out.

Steeped in essentialist language, FDS reclaims hypergamy as women's right to choose 'high value' partners, using dubious evolutionary psychology and biology to argue that women's desire for a financially successful and committed male partner is rooted in nature. They argue that women don't owe angry incels anything, let alone sex and that women's bodies are not a democratic resource, which is true enough. Like male PUAs, they believe in female hypergamy: they just think it's women's God-given right and nature to want a rich man. In a representative Instagram post titled 'Hypergamy is not evil', they write: 'It's not our job to make the dating field accessible to men who don't want to pay the entry fee in the first place.' The same post goes on to state that 'the ideal strategy for women involves selecting a mate with favourable characteristics like an abundance of resources' and concludes by telling men who might not be happy with this state of play to 'shape up or shut up'.[8] The FDS online handbook mixes condemnations of misogyny with eugenicist undertones. In selecting a 'mate', they argue, women need to pay attention to red flags: 'A good test is always: "Are this man's genes worthy of reproducing with mine?"',[9] implicitly flagging entitled incels and other misogynists as substandard genetic material, rather than people whose ideas need to be challenged and who might be able to change.

FDS might be an anonymous dating group for women, but widely followed dating coaches, some of whom have been called 'dark feminine' influencers, are amassing millions of followers by promoting the same crude views under the guise of empowerment. One of the most popular in this movement is SheraSeven (real name Leticia Padua, 1.2 million TikTok followers), dubbed the 'female Andrew Tate',[10] who admonishes women to stop wasting their time on 'dusties' (men without money) and get themselves 'some real lifestyle'. Her advice to women? Go to high-end bars, look conventionally feminine and groomed, and avoid speaking too much to cultivate an air of mystery. Her videos are receiving millions of views, and her catchphrase 'sprinkle sprinkle' has gone viral on TikTok.

Self-styled dating coaches are springing up on Instagram and TikTok and encouraging women to embrace their 'divine feminine' energy and charms to trick 'high value' men who will give them the #princesstreatment in relationships. In the process, they encourage women to conform to conventional feminine beauty standards and adopt subdued behaviour. One of these coaches, who goes by the name AskNelly, has over 100,000 followers on Instagram and runs an online course called Manifesting Mr Right. 'When are we going to stop lying to women? Most men of high socioeconomic status do not want large and in charge, sassy, demanding women … and I'm sorry if that offends you but it's true,' she says, also admonishing women: 'Are you sweet, nurturing and pleasant to be around? Or are you aggressive, domineering and undisciplined?'[11] Behind the superficial you-go-girl empowerment rhetoric, these PUAs promote tradwife attitudes and financial dependence on men, minus the apron, cooking and housework, and with plenty of manicures and Pilates classes. Groups such as FDS may have emerged as a form of self-defence against male supremacists, but they have moulded themselves so closely on what they claim to oppose that one wonders if they are not male supremacists' best allies.

While some of these Instagram coaches are extreme examples, anti-liberal and reactionary feminists offer intellectualised renditions of similar arguments. Andrew Tate propagates the crude discourse of the red pill; Jordan Peterson articulates the scholarly variant of incel ideologies. Similarly, the femosphere possesses intellectual mouthpieces who cloak reactionary perspectives with an intellectual and scientific façade. What they have in common with Instagram dating coaches is their belief in biological essentialism, their use of evolutionary psychology and their lack of hope in any meaningful structural change in gender relations. These self-described anti-liberal feminists advocate for protectionist and individual strategies, which they present as hard-learned life lessons.

Louise Perry in *The Case Against the Sexual Revolution* (2022), for instance, posits that once we accept that there are fundamental differences between men and women rooted in biology and evolution and that consent workshops won't teach men not to rape, we can get on with the more effective business of giving women tips that will minimise their risk of sexual dissatisfaction. These include: getting married and doing everything possible to stay married, only getting drunk with female friends, only sleeping with men who are good 'father material' and not watching porn. Aside from the multiple problems with these suggestions – including the fact that marriage does not protect one from assault and does little to tame 'hard-wired' instincts if one believes in them – what is striking in the argument is the absence of any optimism or hope for anything better. Mary Harrington described her brand of reactionary feminism, which like Perry's acknowledges women's discontent under the current economic and sexual regime, as an attack on 'progress theology'.[12] Her advice to address the contemporary romantic discontent includes promoting heterosexual marriage and making sex 'consequential' by shunning the pill and limiting abortion.

If the best hope for women's happiness is to weed out 'low value' men or stay unhappily married to men at the expense of any collective vision of solidarity for other women, it begs the question: is this the kind of feminism we deserve? Amia Srinivasan cautions against such simplistic readings in *The Right to Sex* (2021). 'A feminism worth having must, not for the first time, expect women to be better – not just fairer and more imaginative – than men have been', she writes.[13] A more ambitious project to address the discontent of both men and women would be a reckoning with societal norms that encourage unrealistic expectations of both sexes. Or putting at the forefront of feminist campaigning demands which have become unfashionable among mainstream feminists: demands for equal pay, for childrearing and care work to be recognised as work and compensated, and for an equal distribution of household chores. Dissatisfied women need social support structures, better policies and a more ambitious feminism that acknowledges its failings and blind spots, not dating coaches who dispense 'high value babe commandments'.

## Feminism and its discontent

If feminism demands us to be better than men have been, many feminists have rightly pointed out that too many men are not interested in being better. Male supremacists who want 'hot blonde sluts', as Srinivasan notes, will not be examining the root of their desires anytime soon, and the disenchantment with sex and heterosexual relationships that many women feel should come as no surprise. In recent years, there have been several panicked headlines about an international 'sex recession', with figures from multiple countries showing that millennials and Gen Z are having less sex than previous generations. A 2021 study showed 40 per cent of Californians aged 18–30 had not had sex in the preceding year.[14] From Britain to Australia,[15] Korea to Japan, and even in France,[16] which can no longer boast romantic exceptionalism, data shows a notable decline in the amount of sex young people are having. The factors behind these trends are no doubt complex, but while male supremacists rage about hypergamous women and a plot against men, many women are increasingly dissatisfied with what's on offer.

While the backlash against sex-positive feminism has been embraced by conservatives and reactionaries who see traditional marriage as a way to re-enchant sex and solve male 'sexual misery' at the same time, recent years have also seen a wider reckoning with the shortcomings of the sexual revolution, one we should not shy away from. Living in the UK, I have found it instructive to watch this shift happen across the Channel in France. 'In countries like France where we think we are free, we tend to be lukewarm,' Harmange tells me. I think she would consider me lukewarm indeed. As a young woman growing up in provincial France like her, purity-related messaging was absent from my life. The 'save-yourself-for-marriage' culture, which trickled down to me from American films, felt quaint. I was steeped in the ideals of liberty, equality and fraternity, which I adhered to with great naivete as a child from a mother who had fled Communist Poland. I liked the idea of being human more than being a woman. I come from the last generation to go to high school without a smartphone and encountered little hostility from boys.

I was socialised in a sex-positive, liberated environment that reductively emphasised agency and choice. As a young woman at university, I often kept feminism at arm's length and did not want to see myself as a victim of men, defined by what they did to me. In Parisian universities and workplaces, the bad encounters with men, the groping by a superior at a newspaper where I interned, the sexual harassment on the metro, were all dismissed and quickly forgotten. For all its blind spots, fourth wave feminism has done much in recent years to allow women to put words on these behaviours. Yet, as #MeToo happened, French icons like Catherine Deneuve were defending men's rights to 'pester' women. Many came to men's rescue: 'A few tweets and it's done … their career is over', Charlotte Gainsbourg lamented.[17] While across the Atlantic, the #MeToo movement encountered swift backlash, in France it failed to fully take off.

There are now signs, however, that French women are no longer lukewarm about the issue. Years after the #MeToo movement first went mainstream internationally, actress Judith Godrèche, who was among Harvey Weinstein's accusers in the US, spoke about the abuse of women and children in French cinema. Norwegian-French actor Aurélien Wiik launched the #MeTooGarçons (#MeTooBoys) hashtag, recounting his own experience of sexual abuse by men in the industry. After more women accused actor Gérard Depardieu of abuse, French president Emmanuel Macron called the accusations a 'man hunt' – sending a powerful signal to abusers and male supremacists alike. No wonder French women are increasingly giving up on men.

The feminist and former porn performer Ovidie, who has starred in and directed indie porn films, says she has voluntarily given up sex, an experience she recounts in her latest book *La chair est triste, hélas* (*The Flesh is Sad, Alas*: untranslated, 2023), as the result of fatigue with sex 'at the service of men and their pleasure'. She also produced a documentary series on the topic of voluntary celibacy, interviewing women who described giving up sex as an escape from patriarchal expectations and sexual disappointment. Editor of French *Elle* magazine Sophie Fontanel's *The Art of Sleeping Alone* (2013) describes giving up heterosexual sex as a form of liberation from societal expectations. The feeling that 1968 revolutionary slogans 'it is forbidden to forbid' and calls to *jouir sans entraves* (which can translate both as 'enjoy yourself without hindrances' or as 'orgasm without hindrances') only served the interests of men and did not offer liberation for all is spreading in France, to the delight of conservative commentators – for instance, columnist Eugénie Bastié who has hailed this era as a new one of 'sexual conservatism', which she sees as a reaction to past 'excesses'.[18]

She is not alone. Feminist historians have also revisited the post-1968 period. French historian Malka Malkovitch has detailed how post-1968 liberation slogans paved the way for widespread abuse of women and children in the 1970s, which was condoned by political and intellectual elites. In early 2020, a French court charged novelist Gabriel Matzneff, who promoted paedophilia in multiple novels for decades and whose work was indulged as a form of creative licence by intellectual elites, with promoting child sexual abuse,[19] at the same time as women accusing him of sexual abuse started being heard after being silenced for many years.[20] In the English-speaking world and beyond, we are also seeing a return of the 1980s 'porn wars', with anti-porn arguments increasingly seeping into the mainstream. Gen Z pop star Billie Eilish calling pornography a 'disgrace' reflects something of a generational shift on the issue.[21]

In recent years, former porn performers who previously defended their work as a form of free sexual expression have come out saying they were coerced. Platforms like OnlyFans, which were touted as putting the power back in the hands of performers, as opposed to big producers like Pornhub, have proved to be equally predatory.[22] There has been renewed interest in the work of previously unpopular anti-porn second-wave feminists, including Andrea Dworkin, bucking the trend of sex-positive feminism. An anti-heterosexual sentiment that was shared by some second-wave feminists has also seen a revival. For example, the idea of political lesbianism, women choosing to no longer sleep with men as a political and feminist choice, has returned in France with the publication of a series of widely commented books on challenging heterosexual sexual scripts, including Louise Morel's *How to Become a Lesbian in Ten Steps* (*Comment devenir lesbienne en dix étapes*, untranslated, 2022). Author and film director Virginie Despentes, a key figure in the movement, has likened 'becoming a lesbian' at age 35 as 'losing 40 kilos' worth of weight'.

Meanwhile, heteropessimism, a term first coined by researcher Asa Seresin to describe performative despair at the state of heterosexual love and its accompanying 'men are trash' jokes, has framed men as an unfixable problem for women.[23]

The revival of political lesbianism may look eccentric given that it did not achieve mainstream appeal a few decades ago in the English-speaking world and that the majority of women are likely to continue being attracted to men. These radical critiques are nonetheless pointing to deep discontent and to the need for braver discussions about sexual politics. Despite feminism's historical polarisation on pornography, there is reluctance among mainstream feminists to engage in the issue, for fear of engaging in protectionist behaviours and skewing conservative. Indeed, second-wave anti-pornography feminists, including Andrea Dworkin and Catharine MacKinnon, formed alliances with the Christian right in the 1980s to pass anti-pornography legislation. The ubiquity of pornography, and the evidently complicated relationship men and women have with it, necessitates a bigger societal conversation than the one currently taking place. Vera-Gray, aware of the conservative turn this can take, says she is 'less interested in framing the issue as one of protection, and more about examining what this does to sexual freedom'. These conversations require nuance, not something that TikTok trends such as 'Cancel Porn' are able to convey.[24]

Similarly, fatigue with lean-in feminism has grown. The 2010s were the definining decade for the frontlining of commercialised, celebrity-endorsed feminism that prioritised the success of privileged white women. This type of feminism, which has received many names, including girlboss feminism, was epitomised by clothing brand Nasty Gal's CEO Sophia Amoruso's autobiography, *#GIRLBOSS*, and the associated Netflix series. The backlash against girlbosses is justified: the CEO of the women's private club The Wing, Audrey Gelman, resigned over accusations of racism and a deleterious workplace culture, one of the casualties of a reckoning with the exclusionary and oppressive politics of this form of feminism.

However, the absence of a widely recognised intersectional and radical alternative to this feminism has left us broadly stuck between the girlboss and what critic Jamie Hood termed the 'anti-woke cool girl'[25] – the kind of woman who gleefully pours scorn on liberal feminism and advocates for the return to a natural social order. We are yet to reimagine an influential radical feminist movement which focuses on class and works alongside racial justice and environmental movements. The concept of intersectionality, originally rooted in the rich tradition of Black feminist activism and put forward by legal scholar Kimberlé Crenshaw to make sense the compounded effects of various oppressions, has gained prominence as an analytical tool in academic circles and some sections of journalism. It has also become a buzzword which has allowed those who use it to continue their work largely unchanged.

We now seem to be in a re-run of the 2010s, with countless columns dedicating to discussing whether *Barbie* is a feminist film and simplistic debates about consent. This is evidenced by a 2024 UK campaign for 'affirmative consent' ('Only Yes Means Yes'), featuring actress Emily Atack. The campaign was forced to backtrack on its original slogan, 'I'm Asking for It', belatedly realising that it was not the bold reappropriation it originally thought it was.[26] Despite widespread understanding that consent is a minimal entry point and a poor concept to capture the forces that coerce us into consenting, campaigns for enthusiastic consent feel like a blast from a decade ago. Meanwhile, self-aware social media trends are doubling down on an ethos of personal responsibility and inviting us to be #thatgirl: get up at 7 am, drink green juices and journal to deal with our discontent.[27]

## Feminist activism in the age of the backlash

This leaves us with the feeling that feminism is no longer transformative and parodies of liberation: the tradwives who create false sisterhood, anti-abortion movements that parade as a remedy against the forces of the market, protectionist impulses which tell us to find a traditionally minded husband, and wellness in lieu of healthcare. Each of these fallacies, however, contains an opportunity for transformative critique. The rise of Gen Z 'puriteens' and the revival of anti-porn discourse are signs of disenchantment but they also offer space for a new sexual politics. New Age anti-feminist empowerment and the individual pursuit of wellness point to the need for the revival of a women-led health movement. True sisterhood and solidarity can fill in a gap that the tradwives are all too ready to step into, at a time when feminist activism has often come to mean online activism, where branding and individualistic empowerment are rewarded by social media platforms' algorithms.[28] The growing popularity of women's circles, which like men's circles tend to veer towards New Age gender essentialism but can take on community-based and even feminist forms, testifies to a desire for a feminism that offers something other than personal advancement.[29] These spaces can channel anger towards action. Harmange's anger, though not my kind of anger, feels more transformative than the wellness-sanctioned 'therapeutic screaming' we're told to practise to let go of our rage.[30]

Crucially, the neoliberal exploitation that much of mainstream feminism has been built on, and the reactionary backlash it has facilitated, tells us there is no feminist way forward without demands for better socio-economic conditions, labour reforms and social support structures which would make childcare viable and domestic work distribution more equal. Alongside women's circles, recent years have seen seemingly inexhaustible fascination with witches, in popular culture, political commentary and on social media where witches congregate under the hashtag #witchesofinstagram. Many commentators have advanced the idea that our growing contemporary passion for witchcraft is proportional to our feelings of helplessness,[31] raising the question of what today's online witches could achieve if they did something else than concoct potions: on Halloween day in 1968, the US stock market plummeted by 13 points after activists from the Women's International Terrorist Conspiracy from Hell (W.I.T.C.H.) descended on Wall Street.[32]

Harmange recognises that mainstream feminism caters primarily to privileged white women, leaving behind working-class women, women of colour, those with disabilities and gender minorities. The exclusion of women of colour from the mainstream feminist movement is something that several generations of feminists have critiqued, including the group behind the 1977 Combahee River Collective, which recognised that gender and race taken separately were inadequate to capture Black women's experience of oppression. The sidelining of Black women's experiences has been stark, including in online abuse. 'The reality is, the sexism and racism Black women face online is not new,' Seyi Akiwowo from Glitch tells me.

> Black women are consistently attacked online, and the abuse is largely ignored. It is a natural result of the legacy of misogynoir, the anti-Black and misogynistic discrimination Black women have uniquely faced for years. We're failing to realise abuse online doesn't just stay in the digital space. It doesn't go away when you switch off your phone.

Before Gamergate, Black women were targets of vicious harassment campaigns orchestrated by male supremacists on 4chan, but few paid attention. They also shaped responses that received little mainstream attention. In June 2014, before Gamergate, a group of male supremacists on 4chan orchestrated a fake campaign called #endfathersday. They blamed the campaign on Black feminists by creating spoof accounts which included words like 'intersectionality'. A group of Black women organised a swift counter-response, using the hashtag #yourslipisshowing and sharing block lists to disrupt the campaign. Lack of attention to these campaigns and Twitter's inaction at the time were warning signs of a culture of online violence that would soon engulf social media.

Mainstream feminism has also skirted around the issue of motherhood and neglected domestic work and childcare in favour of personal advancement and 'smashing the glass ceiling', leaving a gap for movements like tradwives to step in and claim that feminists don't care about motherhood. 'If you are tired, are experiencing different forms of discrimination, have kids, you may not have energy to look for the alternative feminist discourse that is out there, and you might want to turn away from feminism,' Harmange adds. The radicalising power of motherhood is something that reactionary and conspiratorial movements have understood all too well. During the pandemic, QAnon bloomed into a bigger phenomenon by targeting mothers with wild claims about paedophile elites.[33] Feminism has long been ambivalent about motherhood, and second-wave feminists captured the tension. Shulamith Firestone, in *The Dialectic of Sex* (1970), theorised motherhood as a key aspect of women's enslavement, while Adrienne Rich's *Of Woman Born* (1976) described the patriarchal institution of motherhood rather than mothering itself as the site of women's oppression, writing about expectations of women to be self-sacrificial. Needless to say, neoliberal expectations of motherhood and broken childcare systems in many Western countries show that the dream of domestic liberation is still far off.

Canadian academic Andrea O'Reilly has argued for 'matricentric feminism', a feminism for mothers and motherhood, not narrowly defined as a feminism for biological mothers but for whoever engages in mothering work.[34] Recent titles advocating for a radical re-imagining of family structures and motherhood have struck a nerve. Echoing Firestone's writing in her distaste for biological motherhood, Sophie Lewis in *Full Surrogacy Now* (2019) has argued for the abolition of the traditional family unit to reimagine communal forms of gestation and childrearing. 'Surrogacy' as a form of outsourcing of pregnancy and childrearing is already happening across the board, from privileged white people handing over childcare responsibilities to women from ethnic minority backgrounds,[35] to commercial surrogacy which also deepens race and class inequalities.[36] Egalitarian forms of gestation and childrearing, in Lewis' view, are not really about carrying children for others but having community-based and collective forms of care. Lewis' distaste for biological motherhood, which echoes Firestone's description of childbirth as 'not fun' and like 'shitting a pumpkin', can probably feel alienating but hints at an understanding that only a radical transformation of childrearing can truly make parenthood sustainable and fair. A growing strand of feminist thinking is conceptualising women's lived experience of their bodies – from puberty and pregnancy to postpartum and menopause – showing that these need not lead us towards gender essentialism or the belief that there are natural callings our bodies must heed. From British author Lucy Jones' nuanced exploration of 'matrescence' (the period of women's lives where they become mothers) to the work of French philosopher Camille Froidevaux-Metterie, there is a flourishing school of embodied feminism which does not shy away from speaking about the body without reducing women to it, and is giving women new ways to think about their experiences, drawing on the work of previous generations of feminists, including Iris Marion Young.[37]

## The fraught pursuit of visibility

In early 2012, the prominent breast cancer charity Susan G. Komen made headlines with its decision to cease funding Planned Parenthood's breast cancer screenings. Shaunna Thomas and Nita Chaudhary, seasoned in non-profit, policy and community organising, viewed this as a broader trend of regressive politics and an assault on women's rights. The news broke a few months before the start of the campaign to re-elect Barack Obama and while hope was high that he would secure a second term in office. Thomas and Chaudhary perceived that a determined movement was on the march. 'While anti-feminists were very organised, there was not a highly visible organised feminist community that could respond quickly and in real time,' Thomas tells me. This realisation spurred the creation of UltraViolet, a feminist coalition dedicated to crafting impactful online campaigns for social change. Their inaugural petition garnered one million signatures, compelling Susan G. Komen to retract its decision. UltraViolet evolved into a coalition of feminist groups, focusing on different areas: reproductive health, economic security, sexual violence. It focuses on high visibility campaigns, in the wake of #MeToo, successfully campaigning for the dismissal of men accused of sexual violence, including Bill O'Reilly and Les Moonves.

UltraViolet strives to blend grassroots activism with significant mainstream influence through potent campaigns which work on social media. When we speak, Thomas tells me the founders of UltraViolet saw the backlash coming years before Trump. While at the time of our interview she was concerned about the prospect of Trump's re-election in 2024, she also said that 'progressive political leaders are not a guarantee of policies amenable to women's rights' and that 'Democrats have ceded terrain to Republicans' for over a decade. Reversing the tide, amid a slew of regressive legislation aimed at curtailing women's rights and access to healthcare, is, she tells me, a project that does not hinge on the result of an election alone and requires a form of collective and coalition-based activism which achieves wins while giving an equal voice to diverse feminist groups. Ultraviolet, in other words, is seeking to resist feminist fatigue and remind us that feminist organising is critical, and our best hope, but that visibility matters.

Media scholar Sarah Banet-Weiser has shown that 'popular feminism' – which is heavily engaged in discourse and public visibility – drives 'popular misogyny'. As she puts it in her book *Empowered* (2018), 'for every Tumblr page dedicated to female body positivity, there were fat-shaming and body-shaming online comments.' Popular misogynistic backlash is the by-product of popular feminism. Popular feminism is also what allows some feminisms to be more visible than others. The #MeToo movement, originally created by Black feminist Tarana Burke in 2006, became popular only when it was adopted by largely white Hollywood actresses and sidelined the concerns of women of colour and marginalised women around the world. This kind of visibility often ensures structures are not challenged and privileged white women's interests are advanced at the expense of others. As Banet-Weiser argues, political visibility is vital for oppressed groups to be seen and demand change, but popular feminism also runs the risk of pursuing visibility for its own sake. The male supremacist project benefits from growing feelings that we cannot challenge existing structures and inequities, feeding on the feminist movement's draining energy.

Author and feminist activist Sian Norris, who writes about reproductive rights, cautions against some feminist movements' focus on visibility. 'We have to stop engaging in the discourse and recognise the feminist energy that exists around the world.' Instead of bothering to respond to spurious accusations, feminism needs to focus on action. 'I'm not the best example because I spend so much time on social media arguing, but we need to recognise progress where it's happening,' she adds. While the columns of many newspapers in the Global North give the impression there is no more pressing question to solve than deciding once and for all if Taylor Swift is a good feminist, across the world, feminist organisations do vital day-to-day work as rights are being curtailed and are charting the way forward. Organisations in Kenya are continuing to deliver abortion to women amid a murky legal framework.[38] In Argentina, the movement Ni Una Menos, which emerged in 2015 following the murder of a 14-year-old girl at the hands of her boyfriend and which first campaigned against feminicides exemplifies a form of mainstream and intersectional feminist organising which formed alliances with trade unions, the climate movement, Indigenous rights movements and LGBT+ coalitions. The women of Ni Una Menos have campaigned for reforms to alleviate household debt, marched to protest against inflation and used the slogan 'we want ourselves alive and debt free!'[39]

The movement, which was instrumental in the legalisation of abortion in the country,[40] has become a target of male supremacists and the country's ultra-misogynistic president, who upon his election all but dismantled government and public institutions in charge of fighting gender-based violence, racism and discrimination.[41] Elsewhere, feminist organising has faced drawbacks. The 2017 Women's March on Washington, which became the largest single-day march in American history, sparked hopes for sustained feminist activism in the months after Trump's inauguration, before subsequent marches were marred by accusations of antisemitism and racism. The movement lost steam, its pink pussy hats becoming the symbol of everything that sometimes appears wrong with contemporary feminism: co-option by commercial interests, profiling of celebrities, infighting, exclusionary politics and its ultimately non-threatening nature.[42] While male supremacists and anti-feminists are marching forward, feminist movements in many countries are facing existential crises, draining the hope that meaningful social change is possible.

This is happening as the feminist discourse that felt formative for women a decade ago, particularly in the English-speaking world, has fallen out of fashion. The identity-focused feminist publications of the early 2010s, as Michelle Goldberg noted in a *New York Times* piece titled 'The Future is No Longer Female' have closed down.[43] *Bitch* magazine published its last edition in 2022, while its counterpart *Jezebel* announced it would close down after more than 16 years in operation in late 2023, before being bought and revived a few weeks later. Male supremacist and far-right politics which originated from 4chan as Angela Nagle argued in *Kill All Normies* (2017) ascended as the identity-focused feminist discourse which developed on the microblogging platform Tumblr receded, not replaced by an alternative online space favoured by young women and equally defining in its ability to awaken feminist consciousness.[44]

## Wellness and feminist survival

In recent years, the notion of feminist fatigue has received greater attention. Many feminists are rethinking burnout not as something that needs fixing with bubble baths but as a natural by-product of current socio-economic and political structures that needs to be managed when the temptation to disengage can be strong. In 2023, the French feminist group VsCyberH, which fights gender-based harassment, launched the hashtag #PayeTonBurnoutMilitant (#PayForActivistBurnout) and announced it would close its helpline. It cited as a reason the psychological impact on its volunteers, virtually all of whom were women and had spent years listening to and providing support to victims (also mostly women), all the while going without any recognition or respect from the French political class – the French president describing women's accusations against powerful abusers as 'man hunts', for instance. Instead, VsCyberH is now focusing its efforts on lobbying the French government to adopt legislation against digital harms, an example of a shift in priorities to protect activists and achieve change.

Understanding of the political nature of burnout draws on a long history of Black feminist activism. While self-care has become synonymous with $66 vaginal eggs, Audre Lorde described it as an 'act of political warfare' to survive multiple forms of stress and oppression. Black liberation activism implemented structures of self-care – which were structures of community care – for many decades. Maryrose Reeves Allen, who taught physical education at Howard University, established a programme of 'total fitness' for Black women which encompassed various aspects of physical and mental health and challenged white supremacist beauty standards.[45] In June 1983, Spelman College in Atlanta hosted the First National Conference on Black Women's Health Issues, which brought together over 2,000 women and opened a conversation unprecedented in scale about Black women's health and experience of racism and misogyny in the US medical system.[46] The Black Panther movement established free community-based health clinics.[47] Audre Lorde's definition of self-care was rooted in her own experience of breast cancer: wellness, for her, was about self-preservation to be able to continue helping others.

Previous waves of feminism were also marked by women-led health discussions. The women's liberation conference in Boston in 1969 led to the publication of *Our Bodies, Ourselves*, a guide to women's sexual and reproductive health, which included not just practical advice on contraception and abortion but a wider consideration of the political and economic determinants of health. The guide ceased to be updated in 2018 as its funding had gradually dried up. There are, however, emerging signs of a backlash against predatory wellness culture and greater discussion about equity in health. Mainstream media has given greater coverage to women's health. Radical self-care may have been stripped of its radicalism by the neoliberal wellness industry, but the pandemic has shone a light on the disproportionate toll the virus took on people of colour, including Black women. Post-Roe, there has been renewed interest in community care – of the kind that women's healthcare organisations like the Jane Collective provided before the legalisation of abortion.[48]

A series of recent titles have argued in favour of re-politicising wellbeing, Fariha Róisín's *Who Is Wellness For?* (2022), Pooja Lakshmin's *Real Self-Care* (2023) and Tamela J. Gordon's *Hood Wellness* (2024) being just a few examples. This includes 'giving up opportunities, convenience or status so that resources can be distributed to women who are lacking', as Lakshmin wrote in *Ms*.[49] She cites her own experience of giving up her academic job and holding career clinics for aspiring physicians and medical trainees. Artist and activist Tricia Hersey created The Nap Ministry, a non-profit which promotes rest and sleep as a form of racial health justice, with studies showing that Black women get less sleep than their white counterparts.[50] Akiwowo, whose work has focused on self-care in the online world, agrees. 'Self-care doesn't mean doing it alone. It can involve building a community of people with shared values who are committed to supporting each other holding space for you when you are feeling burned out. It requires ongoing commitment,' she says.

(Truly) radical self-care can help us renegotiate our relationship to feminism as we pull back from and return to it. As a woman who benefits every day from the hard work of generations of feminists, I have entertained the 'what has feminism ever done for me?' train of thought. Speaking to women of different generations gives a different perspective: during the writing of this book, a friend (in her 60s) described to me how transformational feminism felt to her in 1970s Britain, echoing the sentiment often expressed by second- and third-wave feminists that they were 'changing the world'. This is a feeling women my generation are finding more difficult to experience, as neoliberal economics and reactionary backlashes have given the status quo an air of inevitability.

Unlike Harmange, I'm a feminist who doesn't hate men, as individuals or as complicit beneficiaries of patriarchal systems. Many, but perhaps not enough, men have disappointed me, and I hope they don't try me. Like many women, I have felt angry: spending too much time on incel forums hasn't helped. Mostly, I have felt concerned about where we are heading and what this means for women. I have been troubled by the thought that we as women might cede to protectionist and individualistic impulses, that we may not, as Srinivasan says, be imaginative. The femosphere may not have the same reach as the manosphere, but it is a growing movement which tries to mould us on that which we need to combat. While men and women can Go Their Own Way, others argue that maybe we can find each other. The final chapter of this book looks at how we can do the unthinkable: find common ground.

# 10

# Finding common ground

Zac Seidler speaks with calm, clarity and passion. He wears thin-rimmed round glasses and a white shirt. A Sydney-based clinical psychologist, he is the director of men's mental health research at the campaign movement Movember. His story is unusual, one he neither shies away from nor places centrally in his experience. While he was at university in 2013, his father, who had suffered from depression for many years, committed suicide. For many years, Seidler and his two brothers saw their father struggle, without fully understanding the extent of his illness. One brother, Jonathan, a writer and journalist who himself was diagnosed with bipolar disorder, explored the history of mental health struggles plaguing different generations of men in his family in his memoir *It's a Shame about Ray* (2022). Growing up with two brothers, Seidler says, 'there was a competitive hierarchy of sorts I had to navigate and it came with emotional literacy and dialogue.' As a child and teen, Seidler pursued drama, an activity that other boys shunned, but he also played sports, mostly with boys. He describes spending a lot of time with girls and boys separately as an early introduction to gender polarisation. 'The way my female friends discussed masculinity was so different from the way boys perceived it.'

While studying psychology at university, he was one of the very few men in his undergraduate programme. 'By the time I was doing my master's degree, it was 25 women and me.' His father's death naturally shaped his interest in men's mental health greatly. 'It's not the reason I do what I do, but it brought it into sharp focus. I saw a gap if I'm honest; the way people looked at it was very black and white.' While he started with the premise that men were not seeking help, his research led him to discover that they were, but the psychological and clinical help on offer was inadequate. He has embarked on a project to establish mental health services for men that account for men's gender-specific problems. At Movember, he leads Men in Mind, an online training programme to help mental health professionals treat men in therapy and address depression and suicidal feelings. Contrary to male supremacist influencers who clamour about male suicide but do little to address the problem beyond selling men self-optimisation programmes, this initiative takes men's mental health seriously.

In his clinical work and research, Seidler has studied first-hand the sway of male supremacist influencers. After conducting interviews with 1,000 young men in the UK, he found that media coverage of anti-feminism has inadvertently fuelled young men's desire for transgression. Mainstream media coverage of Tate has made him less appealing to young men who play a game of 'catch me if you can', jumping to ever more outrageous figures. 'When they see influencers being discussed in the mainstream, the men I work with go "You think this is mainstream? See ya later"', he says. Anti-feminist talking points peddled by mega-influencers mean that young men are swimming in male supremacist rhetoric which normalises violence towards women and coercion. Influencers at the less extreme end of the spectrum like Peterson and Rogan have become such touchstones that, Seidler argues, ignoring them is not an option. Rogan's podcast receives over ten million views per episode, and we're not collectively going to unread Peterson's bestselling book. In this context, 'labelling things as good or bad is unhelpful', says Seidler. He is interested in finding the Goldilocks Zone: the amount of Peterson or Rogan material young men can consume without deriving harm from it. 'If you look at their content, half is probably innocuous, and half is a problem; we need to understand what's protective and what's harmful.'

Seidler feels we need to reclaim the debate about men's mental health from male supremacists, but we also need to understand it as a feminist issue. Feminist movements' refusal to engage with male supremacists is, for Seidler, a dangerous path with consequences for all. He says:

> Part of the feminist movement is not willing to engage with the incel community and empathise, and understand their experience, and if that doesn't happen, I can assure you we will fail and they will become further radicalised. My aim is not to condone behaviour but to understand and analyse it, and understand their complex experience. It's not that it's worse than women, it's that they're struggling. If we want this behaviour to stop, we need to go into the trenches.

Women bear the brunt of men's radicalisation, and ignoring it or retreating into separatist movements – which can provide much-needed safe spaces for some women – will do little to protect women's rights and autonomy as a whole in the long term.

Angelica Ferrara, a feminist scholar and psychologist at Stanford University whose research focuses on men's social connections and friendships, agrees. Addressing some of the underlying problems that men encounter, she argues, is a feminist issue because the consequences of inaction hit women. Across the Global North, she says, there is a 'crisis of male intimacy and connection, as the social needs that men have are being fulfilled by women'. Men's dwindling social networks, far from being a man's problem, is a way in which the patriarchy is sustained as women take on the burden of support. Data on the phenomenon is stark: the number of men who had six or more close friends halved between 1990 and 2021 in the US, a phenomenon that particularly affected single men.[1] In the UK, a 2018 research by Movember found that a quarter of British men had no close friends.

Researchers like Ferrara say that the problem has become especially acute post-pandemic and that male friendships decline in late adolescence and early adulthood. The media has picked up on this, and newspaper opinion sections are dominated by think pieces that use expressions such as 'epidemic of loneliness' and 'crisis of loneliness'. A July 2023 *New York Times* op-ed by Michelle Cottle titled 'Is the cure to male loneliness out on the pickleball court?' urged men to get out of their house and play sports together. It went viral, with the internet mockingly putting forward its own cures for male loneliness, which played on strange male bonding stereotypes, from 'sailing the high seas with your bros' to 'a third computer monitor'.

Loneliness is not necessarily a good metric to use when we talk about men, Ferrara says. 'Men are far less likely to report loneliness accurately because it comes with a particular stigma.' She thinks social isolation is a more accurate description. The factors behind that trend are complex and include a decline of social infrastructure and places where men have historically met, formed bonds and consolidated their power. They range from aristocratic gentlemen's clubs, where the powerful established boundaries in society along gender, ethnicity and class, to working men's clubs, which offered those lower down the social spectrum a place to meet and form class consciousness but also enforce gender norms. The decline of such male spaces has mirrored the greater participation of women in public life, which is a very welcome development, but 'we have not seen a commensurate bouncing back about forming community spaces where men meet that are equitable, accessible and appealing,' says Ferrara, and, one might add, that do not centre around the consumption of alcohol. Today, London's few remaining elite men-only clubs only reflect a broader social truth: that a handful of men shape society and continue to draw lines, including those which exclude other men.

While we can debate whether opening the doors of the Garrick Club in London to women was a great contribution to gender equality outside its symbolic value,[2] Ferrara argues that accessible and socially equitable meeting places for men can foster greater feminist consciousness. Ferrara has a name for the invisible burden that falls on women as they work to sustain men's social networks and shore up the mental health loss that occurs because of their decline – 'men-keeping'. This echoes what sociologist Carolyn Rosenthal called 'kinkeeping' to refer to the work that women put in to keep intergenerational relationships going,[3] from sending 'thank you' cards to older relatives to taking photographs at family gatherings to share with relatives. While data shows that men's networks are shrinking, it is also something that many of us can experience in our own families. Ferrara tells me that her mother has at least eight to ten people she can turn to around her to meet her social needs, while her father has just her mother.

While anecdotes do not amount to data, the data does support the trend. Women, whether as mothers, sisters or partners, are increasingly playing an outsized role in men's lives. Men have become 'emotional gold diggers', as a piece in *Harper's Bazaar* on the topic put it.[4]

Their lack of close friendships also does not give them an opportunity to learn social and emotional skills. 'This can be addressed at every level of society, from individual family units to policy structures,' Ferrara says. 'One of the things parents can do is nurture boys' friendships and show the importance of friendships in boyhood. There is a lot we can do to sustain boys' friendships in late adolescence and not let them die off.' Men's circles, though ranging in quality, are a welcome development for Ferrara: 'Men's willingness to handle their issues outside of women is something to be celebrated.' Both Seidler and Ferrara agree that male spaces are necessary for emotional wellbeing and can foster social consciousness and even feminist awakening. These spaces, however, are controversial due to their exclusionary and misogynistic history. Seidler also thinks 'there is space for men-only spaces if they are done in a respectful and equitable way.'

In the UK, close to 15 years of austerity policies have led to the closure of community centres and public libraries. While there are direct ways in which economic policies impact relationships, including men's relationships, this also plays out in less obviously visible ways. While the decline of men's friendships in late adolescence is partly linked to societal conditioning and the perception that sharing feelings and looking for support are feminine behaviours, Sophie K. Rosa showed in *Radical Intimacy* (2023) the multiple ways in which neoliberalism shapes our social networks and romantic relationships. It does so in very visible ways, with algorithmically driven dating apps, but also more subtly, by making the conditions for some relationships increasingly difficult, due to poverty or lack of social infrastructures, by shaping our desires for certain relationships over others and making the cultivation of some relationships necessary. When professional networking is essential to career advancement in times of economic precarity, when conventional heterosexual relationships are still a marker of social success, and when many are working three jobs in the gig economy to cover their ever-rising rent, finding time for friendships and community connections with no agenda can feel out of reach. Allistone and A Band of Brothers, with its programme that focuses on relationships in the broadest sense and avoids romantic relationships, tries to reprioritise the social bonds that can be forgotten when influencers tell men they need to get the money, the six-pack and the girl.

## Welcoming men into feminism

It is not the easiest time to be teaching men how to become feminists. The work has never been more needed, and yet never before has it faced this amount of sabotage. Equimundo has been working to awaken men to feminist consciousness for over two decades. While men's circles and community programmes sometimes dip their toes in manosphere discourse, Equimundo is firmly feminist and seeks to educate boys and men to become allies of the gender equality cause. It runs educational workshops for men and training programmes for people who work with young men: these can revolve around sports, community, healthcare or workplaces. Caroline Hayes and Brian P. Heilman, who lead research at the organisation, say the male supremacist backlash has made the task difficult and has led to a rethink in strategy.

Given Equimundo's discovery that 40 per cent of men find their online relationships more satisfying than their offline ones, convincing men to join discussion groups to think critically about dominant masculinity is ambitious – particularly young men who have drunk the misogynistic Kool-Aid and are obsessed with what their peers think. Without 'captive audiences' as they call them – in other words, compulsory school or after-school events – it's hard to reach young men. Real-world programmes, they have found, work better than online, but 'the balance between the online and offline world has flipped.' Heilman says that male supremacists' use of the language of empowerment is disrupting their efforts. 'In some ways, they are doing what we're doing: they're trying to get guys to look critically at the way gender works and shapes the world, and trying to free themselves of restrictive world views.'

Like others who try to disengage young men from misogyny, Equimundo is finding that the ideal collides with the reality. 'It's important to consider the spaces that men are already being drawn to, what is holding their attention, what's keeping them there,' Hayes says. 'We can seek to replicate some of the things that do work in terms of engagement, but then look at embedding more positive behavioural outcomes.' In other words, if men spend a lot of time on forums where they compete to strip women with AI tools or search for tips on how to smash their jaws with hammers, is there another space that can be offered to them that involves something healthier yet appealing? Equimundo is using the format of fantasy sports leagues to draw men in. Importantly, what we would like as feminists is not what works for men. When I asked Harmange what men who want to be allies should do, she said men should listen to feminist programmes and read feminist books, but the idea that men are going to tune en masse into intersectional feminist podcasts feels unlikely, to say the least.

The question of whether influencers can be harnessed for good quickly comes up. Seidler wants to partner with what he calls 'risky brands'. If anti-feminist influencers are sucking men into their worldview, he feels our societies need to present men with appealing role models who will offer something that feels equally transgressive, minus the misogyny, which means treading a very fine line. Movember has made partnering with influencers a part of its campaigns.[5] 'We need to engage with the alphas: we need to go into every school and find the top dog and get him on board and it will trickle down,' Seidler says. I ask him about plans put forward by the UK's Labour Party to help schools train 'non-toxic' influencers.[6] He scoffs at the idea, saying that it betrays a lack of understanding of teenage boys' psyches. This is a problem that is 'purposefully avoiding the very confines of what we consider to be appropriate behaviour', he tells me: the idea of nice, progressive, non-threatening feminist influencers appealing to young men, to him, is a pipe dream.

To convert men to feminism, Equimundo has used a 'gender transformative' approach. In other words, it considers feminist awakening as a journey whose starting point has to be acknowledged if change is to take place. 'You have to acknowledge their adherence to certain gender norms, including misogynistic norms; you have to talk about definitions of masculinity and femininity,' Heilman says. 'You have to wade into the manosphere waters, and steer guys in a different direction. It's not going to work to just pretend that none of this exists.' Seidler adds: 'We need to expect and demand more from men, and we need to move the bar up; we need to have a belief system that there is great potential and benefit in encouraging men to live up to a better standard of behaviour.' There are encouraging signs. The percentage of men who had been to therapy in the UK increased from 18 per cent in 2010 to 27 per cent in 2022.[7] More men are also becoming therapists, although they remain under-represented.

While fatherhood has been exploited by MRAs, greater mainstream discussion about the changing nature of fatherhood is also an opportunity for involving men in gender equality. Fathers' roles have changed significantly in the last few decades across many Western countries. Equimundo says that engaging them is helpful because new fatherhood is a time when men rethink their roles and who they want to be. Most fathers now want to be present at the birth of their children, and many take longer parental leave and expect to take on a larger share of caregiving responsibilities than would have been normal 30 years ago. This is not to say that the burden of parenthood is still not disproportionately placed on women but that these societal changes can act as an entry point into reaching men. Heilman says, 'men want childcare, they want paid leave, they want the things that support them as caregivers, even though they may still look up to authoritarian figures.' Derision thrown at men perceived to be present and involved fathers has thus largely backfired. Attacks by Fox News against US Secretary of Transportation Pete Buttigieg when he took paternity leave only managed to dent the channel's 'pro-family' image. In the UK, TV presenter Piers Morgan had to apologise for his comments on #emasculatedBond after sneering at pictures that showed actor Daniel Craig carrying his baby daughter in a sling, while Conservative politician Jacob Rees-Mogg's admission that he had never changed a nappy despite having six children attracted mockery.

## The problem with role models

The question of 'positive role models', like the 'crisis of loneliness', has become something of a social talking point, and it is a divisive issue among researchers and psychologists specialising in masculinity. Men are becoming radicalised, a common argument goes, because they have no positive male role models. Seidler is sceptical. 'The obsession with role modelling to solve masculinity is crazy to me,' he says. 'I see so many men in therapy who come from incredible families and have devoted fathers, and they still get pulled in every direction and have this fractured identity and are pushing the bounds of what is healthy masculinity.' Research on the importance of positive male role models has indeed been very inconsistent in its findings. Beyond Male Role Models, a research project by The Open University (UK) and Action for Children found that vulnerable men needed consistent mentors and regular support services more than present fathers.[8] Commentary about the lack of positive male role models and absentee fathers can lend itself to the stigmatisation of single-parent families and does not account for diverse ranges of family models. 'Positive role models' don't have to mean fathers, or even men. Men can, and should, have positive role models who are women, be they mothers, teachers or mentors.

Discussion about role models has also extended to those in popular culture and the public sphere. While magic can happen in community groups or even some men's circles, 'nobody is channelling an alternative discourse on masculinity into the kind of methodology for engagement that manosphere influencers are using: riling up energy, driving the most vulnerable guys over to subscription models to make income off the conflict,' Heilman says. And no one probably should. There is no progressive Jordan Peterson offering a diagnosis of men's malaise on YouTube that appeals in the same way, but of course the appeal lies in the conflict, the antagonism and the transgressive politics, which is why progressive YouTubers are finding it harder to amass millions of followers. Working in the field of public policy involves a lot of necessary but frustrating discussions about impact and reach, a reflection of the fact that carefully tailored intervention programmes directed at men (and different) groups need to justify their existence and impact to public and private funders, but also of our collective obsession with 'scalability'. Yet in an area as complex as gender politics, it's important to recognise that reach, though important, isn't everything, and that individual and collective shifts cannot always be neatly measured by numbers of likes and shares.

While there are no exact counterparts to PUAs and red pill YouTubers, there are plenty of positive 'role models' in popular culture, sports and the arts who are challenging the dominant models of masculinity. Many of these men are very successful and even popular among young men, but they are not full-time public communicators or influencers. They may be talking about masculinity in interviews, but the rest of the time they play sports, act in films and otherwise engage in their field of excellence. They also face conservative backlash, scrutiny and accusations of hypocrisy. In the UK, England footballer Marcus Rashford has become the most visible figure in a new generation of sports stars who are engaged in social and political discourse. He led a campaign to distribute free school meals during COVID-19, to the dismay of the tabloid press and conservative pundits.

In American football, long a bastion of professional and sexual abuse, 'soft jocks' – macho yet sensitive men like Travis Kelce – are touted as models of new masculinity by progressives and are frequent targets of misinformation campaigns. Actors like Paul Mescal have come to embody sensitive and enlightened masculinity. Straddling the Atlantic divide, the smash hit Apple comedy-drama *Ted Lasso*, in which a wholesome American football coach becomes the manager of a London soccer team, explored issues of men's mental health and portrayed a positive, female-supporting version of manhood in the setting of an elite locker room and won a Peabody award for 'offering the perfect counter to the enduring prevalence of toxic masculinity'.[9]

When former National Football League player and sitcom *Brooklyn Nine-Nine* star Terry Crews spoke about being abused by a Hollywood executive at the height of the #MeToo movement, he became a representative of male #MeToo, a reminder that men are also victims of male violence. He has also spoken about the pain of being immersed in the misogynistic culture of professional football.[10] While Crews has spoken openly in favour of gender equality, others like wrestler and actor Dwayne 'The Rock' Johnson have spoken about their mental health struggles and the pressures of embodying traditional masculinity. Charismatic figures who carry the message are important. 'We need to show young men the guy who's just a little bit older than them who's living a form of masculinity that they want to live and that they might aspire to,' Hayes from Equimundo says. Role models in their lives might not guarantee that men don't turn to outrage merchants, but they can help.

Related to the question of role models has been that of cultural representations. Alice Evans of King's College London studies gender polarisation. She attributes the growing divide between men and women to a few key factors: men's economic resentment, anti-feminist influencers and social media filter bubbles and what she calls feminised public culture, the idea that women are increasingly dominating popular culture and providing other women a discourse about their place in the world, where men do not.[11] In the US, for every six women enrolled at university in 2021, there were four men. The same trend is replicated across many Western countries.[12] In the UK, authors shortlisted for leading literary prizes in very recent years have been predominantly women. Pulitzer-winning novelist Elizabeth Strout told *The Times* that 'all female-dominated' publishing 'might be just as bad' as all male-dominated publishing.[13] A piece in the same paper titled 'Are young male novelists an endangered species?' concluded the societal panic was premature.[14]

While cultural productions by women and featuring women have captured public imagination and achieved greater influence in recent years, to think that we live in a feminised public culture because millennial women write celebrated novels seems like a leap of imagination. Likewise, are we really supposed to think that men are becoming widely disgruntled because they don't have their own Sally Rooney to capture what it is to be a man? Many women might be going into journalism, but men still dominate senior editorial positions.[15] Women might make up a majority of prize-winning authors, but they still only account for less than a quarter of directors and key film executives on top-grossing films.[16] A study by USC Annenberg Inclusion Initiative from

January 2024 found that women led or co-led only 30 per cent of 2023's highest grossing films, down from 44 per cent in 2022.[17]

It does not take a deep examination of the history of literature and the arts, or even recent literary titles, to see there is no dearth of nuanced representations of manhood. Ferrara argues that 'notions of masculinity have evolved through history and geography to encompass and subtract new qualities.' Many human qualities, which are now culturally and socially construed as feminine, were once deemed masculine. To take just one example, eighteenth-century Romantic masculinity afforded men the ability to show immense sensitivity. 'The question that never seems to get asked is: is a prescriptive way to do masculinity helpful to men?' Ferrara adds. Cultural representation, in itself not a guarantee of equitable access to opportunities, inclusion or lack of stereotyping, has nonetheless been an important part of the fight towards gender and racial equality. Being seen and represented in celebrated cultural representations is more than mere symbolism; it is essential for reflecting society and shaping cultural and social perceptions.

The significance of cultural representation is clear for men of colour and men with diverse sexual identities: actor Chadwick Boseman was hailed not only for offering young Black men essential cultural representations with *Black Panther* but also embodying in his personal life a form of Black manhood that 'honours, respects and buttresses a kaleidoscope of other Black masculinities', as scholar Vershawn Ashanti Young put it. While the idea that men are fading into irrelevance in popular culture is a fantasy – though it makes for a compelling headline – it is a fantasy that anti-feminists can easily seize upon to whip up resentment of celebrated cultural productions which feature women and marginalised communities. Films featuring predominantly female casts have been backlash fodder for the last decade. After Gamergate, male supremacists and far-right trolls led a hideous misogynistic and racist hate campaign against actor Leslie Jones during the release of the all-female remake of *Ghostbusters*. Like gaming before, the remake of the popular film offered some an opportunity to stoke men's resentment at the idea that women, in this case a Black woman, was taking something they perceive as theirs.

Any film claiming to make a feminist or progressive statement is ripe for attack. Film and TV have become sites of backlash, because although male-led productions continue to dominate, the success of a small number of productions is enough to enrage those for whom any representation is too much. As could be expected, male supremacists raged at the highest grossing film of 2023 – *Barbie* – which offered them a mirror image of the dystopian world they imagine we live in. What better representation of male supremacy, after all, than the petulant Ken who feels entitled to Barbie's attention, becomes red-pilled in the 'real world' when he discovers patriarchy and seeks to restore a man-led world by turning Barbie's dream house into his 'Mojo Dojo Casa House'? And what better representation of the male supremacist nightmare than Barbie Land: a world dominated by women where men never feel Kenough? The success of the film itself as a cultural production which discusses gender norms was an assault on male supremacist interests.

At the end of the film, radicalised Ken discovers he wasn't so happy in the patriarchy after all. Leading more men to realise that is something increasingly difficult to achieve. We do not live in Barbie Land. We live in the real world, where the success of one film has little bearing on gender equality and representation as a whole. This is not to say it isn't a good idea to broaden what appears in the media. Researchers working in de-radicalisation programmes for young men point to the importance of cultural representations in shaping young men's resentment, particularly the type of content geared towards teenagers. Male supremacist's beliefs in socio-sexual hierarchies may be giving themselves an air of scientific rigour, but they are steeped in pop culture stereotypes about the Jock and the Nerd which have been distilled in films and TV in the last few decades. The 1988 film *Heathers* shows the psychopathic J.D. gun down students, attempt to kill the girl he falls in love with (played by Winona Ryder) and blow himself up in an anticipation of incel violence. In *Buffy the Vampire Slayer* – which promised to offer a feminist discourse in popular culture and has undergone some critical deconstruction in the last few years, due in no small part to several actors accusing director Joss Whedon of abuse and misogyny – the nerdy villain Warren objectifies women, forcibly controls and attempts rape on one and ends up killing two of them.

Appealing teenage shows that move beyond these clichés and feature a diverse cast of young men can only add to the cultural conversation especially as dominant forms of masculinity are challenged by popular culture in a way that may not feel accessible or entirely relatable to men. Similarly, while British 'lads mags' such as *Nuts* and *Zoo*, which reflected the normalised misogyny of their era, closed down a decade ago – at roughly the same time as Gamergate was unfolding, they have not been replaced by a diverse offering that caters to young men's interests while offering a politically progressive discourse or one that challenges dominant masculinity. At a time when anti-feminists and some mainstream conservatives are lamenting the death of manly men, many male celebrities are embodying more nuanced forms of masculinity. Critics have described celebrated actors like Paul Mescal and Timothée Chalamet – among others – as examples of masculine embodiment that challenge dominant masculinity. In 2020, Harry Styles was the first male celebrity to appear on his own on the cover of *Vogue* – he did so wearing a Gucci lace dress, not without backlash from the right and criticism from LGBT+ communities. One could argue that singers and artists playing with gender representations and fluidity are hardly a new phenomenon – David Bowie was appearing on album covers in a satin dress more than 50 years ago. It's unclear how much self-promotional gender-bending and queer-baiting by the celebrities of today actually translates into greater acceptability of gender fluidity for boys but it is part of a broader cultural shift which has been happening over decades.

## Do we forgive?

When I first emailed Neal Allistone to speak about his work with men, he was keen to talk. We exchanged a couple of messages. The first thing he texted after the initial round of introduction was: 'I'll ask a controversial question: don't you think misandry is on the rise too?' Ah, I thought. I had stepped into another den of Men's Rights Activism. I played along. He spoke about his work. He condemned the big influencers sucking men into their racketeering machine and their ideas. When I asked him questions, nothing he said led me to believe he wanted to engage with their arguments. Of course, I can't be sure. When I spoke to him, I could feel the occasional tension and the call of the manosphere – after all he used their language, and language matters – but the overwhelming feeling was that he made, and is making, a conscious effort to turn away from their arguments. 'I choose not to go there,' he told me when I prodded him. Speaking to all the men I interviewed for this book was an exercise in pragmatism and a consideration of what will work to foster change. In a time of polarisation, some researchers and activists are advocating for more compassionate ways of relating to each other, engaging with people who think differently and working constructively within diverse movements, without abandoning accountability.

It is a precarious exercise, conducted in the heat of a debate around 'cancel culture', a tool of political accountability which has come to be understood as the public shaming and ostracisation of whoever steps out of line. It is mostly used by conservatives to stoke fears of censorious mobs, a (sometimes deliberate) misunderstanding of the balance of power and who really has the power to cancel. There has, however, been a greater reckoning among progressives and radicals about the impact of public shaming and whether it is at all useful. Cathy O'Neil in *The Shame Machine* (2022) showed that social media platforms profit off (the act of) shaming because it generates clicks and viral cascades but does little to instil shame in those who ought to feel ashamed.

Black scholar and activist Loretta Ross has advocated for 'call-in culture' to replace 'call-out culture' to allow people to have challenging conversations, build coalitions and encourage others to make positive changes. Calling-in can take on many forms; Ross has, for example, suggested not shaming people on social media but privately messaging them or picking up the phone to discuss grievances (this applies to people who can be given the benefit of the doubt about their intentions). Many others have grappled with how to achieve a 'politics fierce and unapologetic enough truly to change things and smart and expansive enough to change the minds to get there', as Anand Giridharadas writes in his book *The Persuaders* (2022), which features an interview with Ross and other radical political and civic figures.

Speaking to Giridharadas, Ross describes outrage as what happens when there is 'no process for forgiveness with accountability'. She mentions her idea of 'circles of influence' – different people in your life whose beliefs will more or less overlap with yours. Progressives who agree on 90 per cent of things (the 90-percenters circle) can spend their time dividing themselves over the 10 per cent they disagree with, she argues, or they can work towards meaningful change. Ross then considers what it is like to work with the 75-percenters: people who mostly align with you but have significant disagreements, the 50-percenters who only overlap partly or even the 25-percenters, people who are not your allies and may even have views you find abhorrent. The 0-percenters (or the fascists as she describes them) are the only people she does not ally herself with.

Ross has advocated working with people with very divergent views, including those who will never be allies, and challenging but accepting their imperfections if they are well-intentioned and willing to change. In her decades of activism Ross has done work that only a small number of exceptional people are capable of: from accompanying former neo-Nazi Floyd Cochran on a speaking tour to running discussion circles with convicted rapists in prison after one asked for her help.[18] Many times, she has done what 'wasn't her duty, wasn't her mission as she had understood it, wasn't likely to succeed, wasn't deserved, wasn't a justifiable diversion of resources from women, wasn't her theory of change, wasn't, wasn't, wasn't'.[19] Her invitation to call others in comes with a number of caveats, not least that calls for forgiveness are not a way to escape accountability, nor a mechanism for abandoning one's principles or diluting core political aims. Nor are they something that people are ever obliged to do: women from ethnic or religious minority backgrounds who experience racism and misogyny face unique forms of oppression that white women do not and Black women's compassion is not something that white women are entitled to ask for. This kind of bridge-building is something one primarily takes upon oneself rather than demand of others. It can also take on more or less ambitious forms.

Appeals to constructive dialogue can feel hopelessly utopian in our cynical age. Yet, they are at the heart of the Listening Project, part of the Project for the Advancement of Our Common Humanity, a think tank housed at New York University and founded by Dr Niobe Way, a developmental psychologist and former school counsellor who spent years speaking to teenage boys. Its mission is to create dialogue and forge connections. Way's research has shown that boys crave meaningful same-sex connection and intimate friendships, where they can share with trust and without fear of being mocked and betrayed, but they struggle to form these connections, which are – still – culturally viewed as feminine and the subject of homophobic mockery. Friendships decline in late adolescence because of these stereotypes. The 'bromances' long depicted in TV comedy – duos like *Friends*' Chandler and Joey or *Scrubs*' Turk and J.D. (regardless of what one might think of these shows' gender politics) – are still widely liked, perhaps because they show men the types of friendship they wish they had.

Holly Van Hare runs The Listening Project in middle and high schools and says the crisis of connection has intensified since the pandemic. She sees the impact on boys, who are increasingly adversarial and withdrawn, the girls who face the backlash and self-censor, and the difficulties of communication between both genders. 'Girls are increasingly policing their own behaviour,' she says. The Listening Project uses a fairly simple formula: it conducts a general workshop which invites students to consider the impact of cultural expectations on their lives, teaches them a series of interviewing techniques and then sends them off to interview fellow students, teachers, family members and key figures in their community to learn meaningful stories about them, which they turn into a writing project. It provides a speaking space for boys to talk about their exposure to influencers and how it makes them feel. This may sound incredibly simple, but it allows boys to have discussions with their peers and trusted adults which they might find difficult to have with parents. 'There is a real turning point and boys begin to open up when we start to talk about how this affects them and normalise talking about boys' loneliness and friendships.' The aim of the project is to increase 'perceived common humanity' – the ability to see others outside of a series of stereotypes.

Van Hare says the interviewing techniques have possible applications outside of school settings. She suffered from an eating disorder as a girl and has an auto-immune condition, which has led to a 'trying time with the healthcare system' as she puts it. She believes training medical professionals could reduce the sort of patient stereotyping that is driving women and other groups away from medical institutions and into the arms of dubious wellness influencers. This could also benefit men's health. Eating disorders, for instance, are defined by strict and narrow criteria including body mass index and gender assumptions. The perception that eating disorders are a female issue leads to under-diagnosis among boys and men, who are increasingly prone to disordered eating but whose pain can be ignored, a reminder that addressing gender stereotypes serves both women and men's health. Ross, speaking about her work in reproductive justice, recalls working with doctors who shamed and chastised women who attended their clinics for several abortions, sometimes accusing these women of having 'failed' at handling their own contraception, statements which fail to give any consideration to women's specific socio-economic, family and personal circumstances.

Bridge-building is about recognising who you need to work with to achieve change and who the real adversary is. Many men do not possess the feminist consciousness that most feminists, myself included, would hope for. Some do. Many men could do a lot more, and many of those who try to provide an alternative discourse on masculinity and encourage men to be better human beings are, I feel, people to be called in. Thinking about Ross's circles of influence, I wondered where many of the men I spoke to, including those who brandish words like 'misandry', would sit for me. Are they 75-percenters or 50-percenters? In what circle of influence does Will, who if he had his way would take away women's right to their bodily autonomy, sit? Is he the 0-percenter whose worldview is so alien to me that he is unreachable, or is he my 25-percenter?

In discovering Will's radicalisation path, I have wondered how much I hold him responsible for his views. While I find establishing hierarchies of harm generally unhelpful, I have questioned how I feel about knowing an MRA, as opposed to a crude seduction coach: after all, MRAs go to great lengths to present themselves as justice heroes. The fact that they cloak themselves in the mantle of equity does little to dilute any of their core beliefs: if anything, one could argue it makes the enterprise particularly difficult to excuse, that they should know better. I believe Will's desire for justice to be genuine, and in his yearning to undo wrongs, in his scepticism, in his anger too, I see something of my own. I also know the consequences of his belief system for women's freedom and safety.

When I spoke to Will, I felt his fundamental need to be heard. While the male supremacist project writ large is about making sure society doesn't hear women and hears misogynists instead, at an individual level, many men clearly yearn to have their feelings acknowledged. I suspect he wanted to share his story with me because he felt I could give him a fair hearing or maybe he recognised similar vulnerabilities in me. If, as Naomi Klein claims, 'conspiracy theorists get the facts wrong, but they get the feelings right,'[20] I was ready to acknowledge the feeling but hold him accountable for the twisted facts. Moving beyond the feeling is the longer and less straightforward path. Male supremacists might be exploiting anger and grievances, but those same feelings, when redirected towards the real culprits, can be powerful and transformative.

I don't have a duty to pull Will out of his rabbit hole but I would like to believe that if he was willing to challenge his ideas, I would call him in. His radicalisation is not my or any woman's duty to fix, but it is society's to reckon with. I have compassion for Will because I understand all too well the deep feeling that many injustices remain unseen and unaddressed and where those feelings can lead you. I don't have much compassion for the grifters profiteering off others' search for answers, hardships and pain, for the ideologues who know exactly what they're doing, or even for the opportunists who are gleefully cheering on the tradwives. All are cashing in on the backlash. More and more women, and men, are paying the price.

# Epilogue: Coming out into joy

bell hooks had great hope for men. She did not see a way in which women's liberation could be achieved without them. In *The Will to Change* (2004) she spoke poignantly of the need for men to challenge patriarchal systems as well as their desire for love and acceptance. 'It is not true that men are unwilling to change. It is true that many men are afraid to change,' she wrote.[1] Male supremacists are challenging men's will to change, ensuring they stay hooked on the ideology that harms them.

The way male supremacist ideas are spreading and becoming normalised, the way they are acting as an entry point into feverish fascist dreams, the way they have become entangled with the climate emergency and the way in which we are entering new frontiers of AI and technological development that we don't know how to keep up with and regulate all suggest dark horizons. Many people are exploiting the increasingly pervasive feeling that we should stop hoping for meaningful or radical change and retreat into self-preservation.

Many of us also choose 'not to go there' and fight back from different angles. When Allistone said he chooses not to engage with male supremacists, I thought: if only it was that simple. How about, instead of believing in conspiracy theories, we just don't? And then I thought about another meaning to his words. My own susceptibility to a selfish wellness discourse of personal responsibility that distracts me from collective solidarity and tries to capitalise on my attention and weaknesses requires me every day to actively choose to 'not to go there' and recognise it for what it is: a con. It is a constant exercise in disengagement.

It has also been an exercise in connection and community building. My best form of disengagement with the false promises of New Age alt-health has been working with fellow researchers, activists and influencers who are devoting their time and energy to expose unscrupulous wellness influencers' exploitation of pain and injustices so they can perpetuate new ones.

These researchers have displayed clarity of mind, compassion and nuance in their work, never suggesting that people who fall for conspiracy theories are fools but identifying the malign commercial and political interests behind the lies. They have been my (largely online) community. I find following them, talking to them and laughing with them to be a needed antidote to the dark rabbit holes. I have also found diverse community groups and support networks. And I'm not very much on social media.

Researching conspiracy theories and encountering them is a different story. Much of what researchers are recommending needs to happen: greater tech regulation, greater resources in education and digital citizenship, and more nuanced programmes to reach young men. Sometimes these programmes will fail. Sometimes the laws won't make the difference we wanted, but they can make an incremental difference.

And there are bigger successes too. Some have already happened. Argentina's Ni Una Menos showed us what a radical intersectional movement which achieves impact looks like. France became the first country in the world to make abortion a constitutional right thanks to the tireless campaigning of women's rights organisations. Working alongside these organisations, exposing anti-abortion networks and seeing historical legislation be adopted in my home country has given me hope that amid the backlash, there is still joy.

# Notes

## Prologue

1 '"Great replacement theory" and conspiracies about 15-minute cities, cost of living and digital currencies said to be definitely or probably true by one in three in UK', King's College London, 13 June 2023, Available from: https://www.kcl.ac.uk/news/great-replacement-theory-and-conspiracies-about-15-minute-cities-cost-of-living-and-digital-currencies-said-to-be-definitely-or-probably-true-by-one-in-three-in-uk

2 'Women's rights have gone "too far", say majority of Gen Z and millennials, study shows', *The Daily Telegraph*, 9 March 2023, Available from: https://www.telegraph.co.uk/news/2023/03/09/womens-rights-have-gone-far-say-majority-gen-z-millennials-study/

3 'Gender roles and gender identity', Available from: https://pbs.twimg.com/media/FULXdzzWAAAzBLC?format=png&name=large

4 '2022: the year that misogyny was back in fashion', *Rolling Stone*, December 2022, Available from: https://www.rollingstone.co.uk/culture/2022-the-year-that-misogyny-was-back-in-fashion-24905/

5 'What is male supremacism', The Institute for Research on Male Supremacism, Available from: https://www.theirms.org/what-is-male-supremacism

6 While the aggressive anti-feminist backlash we are experiencing is taking place in relatively gender equal countries or those becoming ever more so, in many parts of the world, women live in a state of near complete oppression and erasure, with the return to power of the Taliban in 2021 resulting in a raft of measures to slowly deny women any rights, until they were banned from speaking in public at all.

## Chapter 1

1 'The alt-right has lost control of the "redpill" meme', *The Atlantic*, 13 April 2021, Available from: https://www.theatlantic.com/technology/archive/2021/04/red-pill-meme-alt-right-twitter/618577/

2 Throughout the book there are quotes from personal interviews conducted by the author between October 2022 and March 2024.

3 Bobby Duffy, Rosie Campbell & Gideon Skinner, 'Emerging tensions? How younger generations are dividing on masculinity and gender equality', King's Global Institute for Women's Leadership, February 2024, Available from: https://www.kcl.ac.uk/policy-institute/assets/emerging-tensions.pdf

4 Pierce Alexander Dignam & Deana A. Rohlinger, 'Misogynistic men online: how the red pill helped elect Trump', *Signs: Journal of Women in Culture and Society*, 44(3) (2019), Available from: https://www.journals.uchicago.edu/doi/abs/10.1086/701155?journalCode=signs

5 'Glorification of Plymouth shooter by "incels" prompts calls for action', *The Guardian*, 3 January 2022, Available from: https://www.theguardian.com/uk-news/2022/jan/03/glorification-plymouth-shooter-incels-prompts-calls-for-action

6 'Experts fear rising global "incel" culture could provoke terrorism', *The Guardian*, 30 October 2022, Available from: https://www.theguardian.com/society/2022/oct/30/global-incel-culture-terrorism-misogyny-violent-action-forums

7 'Bondi Junction mall attack: "obvious" killer targeted women, Sydney police say', *BBC News*, 15 April 2024, Available from: https://www.bbc.co.uk/news/world-68814395

8 Anda Iulia Solea & Lisa Sugiura, 'New research highlights the role of TikTok in spreading videos that encourage violence against women', University of Portsmouth, 10 October 2023, Available from: https://www.port.ac.uk/news-events-and-blogs/news/new-research-highlights-the-role-of-tiktok-in-spreading-videos-that-encourage-violence-against-women

9 Paul Elam, 'Challenging the Etiology of Rape,' 14 November 2010, Available from: https://avoiceformen.com/feminist-governance-feminism/challenging-the-etiology-of-rape/. The post itself has since been removed, with the website's editors saying it 'mostly tends to be quoted out of context by dishonest ideologues as "typical" rather than the unusually provocative article that it was.'

10 TheTinMen on Instagram, 6 March 2023, Available from: https://www.instagram.com/p/Cpctcy8tNwC/

11 'Men's rights movement spreads false claims about women', Southern Poverty Law Center, 1 March 2012, Available from: https://www.splcenter.org/fighting-hate/intelligence-report/2012/men%E2%80%99s-rights-movement-spreads-false-claims-about-women

12 'Gillette #MeToo razors ad on "toxic masculinity" gets praise – and abuse', *The Guardian*, 15 January 2019, Available from: https://www.theguardian.com/world/2019/jan/15/gillette-metoo-ad-on-toxic-masculinity-cuts-deep-with-mens-rights-activists

13 'Quand la marque Gillette lance une campagne dangereuse pour les femmes', *Aufeminin*, 20 November 2021, Available from: https://www.aufeminin.com/news-societe/quand-la-marque-gillette-lance-une-campagne-dangereuse-pour-les-femmes-s4032484.html

14 'Daryush "Roosh" Valizadeh', Southern Poverty Law Center, Available from: https://www.splcenter.org/fighting-hate/extremist-files/individual/daryush-roosh-valizadeh

15 'FactCheck: men are more likely to be raped than be falsely accused of rape', *Channel 4 News*, 12 October 2018, Available from: https://www.channel4.

com/news/factcheck/factcheck-men-are-more-likely-to-be-raped-than-be-falsely-accused-of-rape

16 'Who is Andrew Tate?', Hope not Hate, Available from: https://hopenothate.org.uk/andrew-tate/

17 'One in four young men agree with Andrew Tate's views on women, poll finds', *The Independent*, 22 May 2023, Available from: https://www.independent.co.uk/news/uk/home-news/andrew-tate-women-masculinity-romania-b2342084.html

18 'Inside the violent, misogynistic world of TikTok's new star, Andrew Tate', *The Guardian*, 6 August 2022, Available from: https://www.theguardian.com/technology/2022/aug/06/andrew-tate-violent-misogynistic-world-of-tiktok-new-star

19 'Year in search 2022', Google Trends, Available from: https://trends.google.com/trends/yis/2022/US/?hl=en-US

20 Andrew Tate on X, 18 May 2023, Archived: https://archive.ph/VGQF7

21 'I went inside Andrew Tate's Hustler University – where "Gs" celebrate making $11', *The Independent*, 27 January 2023, Available from: https://www.independent.co.uk/news/world/europe/andrew-tate-news-hustler-university-prison-b2270271.html

22 'Children are mimicking a hand gesture linked to misogynist influencer Andrew Tate', ISD, 17 January 2023, Available from: https://www.isdglobal.org/isd-in-the-news/children-are-mimicking-a-hand-gesture-linked-to-misogynist-influencer-andrew-tate/

23 Benjamin Fogel, 'Andrew Tate wants everyone to get in on the grift', *Jacobin*, March 2023, Available from: https://jacobin.com/2023/03/andrew-tate-capitalism-scam-misogyny-alienation-hustle

24 Best of Iman Gadzhi, 'How feminism is destroying men?', YouTube, 20 August 2022, Available from: https://www.youtube.com/watch?v=962e7pFUMsM

25 Iman Gadzhi Extended, 'Q&A – should you drop out of school?', YouTube, 6 July 2020, Available from: https://www.youtube.com/watch?v=Sc0t6iS1Cww

26 Go Left US on X, 25 November 2020, Available from: https://t.co/6kbCHUujaN

27 Bari Weiss, 'Meet the renegades of the intellectual dark web', *The New York Times*, 8 May 2018, Available from: https://www.nytimes.com/2018/05/08/opinion/intellectual-dark-web.html

28 Elise Thomas & Kata Balint, 'Algorithms as a weapon against women: how YouTube lures boys and young men into the "manosphere"', ISD, 27 April 2022, Available from: https://www.isdglobal.org/isd-publications/algorithms-as-a-weapon-against-women-how-youtube-lures-boys-and-young-men-into-the-manosphere/

29 James Pogue, 'Inside the New Right, where Peter Thiel is placing his biggest bets', *Vanity Fair*, May 2022, Available from: https://www.vanityfair.com/news/2022/04/inside-the-new-right-where-peter-thiel-is-placing-his-biggest-bets

30 'Peter Thiel funds recharge capital, targeting women's health and fertility', *The Daily Beast*, 16 June 2023, Available from: https://www.thedailybeast.com/peter-thiel-funds-recharge-capital-targeting-womens-health-and-fertility
31 Joe Rogan on X, 5 April 2013, Archived: https://archive.ph/FziSA
32 JRE Clips, 'Male feminists are weasels', YouTube, 27 July 2018, Available from: https://www.youtube.com/watch?v=V6p-0Vw5uXo
33 Liver King, 'Haters will say Liver King is misogynistic… but they're missing the entire point', YouTube, 23 October 2022, Available from: https://www.youtube.com/watch?v=7lT3G0XBk90
34 'In the Court of the Liver King', *GQ*, 5 May 2022, Available from: https://www.gq.com/story/in-the-court-of-the-liver-king-brian-johnson-ancestral-supplements
35 'In the Court of the Liver King', *GQ*.
36 Liver King, 'Liver King confession… I lied', YouTube, 2 December 2022, Available from: https://www.youtube.com/watch?v=q_Vd7i4ZpgA
37 CVC Wellness on Instagram, 4 May 2024, Available from: https://www.instagram.com/cvcwellness/p/C6jm1ITR3Av/
38 Available from: The InnerFit Lifestyle Program (liveinnerfit.com)
39 'Sperm counts in the West plunge by 60% in 40 years as "modern life" damages men's health', *The Independent*, 25 July 2017, Available from: https://www.independent.co.uk/news/science/sperm-count-west-men-health-drop-60-per-cent-years-modern-life-a7859491.html
40 Max Rosenthal, 'Why did Trump get his testosterone checked?', *Mother Jones*, 15 September 2016, Available from: https://www.motherjones.com/politics/2016/09/donald-trump-testosterone-test-health/
41 'Tucker Carlson has a cure for declining virility', *The New York Times*, 22 April 2022, Available from: https://www.nytimes.com/2022/04/22/health/tucker-carlson-testosterone.html
42 'Healthy frogs can mysteriously reverse their sex', *National Geographic*, 21 March 2019, Available from: https://www.nationalgeographic.com/animals/article/frogs-reverse-sex-more-often-than-thought
43 'Majority of men in Britain show signs of body dysmorphia, study says', *The Independent*, 19 November 2021, Available from: https://www.independent.co.uk/life-style/body-image-dysmorphia-men-women-b1960678.html
44 Sanad AlShareef, Srinivasa Gokarakonda & Raman Marwaha, 'Anabolic steroid use disorder', *StatPearls*, 20 June 2023, Available from: https://www.ncbi.nlm.nih.gov/books/NBK538174/
45 'Body dysmorphia and steroid use on the rise', Priory Group, 24 January 2023, Available from: https://www.priorygroup.com/media-centre/experts-issue-warning-as-body-dysmorphia-and-steroid-use-rise#:~:text=Image%20and%20performance%2Denhancing%20drugs%20(IPEDS)%20are%20becoming%20widely,enhancing%20%E2%80%9Cdrugs%20of%20choice%E2%80%9D

46 AlpacaAurelius on X, 22 January 2023, Archive: https://archive.ph/hLKOB. Note: @AlpacaAurelius is the Twitter handle, though not the display name, of CarnivoreAurelius.

47 AlpacaAurelius on X, 11 February 2023, Available from: https://x.com/AlpacaAurelius/status/1624196637693206531?lang=en

48 Carnivore Aurelius on Instagram, 16 November 2022, Available from: https://www.instagram.com/p/ClAaJ9KOEnv/?img_index=1

49 AlpacaAurelius on X, 4 November 2022, Available from: https://x.com/AlpacaAurelius/status/1588577621935362048

50 'People think this "trad life" carnivore influencer is secretly a woman. He isn't', *Buzzfeed*, 24 January 2023, Available from: https://www.buzzfeednews.com/article/katienotopoulos/carnivore-aurelius-meat-influencer-not-a-woman

51 'Inside the seed oil controversy, where conspiracy meets wellness: "It's engine lubricant folks"', *iNews*, 30 May 2023, Available from: https://inews.co.uk/inews-lifestyle/canola-oil-controversy-conspiracy-wellness-seed-oils-devil-2372490

52 'How raw milk went from a whole foods staple to a conservative signal', *POLITICO*, 10 March 2024, Available from: https://www.politico.com/news/magazine/2024/03/10/the-alt-right-rebrand-of-raw-milk-00145625

53 'Instagram promoted pages glorifying eating disorders to teen accounts', *CNN Business*, 4 October 2021, Available from: https://edition.cnn.com/2021/10/04/tech/instagram-facebook-eating-disorders/index.html

54 'Proud Boys rule book contains masturbation ban', *Rolling Stone*, 23 January 2023, Available from: https://www.rollingstone.com/politics/politics-news/proud-boys-trial-rule-book-masturbation-ban-1234666317/

55 'Masturbation abstinence is popular, and doctors are worried', *NPR*, 3 February 2024, Available from: https://www.npr.org/2026/01/01/1198916105/mens-health-masturbation-abstinence

56 Justin Dubin, Jonathan A. Aguiar, Jasmine S. Lin, Daniel R. Greenberg, Mary Kate Keeter, Richard J. Fantus, et al, 'The broad reach and inaccuracy of men's health information on social media: analysis of TikTok and Instagram', *International Journal of Impotence Research*, 36(3) (2024), Available from: https://www.ncbi.nlm.nih.gov/pmc/articles/PMC9676765/

57 'Men slammed for saying women in relationships shouldn't show off their body', *The Mirror*, 29 April 2022, Available from: https://www.mirror.co.uk/news/weird-news/men-slammed-saying-women-relationships-26829147

58 'Controversial podcaster Myron Gaines is the next Andrew Tate', *New York Post*, 9 June 2023, Available from: https://nypost.com/2023/06/09/controversial-podcaster-myron-gaines-is-the-next-andrew-tate/

59 Louis Bachaud & Sarah E. Johns, 'The use and misuse of evolutionary psychology in online manosphere communities: the case of female mating strategies', *Evolutionary Human Sciences*, 5(28) (2023), Available from: https://www.ncbi.nlm.nih.gov/pmc/articles/PMC10600567/

60 'Nobody should care about a woman's "body count"', *The Atlantic*, 16 September 2023, Available from: https://www.theatlantic.com/ideas/archive/2023/09/body-count-gen-z-andrew-tate-logan-paul/675322/

61 'What is body count and should we care how many people our partner has slept with?', *GQ*, 27 January 2023, Available from: https://www.gq-magazine.co.uk/lifestyle/article/body-count-number-of-sexual-partners

62 'Kevin Samuels, a polarizing YouTube personality, dies at 57', *The New York Times*, 7 May 2022, Available from: https://www.nytimes.com/2022/05/07/us/kevin-samuels-dead.html

63 Laurie A. Rudman, 'Myths of sexual economics theory: implications for gender equality', *Psychology of Women Quarterly*, 41(3) (2017), Available from: https://journals.sagepub.com/doi/abs/10.1177/0361684317714707?journalCode=pwqa

64 Janell C. Fetterolf & Laurie A. Rudman, 'Exposure to sexual economics theory promotes a hostile view of heterosexual relationships', *Psychology of Women Quarterly*, 41(1) (2017), Available from: https://journals.sagepub.com/doi/abs/10.1177/0361684316669697

65 Rivelino on X, 10 February 2024, Archive: https://archive.ph/nNWFQ

66 Gina Cherelus, 'A guide to modern dating terms', *The New York Times*, 11 February 2023, Available from: https://www.nytimes.com/2023/02/11/style/dating-terms-guide-ghosting-rizz.html

67 'This guy used ChatGPT to talk to 5,000 women on Tinder and met his wife', *Gizmodo*, 7 February 2024, Available from: https://gizmodo.com/guy-used-chatgpt-talk-5-000-women-tinder-met-his-wife-1851228179

68 'Why "penny dating" is so manipulative and hurtful', *Psychology Today*, 27 November 2023, Available from: https://www.psychologytoday.com/gb/blog/a-funny-bone-to-pick/202311/the-penny-dating-method-a-manipulative-trend

69 'One in three men believe feminism does more harm than good', Ipsos, 4 March 2022, Available from: https://www.ipsos.com/en-tw/one-three-men-believe-feminism-does-more-harm-good

70 'The state of American men: from crisis and confusion to hope', Equimundo, 2023, Available from: https://www.equimundo.org/wp-content/uploads/2023/05/STATE-OF-AMERICAN-MEN-2023.pdf

## Chapter 2

1 'An account of the Salem witchcraft investigations, trials, and aftermath', UMKC School of Law, Available from: http://law2.umkc.edu/faculty/projects/ftrials/salem/SAL_ACCT.HTM#:~:text=During%20a%20March%2020%20church,.%2C%20would%20join%20the%20accusers

2 'Trump ridiculously claims impeachment is worse than Salem witch trials', *Vox*, 17 December 2019, Available from: https://www.vox.com/policy-and-politics/2018/4/17/17235546/donald-trump-impeachment-witch-hunt-salem

3 'Amber Heard settles defamation case against Johnny Depp', *NBC News*, 19 December 2022, Available from: https://www.nbcnews.com/news/us-news/amber-heard-settles-defamation-case-johnny-depp-rcna62376

4 'Amber Heard: I spoke up against sexual violence – and faced our culture's wrath. That has to change', *The Washington Post*, 18 December 2018, Available from: https://www.washingtonpost.com/opinions/ive-seen-how-institutions-protect-men-accused-of-abuse-heres-what-we-can-do/2018/12/18/71fd876a-02ed-11e9-b5df-5d3874f1ac36_story.html

5 Clara Martiny, Cécile Simmons, Francesca Visser, Rhea Bhatnagar, Isabel Jones & Allison Castillo Small, 'Web of hate: a retrospective study of online gendered abuse in 2022 in the United States', ISD, 30 November 2023, Available from: https://www.isdglobal.org/isd-publications/web-of-hate-a-retrospective-study-of-online-gendered-abuse-in-2022-in-the-united-states/

6 'Harvey Weinstein paid off sexual harassment accusers for decades', *The New York Times*, 5 October 2017, Available from: https://www.nytimes.com/2017/10/05/us/harvey-weinstein-harassment-allegations.html

7 'Has #MeToo gone too far?', *The New York Times*, 13 January 2018, Available from: https://www.nytimes.com/2018/01/13/opinion/sunday/metoo-sexual-harassment.html

8 'Ipsos/NPR examine views on sexual harassment and assault', Ipsos, 31 October 2018, Available from: https://www.ipsos.com/en-us/news-polls/NPR-Sexual-Harassment-and-Assault

9 'Women reveal why they hate #MeToo movement', *Daily Mail*, 6 February 2018, https://www.dailymail.co.uk/femail/article-5354031/Women-reveal-hate-MeToo-movement.html

10 Tim Bower, 'The #MeToo backlash', *Harvard Business Review*, September 2019, Available from: https://hbr.org/2019/09/the-metoo-backlash

11 'Johnny Depp loses libel case over Sun "wife beater" claim', *BBC News*, 2 November 2020, Available from: https://www.bbc.co.uk/news/uk-54779430

12 ThatUmbrellaGuy on X, 10 April 2022, Archived: https://archive.ph/1gRzi

13 'Anti-Amber Heard Twitter campaign one of "worst cases of cyberbullying," report says', *Forbes*, 18 July 2022, Available from: https://www.forbes.com/sites/marisadellatto/2022/07/18/anti-amber-heard-twitter-campaign-one-of-worst-cases-of-cyberbullying-report-says/?sh=66a28a4b7d64

14 'Johnny Depp v. Amber Heard: inside the fan battle on social media', *Rolling Stone*, 3 May 2022, Available from: https://www.rollingstone.com/tv-movies/tv-movie-features/johnny-depp-amber-heard-fan-war-online-social-bots-1345208/

15 'Neo-Nazis are trying to spread hatred through comedy. This isn't funny', *The Guardian*, 19 December 2017, Available from: https://www.theguardian.com/commentisfree/2017/dec/19/neo-nazis-hatred-comedy-racist-daily-stormer

16 'When women are the enemy: the intersection of misogyny and white supremacy', ADL, 20 July 2018, Available from: https://www.adl.org/

resources/report/when-women-are-enemy-intersection-misogyny-and-white-supremacy

17 Renée DiResta, 'How online mobs act like flocks of birds', *Noema*, 3 November 2022, Available from: https://www.noemamag.com/how-online-mobs-act-like-flocks-of-birds

18 'Influencers say they were urged to criticize Pfizer vaccine', *The New York Times*, 26 May 2021, Available from: https://www.nytimes.com/2021/05/26/business/pfizer-vaccine-disinformation-influeners.html

19 'More-troll Kombat', Graphika, 15 December 2020, Available from: https://graphika.com/reports/more-troll-kombat

20 'The Daily Wire spent thousands of dollars promoting anti-Amber Heard propaganda', *Vice*, 19 May 2022, Available from: https://www.vice.com/en/article/3ab3yk/daily-wire-amber-heard-johnny-depp

21 'Mysterious influencer network pushed sexual smears of Harris', *Semafor*, 8 September 2024, Available from: https://www.semafor.com/article/09/08/2024/mysterious-influencer-network-pushed-sexual-smears-of-harris

22 'Amber Heard didn't plagiarize movie quote during trial', *AP News*, 6 May 2022, Available from: https://apnews.com/article/fact-check-amber-heard-talented-mr-ripley-487576135842

23 'No evidence Amber Heard used cocaine in court', PolitiFact, 12 May 2022, Available from: https://www.politifact.com/factchecks/2022/may/12/facebook-posts/no-evidence-amber-heard-used-cocaine-court/

24 'Depp v. Heard trial: how much money YouTubers made from coverage', *Business Insider*, 13 June 2022, https://www.businessinsider.com/how-much-top-law-youtubers-made-during-depp-heard-trial-2022-6

25 CLR Bruce Rivers, 'Criminal lawyer reacts to testimony from Amber Heard and her psychologist', YouTube, 8 May 2022, Available from: https://www.youtube.com/watch?v=kHabg2cEmKw

26 Bruce Rivers, 'Criminal lawyer reacts to testimony from Amber Heard and her psychologist', YouTube, 27 October 2023, Available from: https://www.youtube.com/watch?v=kHabg2cEmKw

27 'Right-wing media declare the death of the #MeToo movement in the wake of Amber Heard judgment', Media Matters for America, 2 June 2022, Available from: https://www.mediamatters.org/sexual-harassment-sexual-assault/right-wing-media-declare-death-metoo-movement-wake-amber-heard

28 'Right-wing media declare the death of the #MeToo movement', Media Matters for America.

29 'Feminism made a Faustian bargain with celebrity culture. Now it's paying the price', *The New York Times*, 20 June 2022, Available from: https://www.nytimes.com/2022/06/20/opinion/roe-heard-feminism-backlash.html

30 Emily Nussbaum, *I Like to Watch* (New York: Random House, 2019).

31 'How Gamergate became a template for malicious action online', *NPR*, 20 August 2019, Available from: https://www.npr.org/2019/

08/30/756034720/how-gamergate-became-a-template-for-malicious-action-online

32 Michael Trice & Liza Potts, 'Building dark patterns into platforms: how GamerGate perturbed Twitter's user experience', MIT Comparative Media Studies Writing, 7 March 2018, Available from: https://cmsw.mit.edu/gamergate-perturbed-twitters-user-experience/

33 Trice & Potts, 'Building dark patterns into platforms'.

34 'Mike Cernovich', Southern Poverty Law Center, Available from: https://www.splcenter.org/fighting-hate/extremist-files/individual/mike-cernovich

35 Stephanie Lamy, *Agora Toxica* (Bordeaux: Editions Du Detour, 2022) (untranslated).

36 Alice E. Marwick, 'Morally motivated networked harassment as normative reinforcement', *Social Media + Society*, 7(2) (2021), Available from: https://journals.sagepub.com/doi/full/10.1177/20563051211021378

37 HuffPost on X, 7 January 2021, Available from: https://t.co/awl5vxrM9W

38 *The New York Times* on X, 7 January 2021, Available from: https://t.co/tOMiYg0z8a

39 'Insurrection Day: when white supremacist terror came to the US Capitol', *The Guardian*, 9 January 2021, Available from: https://www.theguardian.com/us-news/2021/jan/09/us-capitol-insurrection-white-supremacist-terror

40 Aífe Hopkins-Doyle, Aino L. Petterson, Stefan Leach, Hannah Zibell, Phatthanakit Chobthamkit, Sharmaine Binti Abdul Rahim, et al, 'The misandry myth: an inaccurate stereotype about feminists' attitudes toward men', *Psychology of Women Quarterly*, 48(1) (2023), Available from: https://journals.sagepub.com/doi/10.1177/03616843231202708

41 'Why Barbie deserves the backlash', *The Spectator*, 29 July 2023, Available from: https://www.spectator.co.uk/article/why-barbie-deserves-the-backlash/

42 'Concerns about harassment have "morphed into institutional misandry", MP says', *The Independent*, 24 March 2023, Available from: https://www.independent.co.uk/news/uk/christopher-chope-bill-chris-philp-stella-creasy-greg-clark-b2307619.html

43 'How Reddit is used to indoctrinate young men into becoming misogynists', *Vice*, 15 November 2017, Available from: https://www.vice.com/en/article/gyj3yw/how-reddit-is-used-to-indoctrinate-young-men-into-becoming-misogynists

44 Naomi Klein, *Doppelganger* (Penguin: London, 2023)

45 'Mike Cernovich', Southern Poverty Law Center.

46 Bryan B, 'Elon Musk: the way of the future', YouTube, 7 March 2014, Available from: https://www.youtube.com/watch?v=B1OPxitgvmw

47 'Neo-Nazi Andrew Anglin's Twitter account is rife with misogyny', *Rolling Stone*, 30 January 2023, Available from: https://www.rollingstone.com/politics/politics-news/neo-nazi-andrew-anglin-twitter-rife-misogyny-1234671105/

48 'Twitter insiders: we can't protect users from trolling under Musk', *BBC News*, 6 March 2023, Available from: https://www.bbc.co.uk/news/technology-64804007

49 Zoé Fourel & Cooper Gatewood, 'Amplifying far-right voices: a case study on inauthentic tactics used by the Eric Zemmour campaign', ISD, September 2022, Available from: https://www.isdglobal.org/wp-content/uploads/2022/09/Amplifying-far-right-voices_A-case-study-on-inauthentic-tactics-used-by-the-Eric-Zemmour-campaign.pdf

50 'No, that's not Taylor Swift peddling Le Creuset cookware', *The New York Times*, 9 January 2024, Available from: https://www.nytimes.com/2024/01/09/technology/taylor-swift-le-creuset-ai-deepfake.html

51 'Fake and explicit images of Taylor Swift started on 4chan, study says', *The New York Times*, 5 February 2024, Available from: https://www.nytimes.com/2024/02/05/business/media/taylor-swift-ai-fake-images.html

52 'Taylor Swift talks feminism, misogyny in Maxim', *Rolling Stone*, 19 May 2015, Available from: https://www.rollingstone.com/music/music-news/taylor-swift-talks-feminism-misogyny-in-maxim-38970/

53 'Taylor Swift sexual assault case: why is it significant?', *BBC News*, 15 August 2017, Available from: https://www.bbc.co.uk/news/entertainment-arts-40937429

54 'Fake photos of Pope Francis in a puffer jacket go viral, highlighting the power and peril of AI', *CBS News*, 28 March 2023, Available from: https://www.cbsnews.com/news/pope-francis-puffer-jacket-fake-photos-deepfake-power-peril-of-ai/. 'Jon Snow apologizes for the final season of "Game of Thrones" in a ridiculous new deepfake video', *Business Insider*, 14 June 2019, Available from: https://www.businessinsider.com/jon-snow-apologizes-for-game-of-thrones-fake-video-2019-6?r=US&IR=T

55 'Top 10 amazing AI nudifiers to nudify photo online in 2023', *Outsource IT*, 27 August 2023, Available from: https://archive.ph/CyPPc

56 'Bot generated fake nudes of over 100,000 women without their knowledge, says report', *Forbes*, 21 October 2020, Available from: https://www.forbes.com/sites/siladityaray/2020/10/20/bot-generated-fake-nudes-of-over-100000-women-without-their-knowledge-says-report/?sh=70bf36397f6b

57 'Two arrested in Egypt after teenage girl's suicide sparks outrage', *BBC News*, 4 January 2022, Available from: https://www.bbc.com/news/world-middle-east-59868721

58 Mary Franks & Ari Waldman, 'Sex, Lies, and Videotape: Deep Fakes and Free Speech Delusions', *Maryland Law Review*, 78(4) (2019), Available from: https://digitalcommons.law.umaryland.edu/cgi/viewcontent.cgi?article=3835&context=mlr

59 Rana Ayyub, 'I was the victim of a deepfake porn plot intended to silence me', *Huffington Post*, 21 November 2018, Available from: https://www.huffingtonpost.co.uk/entry/deepfake-porn_uk_5bf2c126e4b0f32bd58ba316

60 'Disinformation researchers raise alarms about A.I. chatbots', *The New York Times*, 8 February 2023, Available from: https://www.nytimes.com/2023/02/08/technology/ai-chatbots-disinformation.html

61 'Deepfake it till you make it', Graphika, 7 February 2023, Available from: https://graphika.com/reports/deepfake-it-till-you-make-it

62 'Someone made AI-generated videos backing the coup in Burkina Faso', *Vice*, 27 January 2023, Available from: https://www.vice.com/en/article/v7vw3a/ai-generated-video-burkino-faso-coup

63 'Slovakia's election deepfakes show AI is a danger to democracy', *WIRED*, 3 October 2023, Available from: https://www.wired.co.uk/article/slovakia-election-deepfakes; 'Deepfakes for $24 a month: how AI is disrupting Bangladesh's election', *Financial Times*, 14 December 2023, Available from: https://www.ft.com/content/bd1bc5b4-f540-48f8-9cda-75c19e5ac69c

64 'Attacks on women in politics are on the rise around the world', *Ms.*, 16 January 2022, Available from: https://msmagazine.com/2022/01/16/women-violence-politics-mexico-india-china/

65 '"Rape threats were routine": India's female politicians bombarded with vitriolic online abuse', *The Independent*, 23 January 2020, Available from: https://www.independent.co.uk/news/world/asia/india-woman-politicians-rape-death-threats-abuse-twitter-a9298721.html

66 'Gretchen Whitmer: three men cleared of plotting to kidnap governor', *BBC News*, 15 September 2023, Available from: https://www.bbc.co.uk/news/world-us-canada-66814555

67 'Gavin Plumb's social media history reveals darkening obsession with Holly Willoughby', *Sky News*, 4 July 2024, Available from: https://news.sky.com/story/amp/gavin-plumbs-social-media-history-reveals-darkening-obsession-with-holly-willoughby-13162327

68 Lucina Di Meco, 'Monetising misogyny: gendered disinformation and the undermining of women's rights and democracy globally', She Persisted, February 2023, Available from: https://she-persisted.org/wp-content/uploads/2023/02/ShePersisted_MonetizingMisogyny.pdf

69 Cécile Guerin & Eisha Maharasingam-Shah, 'Public figures, public rage: candidate abuse on social media', ISD, 5 October 2020, Available from: https://www.isdglobal.org/isd-publications/public-figures-public-rage-candidate-abuse-on-social-media/

70 'The likability trap is still a thing', *The New York Times*, 22 November 2019, Available from: https://www.nytimes.com/2019/11/22/us/the-likability-trap-women-politics.html

71 'Why don't more women like Hillary Clinton?', *Financial Times*, 9 June 2016, Available from: https://www.ft.com/content/ab2b473e-2c99-11e6-a18d-a96ab29e3c95

72 'Hillary Clinton faced constant sexism in 2016 campaign, says ex-aide', *The Guardian*, 3 June 2022, Available from: https://www.theguardian.com/us-news/2022/jun/03/hillary-clinton-faced-constant-sexism-in-2016-campaign-says-ex-aide

73 Nina Jankowicz, Jillian Hunchak, Alexandra Pavliuc, Celia Davies, Shannon Pierson & Zoë Kaufmann, 'Malign creativity: how gender, sex, and lies are weaponized against women online', Wilson Center, January 2021, Available from: https://www.wilsoncenter.org/sites/default/files/media/uploads/

documents/Report%20Malign%20Creativity%20How%20Gender%2C%20Sex%2C%20and%20Lies%20are%20Weaponized%20Against%20Women%20Online_0.pdf

74 Cécile Simmons & Zoé Fourel, 'Hate in plain sight: abuse targeting women ahead of the 2022 midterm elections on TikTok and Instagram', ISD, 1 December 2022, Available from: https://www.isdglobal.org/isd-publications/hate-in-plain-sight-abuse-targeting-women-ahead-of-the-2022-midterm-elections-on-tiktok-instagram/

75 'An unrepresentative democracy: how disinformation and online abuse hinder women of color political candidates in the United States', CDT, 27 October 2022, Available from: https://cdt.org/insights/an-unrepresentative-democracy-how-disinformation-and-online-abuse-hinder-women-of-color-political-candidates-in-the-united-states/

76 'The Digital Misogynoir Report: ending the dehumanising of Black women on social media', Glitch, July 2023, Available from: https://glitchcharity.co.uk/wp-content/uploads/2023/07/Glitch-Misogynoir-Report_Final_18Jul_v5_Single-Pages.pdf

77 'Russia's online campaign to destroy Yulia Navalnaya', *WIRED*, 26 February 2024, Available from: https://www.wired.com/story/kremlin-backed-accounts-trying-to-destroy-yulia-navalnaya/

78 '"Sexist" falsehoods target Kamala Harris after Biden drops out,' *France 24*, 23 July 2024, Available from: https://www.france24.com/en/live-news/20240722-sexist-falsehoods-target-kamala-harris-after-biden-drops-out

79 'Elon Musk accused of spreading lies over doctored Kamala Harris video', *The Guardian*, 29 July 2024, Available from: https://www.theguardian.com/technology/article/2024/jul/29/elon-musk-accused-of-spreading-lies-over-kamala-harris-video; Todd Spangler, 'Elon Musk's offer to father a child with Taylor Swift elicits disgust: "You're creepy. Full stop"', *Variety*, 11 September 2024, Available from: https://variety.com/2024/digital/news/elon-musk-father-child-taylor-swift-disgust-creepy-1236140915/

80 '"It could be your next-door neighbour": how female MPs cope with misogynistic abuse', *The Guardian*, 17 February 2023, Available from: https://www.theguardian.com/politics/2023/feb/17/how-female-mps-cope-with-misogynistic-abuse

81 'Jacinda Ardern: political figures believe abuse and threats contributed to PM's resignation', *The Guardian*, 20 January 2023, Available from: https://www.theguardian.com/world/2023/jan/20/jacinda-ardern-speculation-that-abuse-and-threats-contributed-to-resignation

82 Brie D. Sherwin, 'Hocus pocus: modern-day manifestations of witch hunts', *Northwestern Journal of Law and Social Policy*, 19(1) (2023), Available from: https://scholarlycommons.law.northwestern.edu/cgi/viewcontent.cgi?article=1243&context=njlsp

83 'How a conservative activist invented the conflict over critical race theory', *The New Yorker*, 18 June 2021, Available from: https://www.newyorker.com/news/annals-of-inquiry/how-a-conservative-activist-invented-the-conflict-over-critical-race-theory

84 'Texas mifepristone ruling flies in the face of science', American Medical Association, 7 April 2023, Available from: https://www.ama-assn.org/press-center/press-releases/ama-texas-mifepristone-ruling-flies-face-science

85 'Depp v Heard: who trolled Amber?', *Tortoise*, 26 February 2024, Available from: https://www.tortoisemedia.com/2024/02/26/depp-v-heard-who-trolled-amber/

86 'Inside Johnny Depp's epic bromance with Saudi crown prince MBS', *Vanity Fair*, 14 February 2024, Available from: https://www.vanityfair.com/hollywood/johnny-depp-mbs-saudi-arabia

87 'Inside Johnny Depp's epic bromance', *Vanity Fair*.

88 'Isis militants behead two Syrian women for witchcraft', *The Guardian*, 30 June 2015, Available from: https://www.theguardian.com/world/2015/jun/30/isis-militants-behead-syrian-women-witchcraft

89 'Saudi woman executed for "witchcraft and sorcery"', *BBC News*, 12 December 2011, Available from: https://www.bbc.com/news/world-middle-east-16150381

## Chapter 3

1 'Read Justice Alito's initial draft abortion opinion which would overturn Roe v. Wade', *POLITICO*, 2 May 2022, Available from: https://www.politico.com/news/2022/05/02/read-justice-alito-initial-abortion-opinion-overturn-roe-v-wade-pdf-00029504

2 'Orgasmic enlightenment with Kim Anami: Roe vs. Wade. Do I give a shit?', Apple Podcasts, Available from: https://archive.is/s8HmW

3 'Armed and extremist groups are frequenting abortion protests', *TIME*, 8 July 2022, Available from: https://time.com/6194085/abortion-protests-guns-violence-extremists/

4 'Medication abortion "reversal" is not supported by science', ACOG, Available from: https://www.acog.org/advocacy/facts-are-important/medication-abortion-reversal-is-not-supported-by-science; prolifebarbie on Instagram, 1 July 2022, Available from: https://archive.is/YiU2U

5 '10-year-old rape victim forced to travel from Ohio to Indiana for abortion', *The Guardian*, 3 July 2022, Available from: https://www.theguardian.com/us-news/2022/jul/03/ohio-indiana-abortion-rape-victim

6 'Pennyroyal tea for abortion is going viral on TikTok. It could kill you', *Rolling Stone*, 29 June 2022, Available from: https://www.rollingstone.com/culture/culture-news/tiktok-abortion-herbs-misinformation-death-1376101/

7 'Gendered health misinformation', Meedan, October 2022, Available from: https://assets-global.website-files.com/615e270f23c94c3fc683f12c/6360182ce09baba276f9d96d_Gendered%20Health%20Misinformation%20-%20Meedan.pdf

8 https://prolifereplies.liveaction.org/

9 'Aided by right-wing media, anti-choice groups are hijacking Black Lives Matter for their own agenda', Media Matters for America, 22 July 2016,

Available from: https://www.mediamatters.org/rush-limbaugh/aided-right-wing-media-anti-choice-groups-are-hijacking-black-lives-matter-their-own

10 'Fact check: was Planned Parenthood started to "control" the Black population?', *NPR*, 14 August 2015, Available from: https://www.npr.org/sections/itsallpolitics/2015/08/14/432080520/fact-check-was-planned-parenthood-started-to-control-the-black-population

11 'Limbaugh: "original goal of Planned Parenthood was to abort various minorities out of existence"', Media Matters for America, 13 July 2009, Available from: https://www.mediamatters.org/rush-limbaugh/limbaugh-original-goal-planned-parenthood-was-abort-various-minorities-out-existence

12 Clara Martiny, Francesca Visser & Isabel Jones, 'Evaluating platform abortion-related speech policies: were platforms prepared for the post-Dobbs environment?', ISD, October 2022, Available from: https://www.isdglobal.org/wp-content/uploads/2022/10/Evaluating-Platform-Abortion-Related-Speech-Policies.pdf

13 'How an abstinence pledge in the '90s shamed a generation of evangelicals', *The New York Times*, 6 April 2021, Available from: https://www.nytimes.com/2021/04/06/us/abstinence-pledge-evangelicals.html

14 Simone Veil Forever, Archived: https://archive.is/Zgk7X

15 https://progressifmedia.com/

16 'Generation Identity', Hope not hate, Available from: https://hopenothate.org.uk/research-old/investigations/undercover-inside-britains-far-right/generation-identity/

17 'Progressif Media : dans le secret de la fabrique à influenceurs de Bolloré', *Libération*, 5 September 2023, Available from: https://www.liberation.fr/politique/progressif-media-dans-le-secret-de-la-fabrique-a-influenceurs-de-bollore-20230905_2Q4E2OW7YBA6NOV43MFVK67Z3M/

18 'Body politics: the secret history of the US anti-abortion movement', *The Guardian*, 23 July 2022, Available from: https://www.theguardian.com/books/2022/jul/23/body-politics

19 'How "Tucker Carlson Tonight" fuels extremism and fear', *The New York Times*, 30 April 2022, Available from: https://www.nytimes.com/interactive/2022/04/30/us/tucker-carlson-tonight.html?chapter=3

20 'Ramaswamy, the new voice of the "Great Replacement" theory', *The Atlantic*, 13 December 2023, Available from: https://www.theatlantic.com/ideas/archive/2023/12/vivek-ramaswamy-great-replacement-theory/676329/

21 'Exclusive: neo-Nazi marine plotted mass murder, rape campaigns with group, Feds say', *Rolling Stone*, 26 July 2022, https://www.rollingstone.com/politics/politics-news/marine-murder-rape-plot-rapekrieg-1388238/

22 'White supremacists' mixed reactions to Alabama abortion law reflect divide on issue', ADL, 28 May 2019, Available from: https://www.adl.org/resources/blog/white-supremacists-mixed-reactions-alabama-abortion-law-reflect-divide-issue

[23] 'White nationalists are flocking to the US anti-abortion movement', *The Guardian*, 24 January 2022, Available from: https://www.theguardian.com/commentisfree/2022/jan/24/white-nationalists-are-flocking-to-the-us-anti-abortion-movement

[24] 'First Roe, then Obergefell? Far-right activists are eager to turn back the clock', Right Wing Watch, 9 May 2022, Available from: https://www.rightwingwatch.org/post/first-roe-then-obergefell-far-right-activists-are-eager-to-turn-back-the-clock/

[25] 'Rep. Mary Miller says that overturning Roe v. Wade is a "victory for White life"; campaign says she misspoke', *CBS News*, 28 June 2022, Available from: https://www.cbsnews.com/news/mary-miller-victory-for-white-life-roe-v-wade-overturned-donald-trump/

[26] 'Republican uses "Great Replacement" theory to justify abortion ban', *Vice*, 13 April 2023, Available from: https://www.vice.com/en/article/3akqdy/nebraska-steve-erdman-abortion-great-replacement-theory

[27] 'Decriminalise abortion amendment: US groups push anti-abortion agenda in UK', openDemocracy, 19 April 2024, Available from: https://www.opendemocracy.net/en/us-anti-abortion-culture-war-uk-stella-creasy-amendement-/

[28] 'U.S. government's role in sterilizing women of color', Thoughtco, 4 February 2021, Available from: https://www.thoughtco.com/u-s-governments-role-sterilizing-women-of-color-2834600

[29] *18-483 Box v. Planned Parenthood of Indiana and Kentucky, Inc.* (05/28/2019), Available from: https://www.supremecourt.gov/opinions/18pdf/18-483_3d9g.pdf

[30] 'Dorothy Roberts argues that Justice Clarence Thomas's Box v. Planned Parenthood concurrence distorts history', Penn Carey Law (upenn.edu), 6 June 2019, Available from: https://www.law.upenn.edu/live/news/9138-dorothy-roberts-argues-that-justice-clarence

[31] 'A rainbow coalition of haters', *The Atlantic*, 31 January 2024, Available from: https://www.theatlantic.com/ideas/archive/2024/01/republican-strategy-misogyny-matt-gaetz-trump/677302/

[32] 'Hungary's baby-making summit dominated by paranoia, not policy', *POLITICO*, 21 September 2023, Available from: https://www.politico.eu/article/hungarys-baby-making-summit-dominated-by-paranoia-not-policy/

[33] 'Putin says Russian woman should have eight or more children to halt population slump', *Metro*, Available from: https://metro.co.uk/video/putin-says-russian-woman-eight-children-halt-population-slump-3070525/

[34] 'Russian authorities crack down on abortion access amid demographic crisis', *BBC News*, 22 November 2023, Available from: https://www.bbc.co.uk/news/world-europe-67495969

[35] 'Hungary tightens abortion access with listen to "foetal heartbeat" rule', *The Guardian*, 13 September 2022, Available from: https://www.theguardian.com/global-development/2022/sep/13/hungary-tightens-abortion-access-with-listen-to-foetal-heartbeat-rule

36 'Italy's new abortion law is a lesson in how Meloni governs', *The New York Times*, 23 April 2024, Available from: https://www.nytimes.com/2024/04/23/world/europe/italy-abortion-law-meloni.html

37 'Police have demanded records from UK abortion provider 32 times since 2020', *The Guardian*, 23 March 2024, Available from: https://www.theguardian.com/world/2024/mar/23/police-medical-records-abortion-british-pregnancy-advisory-service-bpas

38 'These are the U.S. companies offering abortion-related benefits', *Forbes*, 7 May 2022, Available from: https://www.forbes.com/sites/maggiemcgrath/2022/05/07/these-are-the-us-companies-offering-abortion-related-benefits/; Kavitha Surana, 'Abortion bans have delayed emergency medical care. In Georgia, experts say this mother's death was preventable', *ProPublica*, 16 September 2024, Available from: https://www.propublica.org/article/georgia-abortion-ban-amber-thurman-death

39 'Idaho legislature passes a so-called "abortion trafficking" bill', *NPR*, 30 March 2023, Available from: https://www.npr.org/2023/03/30/1167195255/idaho-trafficking-abortion-minors-interstate-travel-criminalize

40 'Texas man sues women for helping ex-wife get abortion', *BBC News*, 13 March 2023, Available from: https://www.bbc.com/news/world-us-canada-64944416

41 'Texas woman argues unborn baby counts as passenger after fine', *BBC News*, 11 July 2022, Available from: https://www.bbc.com/news/world-us-canada-62124366

42 'Foetal alcohol syndrome case dismissed by Court of Appeal', *BBC News*, 4 December 2014, Available from: https://www.bbc.co.uk/news/uk-30327893

43 'Contraception "should not be legal," says Trump-backed candidate Eubanks', *Newsweek*, 21 May 2022, Available from: https://www.newsweek.com/contraception-should-not-legal-says-trump-backed-candidate-eubanks-1708868

44 'Restoring the Natural Order', European Parliamentary Forum on Population and Development, Available from: https://www.epfweb.org/sites/default/files/2020-05/rtno_epf_book_lores.pdf

45 Neil Datta, 'Tip of the iceberg: religious extremist funders against human rights for sexuality and reproductive health in Europe', European Parliamentary Forum for Sexual and Reproductive Rights, June 2021, Available from: https://www.epfweb.org/sites/default/files/2021-06/Tip%20of%20the%20Iceberg%20June%202021%20Final.pdf

46 'Anti-vax reverse contagion anxiety', Medium, 21 April 2021, Available from: https://matthewremski.medium.com/anti-vax-reverse-contagion-anxiety-81724ea216e0

47 'Pastel QAnon', GNET, 17 March 2021, Available from: https://gnet-research.org/2021/03/17/pastel-qanon/

48 'WHO chief declares end to COVID-19 as a global health emergency', UN News, 5 May 2023, Available from: https://news.un.org/en/story/2023/05/1136367

[49] 'The "Great Reset"', ISD, Available from: https://www.isdglobal.org/explainers/the-great-reset/

[50] 'From 4chan to international politics, a bug-eating conspiracy theory goes mainstream', *NPR*, 31 March 2023, Available from: https://www.npr.org/2023/03/31/1166649732/conspiracy-theory-eating-bugs-4chan

[51] 'Message that opened the Woodstock Festival, 1969', *Integral Yoga Magazine*, Available from: https://integralyogamagazine.org/woodstock-festival/

[52] '"Om-washing": why Modi's yoga day pose is deceptive', *Al Jazeera*, 22 June 2023, Available from: https://www.aljazeera.com/opinions/2023/6/22/om-washing-modis-yoga-day-pose-of-deception

[53] 'Influential moms: examining extremist influencer mothers', GNET, 7 December 2022, Available from: https://gnet-research.org/2022/12/07/influential-moms-examining-extremist-influencer-mothers/

[54] 'UK ad watchdog bans claims that IV drips can treat coronavirus', *The Guardian*, 22 April 2020, Available from: https://www.theguardian.com/media/2020/apr/22/uk-ad-watchdog-bans-claims-that-iv-drips-can-treat-coronavirus

[55] 'Ethnic minorities are bearing the brunt of COVID-19. Here's why', LSE Research, 9 November 2021, Available from: https://www.lse.ac.uk/research/research-for-the-world/race-equity/why-ethnic-minorities-are-bearing-the-brunt-of-covid-19

[56] dr.nicholemorris on Instagram, 18 September 2023, Archived: https://archive.is/uoWNE

[57] dr.nicholemorris on Instagram, 6 January 2023, Archived: https://archive.is/iZD3w

[58] 'Revealed: Monsanto owner and US officials pressured Mexico to drop glyphosate ban', *The Guardian*, 16 February 2021, Available from: https://www.theguardian.com/business/2021/feb/16/revealed-monsanto-mexico-us-glyphosate-ban

[59] '"Smoking gun proof": fossil fuel industry knew of climate danger as early as 1954, documents show', *The Guardian*, 30 January 2024, Available from: https://www.theguardian.com/us-news/2024/jan/30/fossil-fuel-industry-air-pollution-fund-research-caltech-climate-change-denial

[60] Olivia Remes, Carol Brayne, Rianne van der Linde & Louise Lafortune, 'A systematic review of reviews on the prevalence of anxiety disorders in adult populations', *Brain and Behavior*, 6(7) (2016), Available from: https://onlinelibrary.wiley.com/doi/10.1002/brb3.497/abstract;jsessionid=83EDFFA49AF80E29292577FA363F232C.f02t04

[61] 'Polycystic ovary syndrome', Office on Women's Health, Available from: https://www.womenshealth.gov/a-z-topics/polycystic-ovary-syndrome

[62] Maiar Elhariry, Kashish Malhotra, Michelle Solomon, Kashish Goyal & Punith Kempegowda, 'Top 100 #PCOS influencers: understanding who, why and how online content for PCOS is influenced', *Frontiers in Endocrinology*, 13 (2022), Available from: https://www.ncbi.nlm.nih.gov/pmc/articles/PMC9768020/

63 'Jennifer Gunter: "women are being told lies about their bodies"', *The Guardian*, 8 September 2019, Available from: https://www.theguardian.com/lifeandstyle/2019/sep/08/jennifer-gunter-gynaecologist-womens-health-bodies-myths-and-medicine

64 'Birth control TikTok is a symptom of medicine's bigger problem', *WIRED*, 15 August 2022, Available from: https://www.wired.com/story/hormonal-birth-control-tiktok/

65 For the wellness influencer, see getrealgirlfriend on TikTok, Available from: https://www.tiktok.com/@getrealgirlfriend/video/6977749001424620806?q=birth%20control%20is%20poison&t=1714342721774. For the anti-abortion group, see liveactionorg on Instagram, 7 April 2024, Available from: https://www.instagram.com/p/C5cLYuJvped/?img_index=1

66 'Conservative influencers push anti-birth control message', *NBC News*, 1 July 2023, Available from: https://www.nbcnews.com/tech/internet/birth-control-side-effects-influencers-danger-rcna90492

67 Alpha Motivation0 on Instagram, 28 June 2023, Available from: https://www.instagram.com/reel/CuCi2xYgsZr/

68 Urszula Marcinkowska, Amanda C. Hahn, Anthony C. Little, Lisa M. DeBruine & Benedict C. Jones, 'No evidence that women using oral contraceptives have weaker preferences for masculine characteristics in men's faces', *PLOS ONE*, 14(1) (2019), Available from: https://www.ncbi.nlm.nih.gov/pmc/articles/PMC6328097/

69 'Hungary's baby-making summit dominated by paranoia, not policy', *POLITICO*, 21 September 2023, Available from: https://www.politico.eu/article/hungarys-baby-making-summit-dominated-by-paranoia-not-policy/

70 'When women are the enemy: the intersection of misogyny and white supremacy', ADL, 20 July 2018, Available from: https://www.adl.org/resources/report/when-women-are-enemy-intersection-misogyny-and-white-supremacy

71 'Birth control pill history: how Puerto Rican women were used to test the pill', *The Washington Post*, 9 May 2017, Available from: https://www.washingtonpost.com/news/retropolis/wp/2017/05/09/guinea-pigs-or-pioneers-how-puerto-rican-women-were-used-to-test-the-birth-control-pill/

72 'The racist and sexist history of keeping birth control side effects secret', *Vice*, 17 October 2016, Available from: https://www.vice.com/en/article/kzeazz/the-racist-and-sexist-history-of-keeping-birth-control-side-effects-secret

73 'What's driving more women to quit birth control', *Axios*, 25 October 2023, Available from: https://www.axios.com/2023/10/25/birth-control-hormonal-quit-roe

74 'Women are getting off birth control amid misinformation explosion', *The Washington Post*, 21 March 2024, Available from: https://www.washingtonpost.com/health/2024/03/21/stopping-birth-control-misinformation/

75 'Conservative attacks on birth control could threaten access', *The Washington Post*, 5 June 2024, Available from: https://www.washingtonpost.com/health/2024/06/05/birth-control-access-abortion-ban/

76 'New male contraceptive could put a speed limit on sperm', *Huffington Post*, 18 April 2023, Available from: https://www.huffingtonpost.co.uk/entry/male-contraceptive-pill-men-sperm_uk_643e8179e4b0482824b7d232

77 '"None of it's true": wellness blogger Belle Gibson admits she never had cancer', *The Guardian*, 22 April 2015, Available from: https://www.theguardian.com/australia-news/2015/apr/22/none-of-its-true-wellness-blogger-belle-gibson-admits-she-never-had-cancer

78 'The mother is the factory', Science-Based Medicine, 12 November 2009, Available from: https://sciencebasedmedicine.org/the-mother-is-the-factory/

79 Selfhealingmama on Instagram, 29 August 2022, Available from: https://www.instagram.com/reel/Ch2Ri8SA256/

80 'The disinformation dozen', Center for Countering Digital Hate, 24 March 2021, Available from: https://counterhate.com/research/the-disinformation-dozen/

81 kellybroganmd on Instagram, 25 June 2024, Available from: https://www.instagram.com/p/C8pRj-oRqEi/?locale=%E5%A3%9E%E6%9C%BA%3A%40buth2788%E3%80%97MqKoH%7B%3F%3F%3F%3F1%7DgAe8c

82 kellybroganmd on Instagram, 17 June 2024, Available from: https://www.instagram.com/p/C8Uqn_-x7vH/?img_index=1

83 kellybroganmd on Instagram, 2 April 2024, Available from: https://www.instagram.com/p/C5PBjl3pTyK/

84 kellybroganmd on Instagram, 26 March 2024, Available from: https://www.instagram.com/p/C4-8wZIusgh/?img_index=1

85 Lucy Nother, 'Women more likely to use the internet for health reasons, study finds', Investigative Journalism @ UOP, 25 January 2021, Available from: https://medium.com/investigative-journalism-uop/women-are-more-likely-than-men-to-use-the-internet-to-find-health-related-information-book-fff02732f5ee

86 Abigail Aiken, Kathleen Broussard, Dana M. Johnson & Elisa Padron, 'Motivations and experiences of people seeking medication abortion online in the United States', *Perspectives on Sexual and Reproductive Health*, 50(4) (2018), Available from: https://www.ncbi.nlm.nih.gov/pmc/articles/PMC8256438/

87 'That final Barbie line: Greta Gerwig wanted to end the film with a "mic drop kind of joke" that's also "very emotional"', *Variety*, 24 July 2023, Available from: https://variety.com/2023/film/news/barbie-movie-ending-greta-gerwig-gynecologist-last-line-123567835

## Chapter 4

1 antiqueaesthetic on Instagram, 4 May 2022, Archived: https://archive.is/829Ao

2 Google Trends: 'tradwife', Available from: https://trends.google.com/trends/explore?date=today%205-y&q=tradwife&hl=fr

3 https://www.reddit.com/r/RedPillWomen/

4 'I'm a tradwife who lets my husband sleep with other woman while I clean', *Daily Mail*, 24 March 2023, Available from: https://www.dailymail.co.uk/femail/article-11898923/Im-tradwife-lets-husband-sleep-woman-clean.html

5 Sophia Sykes & Veronica Hopner, 'Tradwives: the housewives commodifying right-wing ideology', GNET, 7 July 2023, Available from: https://gnet-research.org/2023/07/07/tradwives-the-housewives-commodifying-right-wing-ideology/

6 'DignifAI: 4Chan campaign uses AI to shame women. She fought back', *Rolling Stone*, 6 February 2024, Available from: https://www.rollingstone.com/culture/culture-news/dignifai-4chan-shame-women-1234961851/

7 Gwenthemilkmaid, on TikTok. Available from: https://archive.ph/eeGBt

8 'Wife Estee Williams gave up her career to be a homemaker and a housewife tradwife', *Daily Mail*, 2 March 2023, Available from: https://www.dailymail.co.uk/femail/real-life/article-11814139/Wife-Estee-Williams-gave-career-homemaker-housewife-Tradwife.html

9 'About the Darling Academy', Available from: https://www.thedarlingacademy.com/about/

10 Kate Power, 'The COVID-19 pandemic has increased the care burden of women and families', *Sustainability: Science, Practice and Policy*, 16 (2020), Available from: https://www.tandfonline.com/doi/full/10.1080/15487733.2020.1776561

11 'The complicated origins of "having it all"', *The New York Times*, 2 January 2015, Available from: https://www.nytimes.com/2015/01/04/magazine/the-complicated-origins-of-having-it-all.html

12 'Black tradwives aim to escape burnout through marriage', *Refinery29*, 21 December 2022, Available from: https://www.refinery29.com/en-us/2022/12/11161942/tiktok-black-tradwives-burnout-marriage-capitalism

13 'Women are suffering from an "exhaustion gap" according to new study', *Forbes*, 15 March 2022, Available from: https://www.forbes.com/sites/kimelsesser/2022/03/14/women-are-suffering-from-an-exhaustion-gap-according-to-new-study/?sh=4a165337b3a2; 'Women do more to fight burnout – and it's burning them out', *Harvard Business Review*, 22 October 2021, Available from: https://hbr.org/2021/10/women-do-more-to-fight-burnout-and-its-burning-them-out

14 Arline T. Geronimus, Margaret T. Hicken, Jay A. Pearson, Sarah J. Seashols, Kelly L. Brown & Tracey Dawson Cruz, 'Do US Black women experience stress-related accelerated biological aging?', *Human Nature*, 21(1) (2010), Available from: https://www.ncbi.nlm.nih.gov/pmc/articles/PMC2861506/

15 'This women's mag is like a Gen Z "Cosmo" for the far right', *Rolling Stone*, 31 May 2023, Available from: https://www.rollingstone.com/culture/culture-features/womens-magazine-gen-z-cosmo-far-right-evie-1234744617/

16 Ayla Stewart, 'Ayla Stewart explains: welcome refugees?? I blame feminism, this is why', YouTube, 15 September 2015, Available from: https://www.youtube.com/watch?v=bTp1Pq6koQs

17 'Ayla Stewart, wife with a purpose', Available from: https://archive.ph/SvPHq

18 Ayla Stewart, 'Feminism – my history with it and my rejection of it', YouTube, 13 September 2015, Available from: https://www.youtube.com/watch?v=__5BCUTzzpQ

19 Blonde in the Belly of the Beast, 'My red pill journey', YouTube, 12 August 2017, Available from: https://www.youtube.com/watch?v=e8E3VjkSDqo

20 Brooke Erin Duffy, Annika Pinch & Megan Sawey, 'The nested precarities of creative labor on social media', *Social Media + Society*, 7(2) (2021), Available from: https://journals.sagepub.com/doi/full/10.1177/20563051211021368

21 'A report on the gender pay gap among influencers found men earned 30% more per post than women did last year', *Business Insider*, 10 March 2022, Available from: https://www.businessinsider.com/report-looks-at-gender-pay-gap-influencer-marketing-data-study-2022-3?r=US&IR=T

22 Jon M. Taylor, 'The case (for and) against multi-level marketing', 1999, Available from: https://www.ftc.gov/sites/default/files/documents/public_comments/trade-regulation-rule-disclosure-requirements-and-prohibitions-concerning-business-opportunities-ftc.r511993-00017%C2%A0/00017-57317.pdf

23 The Direct Selling Association, Available from: dsa.org.uk

24 'doTERRA announces new executive leadership', 21 December 2021, Available from: https://news.doterra.com/NewExecutiveLeadership

25 Frankie Mastrangelo, 'Theorizing #Girlboss culture: mediated neoliberal feminisms from influencers to multi-level marketing schemes', VCU, 2021, Available from: https://scholarscompass.vcu.edu/cgi/viewcontent.cgi?article=7768&context=etd

26 'Why I submit to my husband like it's 1959', *BBC News*, 17 January 2020. Available from: https://www.facebook.com/watch/?v=1011629369209773

27 'The rise and fall of the trad wife', *The New Yorker*, 29 March 2024, Available from: https://www.newyorker.com/culture/persons-of-interest/the-rise-and-fall-of-the-trad-wife

28 Mrs Midwest, '20 "things" I recommend', Archived: https://archive.ph/Vfe0P

29 antiqueaesthetic on Instagram, 7 July 2022, Archived: https://archive.is/39f00

30 'Ted Kaczynski, "Unabomber" who attacked modern life, dies at 81', *The New York Times*, 10 June 2023, Available from: https://www.nytimes.com/2023/06/10/us/ted-kaczynski-dead.html

31 antiqueaesthetic on Instagram, 7 September 2020, Archived: https://archive.ph/XMd4s

32 'Accelerationism', ISD, Available from: https://www.isdglobal.org/explainers/accelerationism/

33 '"Humans weren't always here. We could disappear": meet the collapsologists', *The Guardian*, 11 October 2020, Available from: https://www.theguardian.com/world/2020/oct/11/humans-werent-always-here-we-could-disappear-meet-the-collapsologists

34 '"Humans weren't always here"', *The Guardian*.

35 Allie Beth Stuckey on X, Available from: https://t.co/GAV1VNGc9Q

36 'You don't have to be a tradwife to fight in the culture war', *The Federalist*, 12 June 2023, Available from: https://thefederalist.com/2023/06/12/you-dont-have-to-be-a-tradwife-to-fight-in-the-culture-war/

37 'Why "Mad Men" is bad for women', *Salon*, 23 July 2010, Available from: https://www.salon.com/2010/07/23/mad_men_bad_for_women/

38 'Women's hearts, and souls, return homeward', *The New York Times*, 7 January 2011, Available from: https://www.nytimes.com/2011/01/09/magazine/09fob-wwln-t.html

39 femininedestiny on Instagram, 23 May 2024, Available from: https://www.instagram.com/p/C7TwVtZuCpJ/

40 'ONS survey reveals level of sexual harassment against women', *The Guardian*, 18 March 2021, Available from: https://www.theguardian.com/society/2021/mar/18/ons-survey-finds-one-in-14-women-have-been-victim-of

41 'Young women often face sexual harassment online – including on dating sites and apps', Pew Research Centre, 6 March 2020, Available from: https://www.pewresearch.org/short-reads/2020/03/06/young-women-often-face-sexual-harassment-online-including-on-dating-sites-and-apps/

42 Debby Herbenick, Lucia Guerra-Reyes, Callie Patterson, Yael R. Rosenstock Gonzalez, Caroline Wagner & Nelson Zounlome, '"It was scary, but then it was kind of exciting": young women's experiences with choking during sex', *Archives of Sexual* Behavior, 51(2) (2022), Available from: https://www.ncbi.nlm.nih.gov/pmc/articles/PMC8579901/

43 Killed Women, Available from: https://www.killedwomen.org/

44 wilsonfamilyhomestead on Instagram, 3 September 2022, Available from: https://www.instagram.com/p/CiDPpQBPyyG/

45 'Far-right "tradwives" see feminism as evil. Their lifestyles push back against "the lie of equality"', *The Conversation*, 20 December 2023, Available from: https://theconversation.com/far-right-tradwives-see-feminism-as-evil-their-lifestyles-push-back-against-the-lie-of-equality-219000

46 Robyn Riley, 'Book review: Lady by Roosh V and tips for feminine women', YouTube, 18 March 2019, Available from: https://www.youtube.com/watch?v=hHZJam2SF4U

47 'When women are the enemy: the intersection of misogyny and white supremacy', ADL, Available from: https://www.adl.org/resources/report/when-women-are-enemy-intersection-misogyny-and-white-supremacy

48 'Even those with the vilest of views have the right to be heard', *The Guardian*, 18 March 2018, Available from: https://www.theguardian.com/commentisfree/2018/mar/18/far-right-activists-barred-britain-state-speech

49 'Who is Martin Sellner, the identitarian inspiring Europe's far right?', *Le Monde*, 20 January 2024, Available from: https://www.lemonde.fr/en/m-le-mag/article/2024/01/20/who-is-martin-sellner-the-identitarian-inspiring-europe-s-far-right_6450800_117.html

50 Nancy S. Love, 'Shield maidens, fashy femmes, and tradwives: feminism, patriarchy, and right-wing populism', *Frontiers in Sociology*, 5 (2020), Available from: https://www.ncbi.nlm.nih.gov/pmc/articles/PMC8022555/

51 'The far-right "Barbies" luring Brit girls into the extremist movement with the promise of luxury lifestyles, "star" status and thousands of male admirers', *The Sun*, 9 October 2019, Available from: https://www.thesun.co.uk/news/10041621/extreme-far-right-barbies-women/

52 Eviane Leidig, *The Women of the Far Right: Social Media Influencers and Online Radicalization* (Columbia University Press, 2023), Kindle Edition, p. 57

53 Thaïs d'Escufon on X, 27 February 2024, Available from: https://twitter.com/ThaisEscufon/status/1762465988459520352

54 'The housewives of white supremacy', *The New York Times*, 1 June 2018, Available from: https://www.nytimes.com/2018/06/01/opinion/sunday/tradwives-women-alt-right.html

55 Love, 'Shield maidens, fashy femmes, and tradwives', Available from: https://www.frontiersin.org/journals/sociology/articles/10.3389/fsoc.2020.619572/full

56 'Why the alt-right's most famous woman disappeared', *The Atlantic*, 16 October 2020, Available from: https://www.theatlantic.com/politics/archive/2020/10/alt-right-star-racist-propagandist-has-no-regrets/616725/

57 'Just an empty egg box: how the far-right shames women', *Byline Times*, 27 August 2021, Available from: https://bylinetimes.com/2021/08/27/just-an-empty-egg-box-how-the-far-right-shames-women/

58 '"Alt-right" women are upset that "alt-right" men are treating them terribly', *Salon*, 4 December 2017, Available from: https://www.salon.com/2017/12/04/alt-right-women-are-upset-that-alt-right-men-are-treating-them-terribly/

59 'Lauren Southern: how my tradlife turned toxic', UnHerd, 6 May 2024, https://unherd.com/2024/05/lauren-southern-the-tradlife-influencer-filled-with-regret/

60 Anne Helen Petersen, 'The Edenic allure of Ballerinafarm', Substack, 10 February 2022, Available from: https://annehelen.substack.com/p/the-edenic-allure-of-ballerinafarm

61 '"Ballerina Farm" gave birth two weeks ago. Now it's time for a beauty pageant', *The New York Times*, 30 January 2024, Available from: https://www.nytimes.com/2024/01/30/style/ballerina-farm-mrs-world-hannah-neeleman.html

62 'Utah family shares their life at Ballerina Farm on Instagram', Turning Point USA, 2 September 2021, Available from: https://www.tpusa.com/live/utah-family-shares-their-life-at-ballerina-farm-on-instagram

63 'How to live like Ballerina Farm on a budget', *Evie Magazine*, 26 January 2024, https://www.eviemagazine.com/post/how-to-live-like-ballerina-farm-on-a-budget

64 Megan Agnew, 'Meet the queen of the "trad wives" (and her eight children)', *The Times*, 20 July 2024, Available from: https://www.thetimes.com/magazines/the-sunday-times-magazine/article/meet-the-queen-of-the-trad-wives-and-her-eight-children-plfr50cgk

65 'JD Vance defends "childless cat ladies" comment after backlash', *BBC News*, 26 July 2024, Available from: https://www.bbc.com/news/articles/c147yn4xxx4o

66 Until 1965, French women needed 'marital authorisation' to work outside the home and open a bank account.

67 'They had a fun pandemic. You can read about it in print', *The New York Times*, 7 March 2021, Available from: https://www.nytimes.com/2021/03/07/business/media/the-drunken-canal-media-nyc.html

68 'New York's hottest club is the Catholic Church', *The New York Times*, 9 August 2022, Available from: https://www.nytimes.com/2022/08/09/opinion/nyc-catholicism-dimes-square-religion.html

69 'Why does everyone think you have to be married to be happy?', *The Cut*, 22 September 2023, https://www.thecut.com/article/why-is-everyone-so-eager-for-men-and-women-to-get-married.html

70 'Why tradwives aren't trad enough', UnHerd, 30 January 2020, Available from: https://unherd.com/2020/01/why-tradwife-just-isnt-trad-enough/

## Chapter 5

1 'Unapologetically masculine', Available from: https://coach-gregadams.teachable.com/p/unapologetically-masculine

2 'The rise of Patreon – the website that makes Jordan Peterson $80k a month', *The Guardian*, 14 May 2018, Available from: https://www.theguardian.com/technology/2018/may/14/patreon-rise-jordan-peterson-online-membership

3 'Spotify signs new deal with Joe Rogan reportedly worth up to $250m', *The Guardian*, 2 February 2024, Available from: https://www.theguardian.com/technology/2024/feb/02/spotify-joe-rogan-podcast-contract-details

4 Eva Bujalka, Tim Rich & Stuart Bender, 'The manosphere as an online protection racket: how the red pill monetizes male need for security in modern society', *Fast Capitalism*, 19(1) (2022), Available from: https://fastcapitalism.journal.library.uta.edu/index.php/fastcapitalism/article/view/447

5 Richard Cooper on X, 28 June 2023, Available from: https://x.com/Rich_Cooper/status/1674077977334755328

6 thefreshandfitclips on TikTok, Available from: https://www.tiktok.com/@thefreshandfitclips/video/7216295146973842730

7 Myron Gaines on X, 8 December 2023, Available from: https://twitter.com/unplugfitX/status/1733103768093237382

[8] 'The biggest scams that rocked the crypto world in 2021', *Mashable*, 8 December 2021, Available from: https://mashable.com/article/biggest-cryptocurrency-scams-2021

[9] 'How cryptocurrency revolutionized the white supremacist movement', Southern Poverty Law Center, 9 December 2021, Available from: https://www.splcenter.org/hatewatch/2021/12/09/how-cryptocurrency-revolutionized-white-supremacist-movement

[10] 'Andrew Tate: chats in "War Room" suggest dozens of women groomed', *BBC News*, 31 August 2023, Available from: https://www.bbc.co.uk/news/world-europe-66604827

[11] 'OnlyFans management schemes trace to YouTube's manosphere', *Prism*, 8 January 2024, Available from: https://prismreports.org/2024/01/08/onlyfans-management-schemes-youtube-manosphere/

[12] 'Andrew Tate seemingly coerced women into sex work, leaked texts show', *Rolling Stone*, 25 July 2023, Available from: https://www.rollingstone.com/culture/culture-features/andrew-tate-coerced-women-sex-work-leaked-texts-1234794138/

[13] 'George Mason University's Robin Hanson might be America's creepiest economist', *Slate*, 29 April 2018, Available from: https://slate.com/business/2018/04/economist-robin-hanson-might-be-americas-creepiest-professor.html

[14] 'The redistribution of sex', *The New York Times*, 2 May 2018, Available from: https://www.nytimes.com/2018/05/02/opinion/incels-sex-robots-redistribution.html

[15] 'Jordan Peterson, custodian of the patriarchy', *The New York Times*, 18 May 2018, Available from: https://www.nytimes.com/2018/05/18/style/jordan-peterson-12-rules-for-life.html

[16] 'Sexual market value in the planned economy of inceldom', Available from: https://www.reddit.com/r/badeconomics/comments/8fbdka/sexual_market_value_in_the_planned_economy_of/#lightbox

[17] 'The mainstream pill', Political Research Associates, 1 July 2021, Available from: https://politicalresearch.org/2021/07/01/mainstream-pill

[18] Amia Srinivasan, *The Right to Sex* (London: Bloomsbury, 2022), p. 86.

[19] Alan Finlayson, 'Neoliberalism, the alt-right and the intellectual dark web', *Theory, Culture & Society*, 38(6) (2021), Available from: https://journals.sagepub.com/doi/pdf/10.1177/02632764211036731

[20] 'Bronze Age Mindset', Available from: https://kyl.neocities.org/books/[SOC%20BRO]%20bronze%20age%20mindset.pdf

[21] 'The alt-right manifesto that has Trumpworld talking', *POLITICO*, 23 August 2019, Available from: https://www.politico.com/story/2019/08/23/alt-right-book-trump-1472413

[22] 'Mark Robinson's bizarre ramble: "I absolutely want to go back to the America where women couldn't vote"', *Huffington Post*, 6 March 2024, Available from: https://www.huffingtonpost.co.uk/entry/north-carolina-gop-mark-robinson-women-vote_n_65e7d899e4b0f9d26cacc002

[23] 'A rainbow coalition of haters', *The Atlantic*, 31 January 2024, Available from: https://www.theatlantic.com/ideas/archive/2024/01/republican-strategy-misogyny-matt-gaetz-trump/677302/

[24] '"I need a woman who looks like she got punched": Republicans become more openly pro-abuse', *Salon*, 15 March 2023, Available from: https://www.salon.com/2023/03/15/i-need-a-woman-looks-like-she-got-punched-become-more-openly-pro-abuse/

[25] 'Proud Boys founder Gavin McInnes: "by every metric, men have it worse" than women', Media Matters for America, Available from: https://www.mediamatters.org/sexual-harassment-sexual-assault/proud-boys-founder-gavin-mcinnes-every-metric-men-have-it-worse

[26] 'A new global gender divide is emerging', *Financial Times*, 26 January 2024, Available from: https://www.ft.com/content/29fd9b5c-2f35-41bf-9d4c-994db4e12998

[27] 'Poland's Konfederacja alliance combines far-right views with libertarian economics', *Jacobin*, 15 October 2023, Available from: https://jacobin.com/2023/10/poland-konfederacja-alliance-far-right-libertarian-antisemitism-monarchism-elections

[28] 'How a 4chan wannabe galvanised Spain's far-right election upstarts', *WIRED UK*, 28 April 2019, Available from: https://www.wired.co.uk/article/spain-election-far-right-vox

[29] 'The South Korean election's gender conflict and the future of women voters', Council on Foreign Relations, 8 February 2022, Available from: https://www.cfr.org/blog/south-korean-elections-gender-conflict-and-future-women-voters

[30] 'Meet the incels and anti-feminists of Asia', *The Economist*, 27 June 2024, Online, https://www.economist.com/asia/2024/06/27/meet-the-incels-and-anti-feminists-of-asia

[31] 'Mayor of South Korean city resigns in #MeToo case', *The New York Times*, 23 April 2020, Available from: https://www.nytimes.com/2020/04/23/world/asia/south-korea-busan-mayor-resigns-metoo.html

[32] 'A woman's slaying in Seoul's tony Gangnam district stirs emotions in South Korea', *Los Angeles Times*, 21 May 2016, Available from: https://www.latimes.com/world/asia/la-fg-south-korea-woman-killed-20160521-snap-story.html

[33] Hawon Jung, *Flowers of Fire: The Inside Story of South Korea's Feminist Movement and What It Means for Women's Rights Worldwide* (Dallas: BenBella Books, 2023).

[34] 'Why so many South Korean women are refusing to date, marry or have kids', *The Conversation*, 15 May 2023, Available from: https://theconversation.com/why-so-many-south-korean-women-are-refusing-to-date-marry-or-have-kids-202587

[35] Paul Kirby and Jessica Parker, 'German far right hails "historic" election victory in east', *BBC News*, 1 September 2024, Available from: https://www.bbc.co.uk/news/articles/cn02w01xr2jo

36 Deborah Cole, 'Far-right Freedom party finishes first in Austrian election, latest results suggest', *Guardian*, 30 September 2024, Available from: https://www.theguardian.com/world/2024/sep/29/far-right-freedom-party-winning-austrian-election-first-results-show

37 'Grilling, guys and the great gender divide', *Forbes*, 1 July 2010, Available from: https://www.forbes.com/2010/07/01/grilling-men-women-barbecue-forbes-woman-time-cooking.html?sh=402b724abad6

38 'Soy boy: what the right's new masculinity insult is all about', *Daily Dot*, 27 October 2017, Available from: https://www.dailydot.com/unclick/soy-boy-alt-right-insult/

39 Jennie King, Lukasz Janulewicz & Francesca Arcostanzo, 'Deny, deceive, delay: documenting and responding to climate disinformation at COP26 and beyond', ISD, 9 June 2022, Available from: https://www.isdglobal.org/isd-publications/deny-deceive-delay-documenting-and-responding-to-climate-disinformation-at-cop26-and-beyond-full/

40 'Kudlow: Biden's Green New Deal means no meat for the 4th of July, have grilled Brussels sprouts instead', 23 April 2021, *Fox Business*, Available from: https://www.foxbusiness.com/media/kudlow-bidens-climate-plan-means-no-meat-for-the-4th-of-july-have-grilled-brussel-sprouts-instead

41 Samantha Stanley, Cameron Day & Patricia Brown, 'Masculinity matters for meat consumption: an examination of self-rated gender typicality, meat consumption, and veg*nism in Australian men and women', *Sex Roles*, 88 (2023), Available from: https://link.springer.com/article/10.1007/s11199-023-01346-0

42 Silvia Pastorino, 'Meat and dairy-reduction policies would help meet net zero targets and improve population health in the UK', LSHTM, 5 June 2023, Available from: https://www.lshtm.ac.uk/newsevents/expert-opinion/meat-and-dairy-reduction-policies-would-help-meet-net-zero-targets-and

43 'Marjorie Taylor Greene warns of meat grown in a "peach tree dish" while peddling Bill Gates conspiracy', *The Independent*, 30 May 2022, Available from: https://www.independent.co.uk/news/world/americas/us-politics/marjorie-taylor-green-bill-gates-meat-b2090463.html

44 Cécile Simmons, 'Mainstreaming climate scepticism: Analysing the reach of fringe websites on Twitter', ISD, 15 March 2023, Available from: https://www.isdglobal.org/digital_dispatches/mainstreaming-climate-scepticism-analysing-the-reach-of-fringe-websites-on-twitter/

45 'What does a Jordan Peterson conference say about the future of climate change? Apparently we're headed towards "human flourishing"', *The Guardian*, 9 November 2023, Available from: https://www.theguardian.com/environment/2023/nov/09/what-does-a-jordan-peterson-conference-say-about-the-future-of-climate-change-apparently-were-headed-towards-human-flourishing

46 '"Word salad of nonsense": scientists denounce Jordan Peterson's comments on climate models', *The Guardian*, 27 January 2022, Available from: https://www.theguardian.com/environment/2022/jan/27/word-salad-of-nonsense-scientists-denounce-jordan-petersons-comments-on-climate-models

47 Jonas Anshelm & Martin Hultman, 'A green fatwā? Climate change as a threat to the masculinity of industrial modernity', *NORMA*, 9(2) (2013), Available from: https://www.tandfonline.com/doi/full/10.1080/18902138.2014.908627
48 Cara Daggett, 'Petro-masculinity: fossil fuels and authoritarian desire', *Millennium: Journal of International Studies*, 47(1) (2018), Available from: https://journals.sagepub.com/doi/full/10.1177/0305829818775817
49 'With United We Roll rally, Canada's right revs up its engines', *The Washington Post*, 21 February 2019, Available from: https://www.washingtonpost.com/opinions/2019/02/21/with-united-we-roll-rally-canadas-right-revs-up-its-engines/
50 'Poll of almost 500 global climate scientists reveals many are having their work hindered by online abuse', Global Witness, Available from: https://www.globalwitness.org/en/campaigns/digital-threats/global-hating/
51 'Alexandria Ocasio-Cortez recounts horror of seeing herself in "deepfake porn"', *The Guardian*, 9 April 2024, Available from: https://www.theguardian.com/us-news/2024/apr/09/alexandria-ocasio-cortez-deepfake-porn
52 *COP, Look, Listen*, Issue 6, Available from: https://caad.info/wp-content/uploads/2022/11/GSCC-Mail-COP-LOOK-LISTEN_-Private-jet-disinfo-violent-threats-and-the-return-of-climate-hoax-content.pdf
53 'Accelerationism', ISD, 20 September 2022, Available from: https://www.isdglobal.org/explainers/accelerationism/
54 'Eco-fascist "Pine Tree Party" growing as a violent extremism threat', *HS Today*, 27 September 2020, Available from: https://www.hstoday.us/subject-matter-areas/counterterrorism/eco-fascist-pine-tree-party-growing-as-a-violent-extremism-threat/#Endnote9
55 'Many of the world's poorest countries are the least polluting but the most climate-vulnerable. Here's what they want at COP27', *PBS NewsHour*, 2 November 2022, Available from: https://www.pbs.org/newshour/science/many-of-worlds-poorest-countries-are-the-least-polluting-but-the-most-climate-vulnerable-heres-what-they-want-at-cop27
56 'Women in science, not in silence: pioneering change in the global climate crisis', UNESCO, 2 February 2024, Available from: https://www.unesco.org/en/articles/women-science-not-silence-pioneering-change-global-climate-crisis#:~:text=As%20many%20as%2080%20per,aftermath%20of%20a%20natural%20disaster
57 Timothy Q. Donaghy, Noel Healy, Charles Y. Jiang & Colette Pichon Battle, 'Fossil fuel racism in the United States: how phasing out coal, oil, and gas can protect communities', *Energy Research & Social Science*, 100 (2023), Available from: https://www.sciencedirect.com/science/article/pii/S2214629623001640
58 'In America's oil country, men losing their jobs are suffering in silence', *The Guardian*, 20 October 2020, Available from: https://www.theguardian.com/us-news/2020/oct/20/unemployment-men-lose-job-self-esteem

59 'Death in the oilfields', The Center for Public Integrity, 21 December 2018, Available from: https://apps.publicintegrity.org/blowout/us-oil-worker-safety/

## Chapter 6

1 Julia Davidson, Sonia Livingstone, Sam Jenkins, Anna Gekoski, Clare Choak, Tarela Ike, et al, 'Adult online hate, harassment and abuse: a rapid evidence assessment', June 2019, Available from: https://assets.publishing.service.gov.uk/media/5d110e2640f0b6200bb2b2da/Adult_Online_Harms_Report_2019.pdf

2 Kovila Coopamootoo, 'Online safety tech failing women – despite them being most at risk', King's College London, 15 August 2023, Available from: https://www.kcl.ac.uk/news/online-safety-tech-failing-women-despite-them-being-most-at-risk

3 'Safety by design', eSafety Commissioner, Available from: https://www.esafety.gov.au/industry/safety-by-design/principles-and-background

4 'Taylor Swift deepfakes originated from AI challenge, report says', *Bloomberg*, 5 February 2024, Available from: https://news.bloomberglaw.com/artificial-intelligence/taylor-swift-deepfakes-originated-from-ai-challenge-report-says

5 maplecocaine on X, 3 January 2019, Available from: https://twitter.com/maplecocaine/status/1080665226410889217?lang=en

6 'You can now become Twitter's main character for literally anything', *Vice*, 25 October 2022, Available from: https://www.vice.com/en/article/93ag7a/twitter-main-character-discourse

7 'Global top websites by monthly visits 2023', Statista, Available from: https://www.statista.com/statistics/1201880/most-visited-websites-worldwide/

8 'The children of Pornhub', *The New York Times*, 4 December 2020, Available from: https://www.nytimes.com/2020/12/04/opinion/sunday/pornhub-rape-trafficking.html

9 Fiona Vera-Gray, Clare McGlynn, Ibad Kureshi & Kate Butterby, 'Sexual violence as a sexual script in mainstream online pornography', *The British Journal of Criminology*, 61(5) (2021), Available from: https://academic.oup.com/bjc/article/61/5/1243/6208896?login=false

10 Alessia Tranchese & Lisa Sugiura, '"I don't hate all women, just those stuck-up bitches": how incels and mainstream pornography speak the same extreme language of misogyny', *Violence against Women*, 27 (2021), Available from: https://pubmed.ncbi.nlm.nih.gov/33750244/

11 'Sexual choking: strangulation during sex has been "mainstreamed" but risks brain damage', *Sydney Morning Herald*, 3 December 2022, Available from: https://www.smh.com.au/national/strangulation-during-sex-has-been-mainstreamed-but-risks-brain-damage-experts-warn-20221129-p5c216.html

12 'Half of adults in UK watched porn during pandemic, says Ofcom', *The Guardian*, 9 June 2021, https://www.theguardian.com/media/2021/jun/09/half-british-adults-watched-porn-pandemic-ofcom

13 'British police launch first investigation into virtual rape in metaverse', *Euronews*, 4 January 2024, Available from: https://www.euronews.com/next/2024/01/04/british-police-launch-first-investigation-into-virtual-rape-in-metaverse

14 'Researchers find a way to make VR headsets more realistic', *The Economist*, 1 February 2023, Available from: https://www.economist.com/science-and-technology/2023/02/01/researchers-find-a-way-to-make-vr-headsets-more-realistic

15 'I'm with the banned', Medium, 21 July 2016, Available from: https://medium.com/welcome-to-the-scream-room/im-with-the-banned-8d1b6e0b2932#.mzp91p5rd

16 'The disinformation dozen', Center for Countering Digital Hate, Available from: https://counterhate.com/wp-content/uploads/2022/05/210324-The-Disinformation-Dozen.pdf

17 Alexander Howard, 'Has the tide turned for Telegram, TikTok and X?', *The New York Times*, 10 September 2024, Available from: https://www.nytimes.com/2024/09/10/opinion/telegram-tiktok-x-social-media.html

## Chapter 7

1 'Far-right exploitation of Covid-19', ISD, 12 May 2020, Available from: https://www.isdglobal.org/wp-content/uploads/2020/05/20200513-ISDG-Weekly-Briefing-3b.pdf

2 Merrill Fabry, 'Here's how the first fact-checkers were able to do their jobs before the internet', *TIME*, 24 August 2017, Available from: https://time.com/4858683/fact-checking-history/

3 Naomi Klein, 'The Great Reset conspiracy smoothie', 8 December 2020, Available from: https://naomiklein.org/the-great-reset-conspiracy-smoothie/

4 'Why are conspiracy theories so compelling?', University of Nottingham, 24 May 2023, Available from: https://www.nottingham.ac.uk/alumni/why-are-conspiracy-theories-so-compelling

5 'Britain has had enough of experts, says Gove', *Financial Times*, 3 June 2016, Available at: https://www.ft.com/content/3be49734-29cb-11e6-83e4-abc22d5d108c

6 'How conspiracy theories infected British politics', *POLITICO*, 20 September 2023, Available from: https://www.politico.eu/article/conspiracy-theories-covid-vaccines-are-rife-in-british-politics/

7 'On coronavirus, Americans still trust the experts', *The New York Times*, 27 June 2020, Available from: https://www.nytimes.com/2020/06/27/upshot/coronavirus-americans-trust-experts.html

8 'How the world dates online', Statista, Available from: https://www.statista.com/chart/24165/online-dating-penetration-rate-revenue-selected-countries/

9 'Where are all the good men?', Available from: https://www.reddit.com/r/WhereAreAllTheGoodMen/

10 'Dating apps rife with sexual violence, Australian study reveals, amid calls for better user safeguards', *The Guardian*, 4 October 2022, Available from: https://www.theguardian.com/australia-news/2022/oct/04/dating-apps-rife-with-sexual-violence-new-study-reveals-amid-calls-for-better-user-safeguards

11 'Sharp surge in rapes and assaults linked to dating apps', *The Daily Telegraph*, 4 January 2021, Available from: https://www.telegraph.co.uk/news/2023/01/04/sharp-surge-rapes-assaults-linked-dating-apps/

12 'Plenty of Fish's "Dick Pics" and why dating apps are taking their ads to the subway', *The Drum*, 2 June 2023, Available from: https://www.thedrum.com/news/2023/06/02/exclusive-why-are-plenty-fish-and-other-dating-apps-taking-their-ads-the-subway

13 Katherine Dean & Sarah Davidge, 'Influencers and attitudes: how will the next generation understand domestic abuse?', Women's Aid, 2023, Available from: https://www.womensaid.org.uk/wp-content/uploads/2023/10/CYP-WWF-FINAL-SMALL.pdf

14 Fiona Vera-Gray & Liz Kelly, 'Contested gendered space: public sexual harassment and women's safety work', *International Journal of Comparative and Applied Criminal Justice*, 44(4) (2020), Available from: https://www.tandfonline.com/doi/full/10.1080/01924036.2020.1732435

15 Rebecca Lewis, 'Alternative influence: broadcasting the reactionary right on YouTube', Data & Society (September 2018), Available from: https://datasociety.net/wp-content/uploads/2018/09/DS_Alternative_Influence.pdf

16 'Hasan Piker is Twitch's top streamer', *The New York Times*, 10 November 2020, Available from: https://www.nytimes.com/2020/11/10/style/hasan-piker-twitch.html

17 Andrew Marantz, 'The stylish socialist who is trying to save YouTube from alt-right domination', *The New Yorker*, 19 November 2018, Available from: https://www.newyorker.com/culture/persons-of-interest/the-stylish-socialist-who-is-trying-to-save-youtube-from-alt-right-domination

18 ContraPoints, 'The witch trials of J.K. Rowling', YouTube, 18 April 2023, Available from: https://www.youtube.com/watch?v=EmT0i0xG6zg

19 'Could these subreddits save incels?', *Vice*, 22 March 2023, Available from: https://www.vice.com/en/article/jg5xbg/could-these-subreddits-save-incels

20 'The normie gets the girl', Date Psychology, 28 June 2023, Available from: https://datepsychology.com/the-normie-gets-the-girl/

21 'Women don't find Gigachad attractive', Date Psychology, 12 September 2022, Available from: https://datepsychology.com/women-dont-find-gigachad-attractive/

22 'What is a high body count?', Date Psychology, 29 January 2024, Available from: https://datepsychology.com/what-is-a-high-body-count/

23 'How attractive are red pill influencers? Ratings from a large sample', Date Psychology, 16 January 2024, Available from: https://datepsychology.com/how-attractive-are-red-pill-influencers-ratings-from-a-large-sample/

24 Louis Bachaud & Sarah Johns, 'The use and misuse of evolutionary psychology in online manosphere communities: the case of female mating strategies', *Evolution and Human Behavior*, 5(28) (2023), Available from: https://www.ncbi.nlm.nih.gov/pmc/articles/PMC10600567/

25 William Costello on X, 3 June 2022, Available from: https://x.com/CostelloWilliam/status/1532678653674414080

26 Sarah E Hill on Instagram, 7 March 2024, Available from: https://www.instagram.com/p/C4OP9rbgXLc/?hl=en

27 'Don't accept his proposal until you're off birth control – you might be choosing the wrong husband', *Evie Magazine*, 15 August 2023, Available from: https://www.eviemagazine.com/post/dont-accept-proposal-until-off-birth-control-choosing-wrong-husband

28 'How women drove evolution: Cat Bohannon on her radical new history of humanity', Science and nature books, *The Guardian*, 30 September 2023, Available from: https://www.theguardian.com/books/2023/sep/30/how-women-drove-evolution-cat-bohannon-on-her-radical-new-history-of-humanity

29 Michael Caulfield, 'Recalibrating our approach to misinformation', *EdSurge*, 19 December 2018, Available from: https://www.edsurge.com/news/2018-12-19-recalibrating-our-approach-to-misinformation

30 Caulfield, 'Recalibrating our approach to misinformation'.

31 Timothy Caulfield, 'Does debunking work? Correcting COVID-19 misinformation on social media', in Colleen Flood, Vanessa MacDonnell, Jane Philpott, Sophie Thériault & Sridhar Venkatapuram (eds) *Vulnerable: The Law, Policy and Ethics of COVID-19* (Ottawa: University of Ottawa Press, 2020), pp. 183–200, Available from: https://www.ualberta.ca/law/media-library/faculty-research/hli/media/images/caulfield-debunking-works-vulnerable-caulfield.pdf

32 'Gen Zers still really want to be influencers', *Morning Consult*, 4 October 2023, Available from: https://pro.morningconsult.com/analysis/gen-z-interest-influencer-marketing

33 'Influencer among UK children's top 10 dream jobs, research', *Marketing Report*, 19 April 2024, Available from: https://marketingreport.one/news/influencer-among-uk-childrens-top-10-dream-jobs-research.html

34 'Sex education review launched by Sunak', *The Times*, 8 March 2023, Available from: https://www.thetimes.co.uk/article/uk-sex-education-review-rishi-sunak-inquiry-2023-f57556grq

35 'Kaitlyn Regehr features on Today in Focus', University of Kent, 30 September 2019, Available from: https://blogs.kent.ac.uk/arts-news/2019/09/30/kaitlyn-regehr-features-on-today-in-focus/

36 'Breaking point: securing the future of sexual health services', Local Government Association, 15 November 2022, Available from: https://www.local.gov.uk/publications/breaking-point-securing-future-sexual-health-services#skyrocketing-attendance

37 'UK government has only spent half the sex education training money it promised', *Vice*, 1 June 2022, Available from: https://www.vice.com/en/article/jgmy9k/sex-education-training-england

38 'Sex education is a "postcode lottery" for young people', *Vice*, 26 April 2022, Available from: https://www.vice.com/en/article/4aw9xj/sre-postcode-lottery-england

## Chapter 8

1 Pankaj Mishra, 'Jordan Peterson & fascist mysticism', *The New York Review of Books*, 19 March 2018, Available from: https://www.nybooks.com/online/2018/03/19/jordan-peterson-and-fascist-mysticism/

2 'Life coaches in the US – market size, industry analysis, trends and forecasts (2024–2029)', IBISWorld, November 2023, Available from: https://www.ibisworld.com/united-states/market-research-reports/life-coaches-industry/#TableOfContents

3 'Four in ten Australians regularly feel lonely according to new Telstra report', Telstra, 7 October 2021, Available from: https://www.telstra.com.au/aboutus/media/media-releases/telstra-loneliness-report-2021

4 'The loneliness epidemic persists: a post-pandemic look at the state of loneliness among U.S. adults', Cigna Group, Available from: https://newsroom.thecignagroup.com/loneliness-epidemic-persists-post-pandemic-look

5 'The state of American men: from crisis and confusion to hope', Equimundo, 2023, Available from: https://www.equimundo.org/wp-content/uploads/2023/05/STATE-OF-AMERICAN-MEN-2023.pdf

6 'Men's think-tank leader receives $20 million from Melinda Gates', *National Post*, 29 May 2024, Available online: https://nationalpost.com/news/world/mens-think-tank-leader-receives-20-milllion-from-melinda-gates

7 'A gender gap at the gym is keeping women from working out', *Glamour*, 5 March 2019, Available from: https://www.glamour.com/story/a-gender-gap-at-the-gym-is-keeping-women-from-working-out

8 'In the company of men – and Zen: a male-only wellness retreat in Wiltshire', *The Guardian*, 10 June 2023, Available from: https://www.theguardian.com/travel/2023/jun/10/male-only-wellness-retreat-in-wiltshire

9 'The vegan wellness retreat run by 6′ 6″ rugby player who once killed a chicken with his bare hands', *The Daily Telegraph*, 13 June 2023, Available from: https://www.telegraph.co.uk/travel/activity-and-adventure/vegan-men-mental-health-retreat-anthony-mullally/

10 'History of the ManKind Project', Available from: https://mankindproject.org/history/

11 'Qu'est-ce que le "Mankind Project", ce groupe masculiniste soupçonné de dérives sectaires?', *Marianne*, 7 November 2022, Available from: https://www.marianne.net/societe/laicite-et-religions/quest-ce-que-le-mankind-project-ce-groupe-masculiniste-soupconne-de-derives-sectaires

12 'What is toxic masculinity?', *The New York Times*, 22 January 2019, Available from: https://www.nytimes.com/2019/01/22/us/toxic-masculinity.html

## Chapter 9

1 Pauline Harmange, 'Et puis, épuisée', Available from: https://paulineharmange.fr/2019/07/epuisee/

2 'La Pause Simone: J'ai pris un café avec Typhaine D, créatrice de "la féminine universelle"', *Femme Actuelle*, 27 March 2024, Available from: https://www.femmeactuelle.fr/actu/news-actu/la-pause-simone-j-ai-pris-un-cafe-avec-typhaine-d-creatrice-de-la-feminine-universelle-2172957

3 'Womad: the new face of feminism in Korea?', *Berkeley Political Review*, 9 September 2019, Available from: https://bpr.berkeley.edu/2019/09/08/womad-the-new-face-of-feminism-in-korea/

4 'Talking about men: what is and isn't allowed', Reddit thread, Available from: https://archive.is/lmKbN

5 ZUBY on X, 1 October 2023, Available from: https://twitter.com/ZubyMusic/status/1708256237698093432

6 Hannah Rae Evans & Adam Lankford, 'Femcel discussions of sex, frustration, power, and revenge', *Archives of Sexual Behavior*, 53 (2024), Available from: https://link.springer.com/article/10.1007/s10508-023-02796-z

7 'India lodged average 86 rapes daily, 49 offences against women per hour in 2021: NCRB data', *The Hindu*, 31 August 2022, Available from: https://www.thehindu.com/news/national/india-lodged-average-86-rapes-daily-49-offences-against-women-per-hour-in-2021-government-data/article65833488.ece

8 The Female Dating Strategy on Instagram, 27 May 2022, Available from: https://www.instagram.com/p/CeCRqmTpaDo/?img_index=3

9 *Female Dating Strategy Handbook*, Archived: https://archive.org/details/fds-handbook-v-1.35

10 '"The female Andrew Tate": the new influencer dating doctrine is extreme – but I can see why it's popular', *The Guardian*, 9 August 2023, Available from: https://www.theguardian.com/commentisfree/2023/aug/09/female-andrew-tate-influencer-dating-debt-man-bills

11 Nelly Sudri on Instagram, 11 December 2023, Available from: https://www.instagram.com/ask.nelly/reel/C0uDyGvpMJJ/

12 '*Feminism against Progress* by Mary Harrington: review', *The New Statesman*, 18 March 2023, Available from: https://www.newstatesman.com/culture/books/book-of-the-day/2023/03/feminist-case-against-progress

13 Amia Srinivasan, *The Right to Sex* (London: Bloomsbury, 2022).

14 'Young people are having less sex than their parents did at their age. Researchers explore why', *KFF Health News*, 22 May 2023, Available from: https://kffhealthnews.org/news/article/young-people-less-sex-than-parents-did-at-their-age-generational-shift-asexual/

15 'British people "having less sex" than previously', *BBC News*, 8 May 2019, Available from: https://www.bbc.com/news/health-48184848

16 'Why do people in France say they're having less sex?', *RFI*, 11 February 2024, Available from: https://www.rfi.fr/en/france/20240211-why-do-people-in-france-say-they-are-having-less-sex

17 'Charlotte Gainsbourg: "Everything now is so politically correct. So boring"', *The Guardian*, 26 October 2019, Available from: https://www.theguardian.com/culture/2019/oct/26/charlotte-gainsbourg-everything-now-so-politically-correct-boring

18 Eugénie Bastié on X, 9 February 2024, Available from: https://twitter.com/EugenieBastie/status/1755683169020367034

19 'Gabriel Matzneff, who wrote for years about pedophilia, is charged', *The New York Times*, 12 February 2020, Available from: https://www.nytimes.com/2020/02/12/world/europe/gabriel-matzneff-pedophilia-charge.html

20 'France's intellectual elite protected my abuser Gabriel Matzneff – I want to know why', *The Times*, 28 September 2021, Available from: https://www.thetimes.co.uk/article/frances-intellectual-elite-protected-my-abuser-gabriel-matzneff-i-want-to-know-why-75jlsh6rk

21 'Billie Eilish says watching porn as a child "destroyed my brain"', *The Guardian*, 15 December 2021, Available from: https://www.theguardian.com/music/2021/dec/15/billie-eilish-says-watching-porn-gave-her-nightmares-and-destroyed-my-brain

22 'The "e-pimps" of OnlyFans', *The New York Times*, 16 May 2022, Available from: https://www.nytimes.com/2022/05/16/magazine/e-pimps-onlyfans.html

23 Asa Seresin, 'On Heteropessimism', *The New Inquiry*, 9 October 2019, Available from: https://thenewinquiry.com/on-heteropessimism/

24 'TikTok's "Cancel Porn" movement is more complicated than it seems', *Vox*, 2 March 2021, Available from: https://www.vox.com/the-goods/2021/3/2/22308197/cancel-porn-tiktok-onlyfans-sex-work

25 'The Girlboss and the anti-woke cool girl', *The Drift*, 31 January 2022, Available from: https://www.thedriftmag.com/the-girlboss-and-the-anti-woke-cool-girl/

26 'Affirmative consent campaign calls for sexual assault law change in England and Wales – but this approach has pitfalls, too', *The Conversation*, 13 March 2024, Available from: https://theconversation.com/affirmative-consent-campaign-calls-for-sexual-assault-law-change-in-england-and-wales-but-this-approach-has-pitfalls-too-225317

27 'I tried to be TikTok's "that girl" for a week', *Vice*, 9 September 2021, Available from: https://www.vice.com/en/article/5db8ek/tiktok-youtube-viral-trend-that-girl-internet-genz-challenge

28 Christina Scharff, 'Feminism is trending: digital feminist activism, labour and subjectivity', King's College London, Available from: https://www.kcl.ac.uk/research/feminism-is-trending-digital-feminist-activism-labour-and-subjectivity

29 Verta Taylor & Leila Rupp, 'Women's culture and lesbian feminist activism: a reconsideration of cultural feminism', *Signs: Journal of Women in Culture and Society*, 19(1), Available from: https://www.journals.uchicago.edu/doi/abs/10.1086/494861?journalCode=signs#:~:text=2%20In%20Echols%27s%20words%2C%20%22radical,%22%20(1989%2C%206)

30 'Ritual raging: why so many women are turning to therapeutic screaming', *Dazed*, 27 March 2024, Available from: https://www.dazeddigital.com/beauty/article/57598/1/the-rise-of-therapeutic-screaming-primal-scream-arthur-janov

31 Bianca Bosker, 'Why is witchcraft on the rise?', *The Atlantic*, 1 March 2020, Available from: https://www.theatlantic.com/magazine/archive/2020/03/witchcraft-juliet-diaz/605518/

32 Mary McGill, 'Wicked W.I.T.C.H: the 60s feminist protestors who hexed patriarchy', *Vice*, 28 October 2016, Available from: https://www.vice.com/en/article/wicked-witch-60s-feminist-protestors-hexed-patriarchy/

33 'QAnon moms: parenting influencers embrace sex-trafficking conspiracies', *Rolling Stone*, 2 September 2020, Available from: https://www.rollingstone.com/culture/culture-features/qanon-mom-conspiracy-theory-parents-sex-trafficking-qamom-1048921/

34 Andrea O'Reilly, 'Ain't I a feminist? Matricentric feminism, feminist mamas, and why mothers need a feminist movement/theory of their own', Mom Museum (2015), Available from: https://mommuseum.org/aint-i-a-feminist-matricentric-feminism-feminist-mamas-and-why-mothers-need-a-feminist-movementtheory-of-their-own/

35 Eve Mefferd & Dawn Dow, 'The US child care system relies on women of color, but structural barriers systematically disadvantage them', Urban Institute, 14 June 2023, Available online: https://www.urban.org/urban-wire/us-child-care-system-relies-women-color-structural-barriers-systematically-disadvantage

36 EN Glenn, 'From servitude to service work: historical continuities in the racial division of paid reproductive labor', *Signs: Journal of Women in Culture and Society*, 18(1) (University of Chicago Press, 1992).

37 Iris Marion Young, 'Throwing like a girl: a phenomenology of feminine body comportment motility and spatiality', *Human Studies*, 3 (1980), Available from: https://warwick.ac.uk/fac/arts/english/currentstudents/undergraduate/modules/fulllist/special/transnational/iris_marion_young.pdf

38 'Kenya's pro-choice movement faces emboldened threats in a post-Roe world', *Byline Times*, 22 July 2022, Available from: https://bylinetimes.com/2022/07/22/kenyas-pro-choice-movement-faces-emboldened-threats-in-a-post-roe-world/

39 Jo Littler & Verónica Gago, 'We want ourselves alive and debt free!', *Soundings: A Journal of Politics and Culture*, 80 (Spring 2022), Available from: https://muse.jhu.edu/pub/248/article/856493

40 'Argentina legalizes abortion, a milestone in a conservative region', *The New York Times*, 30 December 2020, Available from: https://www.nytimes.com/2020/12/30/world/americas/argentina-legalizes-abortion.html

41 'In Argentina, feminists and LGBT groups challenge Javier Milei', *Le Monde*, 9 March 2024, Available from: https://www.lemonde.fr/en/international/article/2024/03/09/in-argentina-javier-milei-challenged-by-feminists-and-lgbt-groups_6599688_4.html

42 '"Nobody needs another pink hat": Why the Women's March is struggling for relevance', *The Washington Post*, 12 January 2020, Available online: https://www.washingtonpost.com/local/the-womens-march-sparked-a-resistance-three-years-later-its-a-movement-struggling-to-find-relevance/2020/01/11/344ccf22-3323-11ea-a053-dc6d944ba776_story.html

43 Michelle Goldberg, 'The future isn't female any more', *The New York Times*, 17 June 2022, Available from: https://www.nytimes.com/2022/06/17/opinion/roe-dobbs-abortion-feminism.html

44 Briony Hannell, 'How Tumblr raised a generation of feminists', *The Conversation*, 26 February 2024, Available from: https://theconversation.com/how-tumblr-raised-a-generation-of-feminists-223483

45 Kimberly Brown Pellum, 'Teaching Black women's self-care during Jim Crow', *JSTOR Daily*, 6 October 2021, Available from: https://daily.jstor.org/teaching-black-womens-self-care-during-jim-crow/

46 'Three days that changed the thinking about Black women's health', *The New York Times*, 11 November 2023, Available from: https://www.nytimes.com/2023/11/11/headway/black-women-health.html

47 Mary T. Bassett, 'Beyond berets: the Black Panthers as health activists', *American Journal of Public Health*, 106(10) (2016), Available from: https://www.ncbi.nlm.nih.gov/pmc/articles/PMC5024403/

48 'A brief history of the Jane Collective', *Hey Alma*, 24 May 2022, Available from: https://www.heyalma.com/a-brief-history-of-the-jane-collective/

49 'For women in America, the fight for "real selfcare" never ends', *Ms.*, 20 March 2023, Available from: https://msmagazine.com/2023/03/20/women-real-self-care/

50 César Caraballo, Shiwani Mahajan, Javier Valero-Elizondo, Daisy Massey, Yuan Lu, Brita Roy, et al, 'Evaluation of temporal trends in racial and ethnic disparities in sleep duration among US adults, 2004–2018', *JAMA Network Open*, 5(4) (2022), Available from: https://jamanetwork.com/journals/jamanetworkopen/fullarticle/2790797

## Chapter 10

1 'American men suffer a friendship recession', The Survey Center on American Life, 6 July 2021, Available from: https://www.americansurveycenter.org/commentary/american-men-suffer-a-friendship-recession/

2 '"It's beyond satire": tumultuous week at Garrick Club as members speak out', *The Guardian*, 23 March 2024, Available from: https://www.theguardian.com/uk-news/2024/mar/23/its-beyond-satire-tumultuous-week-at-garrick-club-as-members-speak-out

3 Carolyn J. Rosenthal, 'Kinkeeping in the familial division of labor', *Journal of Marriage and Family*, 47(4) (1985), Available from: https://www.google.co.uk/url?sa=t&rct=j&q=&esrc=s&source=web&cd=&ved=2ahUKEwjFuInT7JqHAxWNT6QEHeifAtsQFnoECBoQAQ&url=https%3A%2F%2Fwww.jstor.org%2Fstable%2F352340&usg=AOvVaw1j9xhcUAvL5Vq5ktXXO7Kv&opi=89978449

4 'How men became "emotional gold diggers" – men have no friends and women bear the burden', *Harper's Bazaar*, 2 May 2019, Available from: https://www.harpersbazaar.com/culture/features/a27259689/toxic-masculinity-male-friendships-emotional-labor-men-rely-on-women/

5 'Top YouTubers partner with Movember to support young men', Movember, 17 October 2022, Available from: https://us.movember.com/story/top-youtubers-partner-with-movember-to-support-young-men

6 'Labour to help schools develop male influencers to combat Tate misogyny', *The Guardian*, 26 February 2024, Available from: https://www.theguardian.com/education/2024/feb/26/labour-to-help-schools-develop-male-influencers-to-combat-tate-misogyny

7 'Men's Health Week: changing attitudes to mental health and therapy', BACP, 16 June 2022, Available from: https://www.bacp.co.uk/news/news-from-bacp/2022/16-june-mens-changing-attitude-to-mental-health-and-therapy/

8 'You don't have to be male to be a role model for men', *The Conversation*, 9 February 2017, Available from: https://theconversation.com/you-dont-have-to-be-male-to-be-a-role-model-for-men-71296

9 Peabody Awards, Available from: https://peabodyawards.com/award-profile/ted-lasso/

10 'Terry Crews: Marvel, toxic masculinity and life after #metoo', *The Guardian*, 22 May 2018, Available from: https://www.theguardian.com/culture/2018/may/22/terry-crews-marvel-toxic-masculinity-and-life-after-metoo

11 Alice Evan, 'What prevents & what drives gendered ideological polarisation?', Substack, 27 January 2024, Available from: https://www.ggd.world/p/what-prevents-and-what-drives-gendered

12 'Women on the move: the gender dimensions of academic mobility', IIE, Available from: https://www.iie.org/publications/women-on-the-move-the-gender-dimensions-of-academic-mobility

13 'Elizabeth Strout warns of the dangers of women writers dominating fiction', *The Times*, 24 October 2021, Available from: https://www.thetimes.co.uk/article/elizabeth-strout-warns-of-the-dangers-of-women-writers-dominating-fiction-z93tqkh6g

14 'Are young male novelists really an endangered species?', *The Times*, 4 April 2022, Available from: https://www.thetimes.com/culture/books/article/are-young-male-novelists-really-an-endangered-species-9sgqxzvh6

15 '"Glass newsroom" concerns in new journalism gender gap report', *Press Gazette*, 16 November 2021, Available from: https://pressgazette.co.uk/news/glass-newsroom-journalism-gender-gap/

16 Martha Lauzen, 'The Celluloid Ceiling: employment of behind-the-scenes women on top grossing U.S. films in 2022', Center for the Study of Women in Television and Film, 2023, Available from: https://womenintvfilm.sdsu.edu/wp-content/uploads/2023/01/2022-celluloid-ceiling-report.pdf

17 'Study shows "catastrophic" 10-year low for female representation in film', *The Guardian*, 21 February 2024, Available from: https://www.theguardian.com/film/2024/feb/21/female-representation-film-usc-annenberg-study

[18] 'Up from hatred', *Los Angeles Times*, 10 August 1997, Available from: https://www.latimes.com/archives/la-xpm-1997-aug-10-tm-21338-story.html

[19] Anand Giridharadas, *The Persuaders: Winning Hearts and Minds in a Divided Age* (London: Allen Lane, 2022), p. 43.

[20] Naomi Klein, *Doppelganger* (New York: Farrar, Straus and Giroux, 2023).

## Epilogue

[1] bell hooks, *The Will to Change: Men, Masculinity, and Love* (New York: Washington Square Press, 2004).

# Further reading

Akiwowo, Seyi. (2022) *How to Stay Safe Online*, London: Penguin.
Bates, L. (2020) *Men Who Hate Women*, London: Simon & Schuster.
Beres, D., Remski, M. and Walker, J. (2023) *Conspirituality*, London: Hachette.
Ebner, J. (2020) *Going Dark*, London: Bloomsbury.
Klein, N. (2023) *Doppelganger*, London: Allen Lane.
Reeves, R. (2022) *Of Boys and Men*, London: Swift Press.

# Index

## G

## J



## K



## L

## N



## O



## P

## S

## T

## U



## V

www.ingramcontent.com/pod-product-compliance
Lightning Source LLC
Chambersburg PA
CBHW031142020426
42333CB00013B/481

* 9 7 8 1 4 4 7 3 7 4 8 4 8 *